Imagining Religion

Chicago Studies in the History of Judaism

Jacob Neusner, William Scott Green,
and Calvin Goldscheider, Editors

Jonathan Z. Smith

Imagining Religion

From Babylon to Jonestown

The University of Chicago Press

Chicago and London

The University of Chicago Press, Chicago 60637

The University of Chicago Press, Ltd., London

9 8 7 6 5   12 11 10 09 08 07 06 05 04 03

Library of Congress Cataloging-in-Publication Data

Smith, Jonathan Z.
  Imagining Religion.

  (Chicago studies in the history of Judaism.)
  1. Religion—Addresses, essays, lectures.
2. Judaism—Addresses, essays, lectures.
I. Title. II. Series.
BL50.S578   200   82-2734
ISBN #   0-226-76360-9   AACR2

For Frances and David Bergstein

who have lived much of what is imagined in these pages

Contents

Acknowledgments

Chapter 1 was delivered as a centennial address for the Society of Biblical Literature (1978) and published in W. S. Green, ed., *Approaches to Ancient Judaism* (Missoula, 1980), 2:1–25, © Brown University.

Chapter 2 was given as the initial presentation to the reconstituted History of Judaism section of the American Academy of Religion (1979). It will appear in W. S. Green, ed., *Approaches to Ancient Judaism,* vol. 4.

Chapter 3 was delivered at a meeting of the Max Richter Conversation on Ancient Judaism, Brown University (1977) and was published in W. S. Green, ed., *Approaches to Ancient Judaism* (Missoula, 1978), 1:11–28, © Brown University. It is printed here in revised form.

Chapter 4 incorporates part of my Arthur O. Clark Lectures at Pomona College (1974) and was delivered in its present form as a Woodward Court Lecture at the College of the University of Chicago. It was published in the twentieth anniversary issue of *History of Religions* 20 (1980): 112–27, © University of Chicago. It is printed here in revised form.

Chapter 5 was first presented at a colloquium sponsored by the Institute for Religious Studies, University of California at Santa Barbara (1980), and appears here for the first time.

Chapter 6 incorporates part of my Arthur O. Clark Lectures at Pomona College (1974) and was published in *History of Religions* 16 (1976): 1–19, © University of Chicago. It is printed here in revised form.

Chapter 7 was first delivered as a Woodward Court Lecture at the College of the University of Chicago (1980), and appears here for the first time.

The Hare Hongi translation of "A Maori Cosmogony" in Appendix 1 is reprinted, with permission, from the *Journal of the Polynesian Society* 16 (1907): 109–19, © The Polynesian Society.

The J. Prytz Johansen translation of the first part of the same Maori text is reprinted in Appendix 1 with permission from J. Prytz Johansen, *Studies in Maori Rites and Myths,* in the series Historisk-filosofiske Meddelelser udgivet af Det Kongelige Danske Videnskabernes Selskab, 37:4 (1958): 52–53, © Det Kongelige Danske Videnskabernes Selskab.

The transcript of the "White Night" tape recording from Jonestown is reprinted in Appendix 2 with permission from *The New York Times*, 15 March 1979, © 1979 by The New York Times Company. Reprinted by permission.

Introduction

If we have understood the archeological and textual record correctly, man has had his entire history in which to imagine deities and modes of interaction with them. But man, more precisely western man, has had only the last few centuries in which to imagine religion.[1] It is this act of second order, reflective imagination which must be the central preoccupation of any student of religion. That is to say, while there is a staggering amount of data, of phenomena, of human experiences and expressions that might be characterized in one culture or another, by one criterion or another, as religious—*there is no data for religion*. Religion is solely the creation of the scholar's study. It is created for the scholar's analytic purposes by his imaginative acts of comparison and generalization. Religion has no independent existence apart from the academy. For this reason, the student of religion, and most particularly the historian of religion, must be relentlessly self-conscious. Indeed, this self-consciousness constitutes his primary expertise, his foremost object of study.

For the self-conscious student of religion, no datum possesses intrinsic interest. It is of value only insofar as it can serve as exempli gratia of some fundamental issue in the imagination of religion. The student of religion must be able to articulate clearly why "this" rather than "that" was chosen as an exemplum. His primary skill is concentrated in this choice. This effort at articulate choice is all the more difficult, and hence all the more necessary, for the historian of religion who accepts neither the boundaries of canon nor of community in constituting his intellectual domain, in providing his range of exempla.

Implicit in this effort at articulate choice are three conditions. First, that the exemplum has been well and fully understood. This requires a mastery of both the relevant primary material and the history and tradition of its interpretation. Second, that the exemplum be displayed in the service of some important theory, some paradigm, some fundamental question, some central element in the academic imagination of religion. Third, that there be some method for explicitly relating the exemplum to the theory, paradigm, or question and some method for evaluating each in terms of the other.

The first three essays brought together in this volume attempt to fulfill this agendum with respect to data drawn from the study of Judaism. The interest of the historian of religion in these materials cannot depend on apologetic, historical, or demographic reasons. That is to say, the interest in Judaism for the imagination of religion cannot be merely because it is "there," because it has played some role in our collective invention of western civilization, or because some students of religion happen to be Jews. Rather, it is because of the peculiar position of Judaism within the larger framework of the imagining of western religion: close, yet distant; similar, yet strange; "occidental," yet "oriental"; commonplace, yet exotic. This tension between the familiar and the unfamiliar, at the very heart of the imagining of Judaism, has enormous cognitive power. It invites, it requires comparison. Judaism is foreign enough for comparison and interpretation to be necessary; it is close enough for comparison and interpretation to be possible.[2] By virtue of its tensive situation between the near and the far, Judaism provides an important test case for central methodological issues such as definition and comparison besides illuminating the larger areas of imagination, self-consciousness, and choice crucial to the academic study of religion.[3]

The second group of essays (chaps. 4–7) plays with the same tension, but from another point of view. In this, I have been much influenced by a passage in *An Inquiry into the Original of Our Ideas of Beauty and Virtue* by that remarkable figure of the eighteenth century Scottish Enlightenment, Francis Hutcheson:

> The late ingenious author [Lord Shaftesbury] has justly observed the absurdity of the monstrous taste which has possessed both the readers and writers of travels. They are sparing enough in account of the natural affections, the families, associations and friendships of the [American] Indians . . . indeed, of all their normal pursuits. They say, "These are but common stories. No need to travel to the Indies for what we see in Europe every day." The entertainment, therefore, in these ingenious studies consists chiefly in exciting horror and making men stare. The ordinary employment of the bulk of the Indians . . . has nothing of the prodigious, but a human sacrifice, a feast upon enemies' carcasses can raise a horror and admiration of the wondrous barbarity of the Indians.[4]

This extract, it seems to me, states with precision the most interesting dilemma of choice confronting the student of religion. Does one focus on those things which "excite horror and make men stare," or does one concentrate on "common stories," on "what we see in Europe every day"? It is a tension between religion imagined as an *exotic* category of human experience and expression, and religion imagined as an *ordinary* category of human expression and activity.

It has been my continued presupposition that the latter choice for imagination is the more productive for the development of history of religions as an academic enterprise. And therefore, that characteristic history of religions materials such as myths are best approached as "common stories," as pieces of prosaic discourse rather than as multivalent, condensed, highly symbolic speech. In short, I hold that there is *no privilege* to myth or other religious materials. They must be understood primarily as texts in context, specific acts of communication between specified individuals, at specific points in time and space, about specifiable subjects. Kenneth Burke's definition of a proverb as a "strategy for dealing with a situation" provides an important insight when extended to these materials.[5] For the historian of religion, the task then becomes one of imagining the "situation," of constructing the context, insofar as it is relevant to his interpretative goals. This implies, as well, that there is no privilege to the so-called exotic. For there is no primordium—it is all history. There is no "other,"—it is all "what we see in Europe every day."

Nevertheless, the historian of religion, like the anthropologist, will continue to gain insight from the study of materials and cultures which, at first glance, appear uncommon or remote. For there is extraordinary cognitive power in what Victor Shklovsky termed "defamiliarization"—making the familiar seem strange *in order to enhance our perception of the familiar.*[6] The success of any historian of religion's work depends upon a judgment as to whether this enhancement has taken place.

The essays collected together in this volume are as well the efforts of a teacher. Each was written during my tenure as dean of the College of the University of Chicago. Each had its origin in a specific classroom situation as I attempted to describe, through concrete example, the particular angle of vision of the historian of religion. As such, each essay has a double pedagogic intent: to cast light upon a specific religious phenomenon and to do so in such a way that the characteristic preoccupations and strategies of the historian of religion be better revealed.

Once again, Jacob Neusner has served as the editor of the series in which my work appears. Jack has been my valued conversation partner for more than twenty years. What is more important, through his efforts at organizing meetings, his various publication endeavors, his unfailing sponsorship of younger colleagues, he has been the single most vital force in the academic study of religion in this country. I owe much to him as I do to the incisive criticism and constant stimulation of my dear friend Hans Penner. In some profound sense, I have never left that magical year when Jack, Hans and I were colleagues at Dartmouth College.

This volume is dedicated to two remarkable individuals who allowed me to join their family some fifteen years ago. They have both taught me much that cannot be acknowledged in footnotes.

1 Fences and Neighbors: Some Contours of Early Judaism

In February, 1948, that remarkable French poet, Francis Ponge, noted in his journal, later to be published under the title, *Méthodes:*

> Analogies are interesting, but less so than differences. What is important is to grasp, through analogies, the differential quality. When I say that the inside of a walnut is similar to a praline, it is interesting. But even more interesting is their difference. To make one feel analogies, that is something. To name the differential quality of a walnut, that is purpose, that is progress.[1]

My task, in this essay, is to inquire whether we have made some "progress" in "naming the differential quality" of what has been termed early Judaism. To do so will require a detour. This is necessary because the problem is not one of data. There are more than enough materials, more indeed than are available for most religious traditions. Materials gathered, for the most part, in convenient and accessible collections. Rather, the central problems for the student of religion are those of theory and method.

The passage from Ponge does not serve only as the motto for this endeavor, it signals the difficulties as well. In what respects is it interesting to compare and contrast the walnut and the praline? Shall they be compared with respect to color, or texture, or taste? Is the difference best stated as being between a walnut and a pecan inasmuch as most pralines are fashioned from the latter? Or, is the difference best stated as being between a natural, raw nut and a manufactured, cooked product? Is the difference a factor of the oils in each nut, our chemistry of taste, or is it due to the large quantities of sugar added to the praline during its manufacture? Is the praline well established as a taxon? Individual specimens of pralines differ widely. The proportion of brown to white sugar, the possible addition of vinegar or lemon juice, cream or butter represent a far wider range of possibilities and variations than exists within the taxon of walnut or pecan as members of the same botanical family, the *Juglandaceae,* a complex group which contains three subfamilies, eight genera and fifty-seven species. It may be necessary to confront the issue of internal comparisons between pralines before moving on to external comparisons between walnuts and pralines. These problems are only surface issues. There are deeper and more difficult questions which strike at the heart of the enterprise.

There are several types of ordering systems which seek to define categories in order to yield entities which may be compared. The most frequent, and least useful, is some artificial and unscientific system of classification which makes no pretense of revealing anything about its subject matter, whose major justification is the relative ease with which information may be located or recalled. The most familiar example is the sort of classification employed in libraries, whether they use the Dewey Decimal or the Library of Congress categories or the sequential assignment of accession numbers or arbitrary computer codes. Another would be the artificial alphabetical arrangements employed by directories, indexes, encyclopaedia, and lexica.[2] Indeed, in the new edition of the *Encyclopaedia Britannica,* the article, "Judaism, History of" occurs immediately before the article, "Juglandales," the botanical order to which both the walnut and pecan belong. Yet there is no implication that these two topics are related or comparable in any other sense than that the combination of their initial consonants and vowels happens to be the same.

The botanical article on the *Juglandaceae* in the *Britannica* depends upon the most widely used scientific system of ordering, the taxonomy.[3] When properly constructed, its central feature is hierarchy. Taxa at the same level differ from and exclude one another. Taxa at a higher level include the lower taxa as being similar. The lowest division, the *infima species,* is, thus, the most different. The highest, the *summum genus,* is the most inclusive. Biological taxonomies enumerate a graded series of hierarchical categories—kingdom, phylum, class, order, family, genus, species—which are related and distinguished on the basis of morphological and/or genetic features. Thus, on the level of species, the white walnut (*J. cinerea*) and the black walnut (*J. nigra*) differ from each other, but are included in the same genus. The walnuts differ from the willows and birches at the level of genus, but are included in the same class (*Dicotyledonae*). The walnuts and the algae differ at every level, save for their inclusion in the plant kingdom.

In both theory and practice, taxonomies are determined by *monothetic* procedures and presuppositions, the quest for a single item of discrimination, the *sine qua non*—the *that without which* a taxon would not be itself but some other. As such, taxonomy closely resembles the "Logical Tree" of Porphyry which focuses on features and attributes and asks a set of binary questions with respect to a graded series of singular features. For example:

Does it have chlorophyll or not?
If it has chlorophyll, does it have true flowers or not?
If it has true flowers, are its ovules in a closed ovary or not?
If its ovules are in a closed ovary, does the embryo have two cotyledons or not?
If the embryo has two cotyledons, are the flowers bisexual or not?
If its flowers are bisexual, are they in spike form or not?
If its flowers are in spike form, are there secondary, sterile catkins in addition to the fertile flowers or not?
If it has secondary, sterile catkins, do the fertile flowers have a corolla or not?
If there is no corolla, is there a four-toothed calyx or not?

At this point in the series, the unique walnut family has been reached and one may ask the final discriminatory question:

If it has a four-toothed calyx, does it have petals or not?

If it has petals, it *must* be a walnut; if it lacks petals, it *must* be a pecan.[4]

In this example, I have remained faithful to the preoccupations of Linnaeus in posing the binary questions in terms of the plant's reproductive organs. Quite different, but no less definitive, agenda can and have been generated by ordering the questions according to other sets of differentia such as wood anatomy or the morphology of pollen grains.[5] But the intention remains the same: the definition of a walnut by means of the progressive and orderly reduction of its characteristics to a single and decisive trait. In the Linnaean system, this would be the possession of a four-toothed calyx with petals. This is a specification of the walnut's absolute uniqueness with respect to the wider, but nonetheless similar set of Juglandales. It is a specification which lacks ambiguity. The same cannot be said for the more familiar, lexical definition such as that given for walnut in a popular dictionary, "a tree which yields both valuable timber and a distinctively flavored nut."[6] This statement could be applied with equal accuracy both to related species (e.g., the hickory) and unrelated species (e.g., the chestnut).

The classical system of taxonomy was a monothetic, definitional enterprise which held that all members of a given taxon invariably shared common features while differing from other, closely adjacent taxa by a single, definitive feature. This system had its roots in classical Greek theories of logic and definition and is associated with the eighteenth century works of Linnaeus.[7] In the nineteenth century, the Linnaean system was perturbed by evolutionary theories which seemed to hold forth the possibility of a more "natural" system of classification. Time was factored into the system, and the logical definition of class by the possession of common and distinctive attributes was replaced by an historical definition of class as descended from a common ancestor. The logical *prior* gave way to the historical *primordium*. While the notion of common was maintained, it became something of a mirage, for there was neither a theoretical basis nor an empirical warrant for the assumption that any given ancestral trait would persist in any given descendant. Variability, especially as related to geographic populations, introduced further complications at the level of species and subspecies. Successive taxonomic proposals have wrestled with these dilemmas.[8]

Perhaps the most promising development in recent years has been the return to the suggestion made by Michel Adanson in 1763 in controversy with Linnaeus over the question of the mutability of species.[9] Adanson argued that the members of a given taxon *need not* possess all of the defining characteristics of that taxon and that there was no a priori justification for deciding what characteristics were most definitive.[10] Although the state of the art in the eighteenth century was not such that Adanson could have put it this way, what he was suggesting was something like a statistical approach to classification.

This possibility lay dormant until 1959, when it was revived in a theoretical proposal by Morton Beckner, and was formulated in a pragmatic and definitive statement in 1963 in Robert Sokol and Peter Sneath's *Principles of Numerical Taxonomy.*[11]

What was proposed was a new, self-consciously *polythetic* mode of classification which surrendered the idea of perfect, unique, single differentia—a taxonomy which retained the notion of necessary but abandoned the notion of sufficient criteria for admission to a class. In this new mode, a class is defined as consisting of a set of properties, each individual member of the class to possess "a large (but unspecified) number" of these properties, with each property to be possessed by a "large number" of individuals in the class, but no single property to be possessed by every member of the class.[12] If the class contained a large population, it would be possible to arrange them according to the properties they possessed in common in such a way that each individual would most closely resemble its nearest neighbor and least closely resemble its farthest. The probability would be high that the individuals at either extreme would scarcely resemble one another, that is, they may have none of the properties of the set in common. In such a system, there will always be borderline cases. Indeed, this is to be welcomed as a stimulus to further research.

To state this more concretely. Imagine a group of six individuals, each possessing three characteristics of a set, A–H. Individual 1 has characteristics A, B, C; individual 2 has B, C, D; individual 3 has A, B, D; individual 4 has A, C, D; individuals 5 and 6 have characteristics F, G, H in common. Individuals 1–4 would be formed into a polythetic group sharing a number of characteristics, although no one characteristic is found in all four individuals. Hence, no one characteristic is definitive. Individuals 5 and 6 form a classic monothetic set with the only question remaining the determination as to whether characteristic F or G or H is definitive.[13]

Much depends on the precision with which what was left deliberately vague above can be defined. What constitutes a "large (but unspecified)" number of properties? What constitutes a "large number" of individuals? There are complex procedural issues of scaling, weighting, and measurements of degrees of affinity which may be addressed by a variety of statistical devices. There are also pragmatic problems in cluster-type analyses of large populations for a large number of characteristics, but statistical methods and computer technology have largely overcome these.[14]

One can point to an impressive body of scholarship within and without the biological sciences in which polythetic classification has been successfully employed.[15] Within the study of religion, there is no lack of potential elements for polythetic classification. For example, the *Cross-Cultural Summary,* edited by R. B. Textor, yields more than twenty thousand statistically significant correlations for a sample of some sixty societies.[16]

II

All of the issues raised with respect to biological classification recur in the study of religion and its taxonomic agenda: the attempt to distinguish religion from other taxa of human experience and expression, the attempt to distinguish various taxa within religion, the attempt to distinguish various taxa within a particular religion. Each of these issues must be faced before beginning to address the task of "naming the differential quality" of early Judaism.[17]

The first level of inquiry, that of the distinction of religion, has usually been attempted in a monothetic fashion. Scholars have engaged in the quest for the unique and definitive *sine qua non,* the "that without which" religion would not be religion but rather an instance of something else. In the main, the results of this enterprise have not been convincing; they have failed to achieve consensus. They have been poorly formulated and violate the ordinary canons of definition.[18] But this is less disturbing than the fact that the presuppositions of the monothetic enterprise have been deliberately tampered with for apologetic reasons.

Central to the monothetic procedure is the goal of achieving the unique and definitive, as well as the necessary corollary that this uniqueness is both ordinary and reciprocal. In terms of the previous botanical example: the walnut is unique in possessing bisexual flowers in spiked form with four-toothed calyxes, lacking corolla, but with petals. These characteristics make the walnut unique with respect to the closely adjacent pecan as well as all other species. But the pecan is likewise unique with respect to the closely related walnut as well as all other species. None of this is admitted by students of religion. Some special uniqueness is claimed for religion as well as for particular religious traditions, and this uniqueness is conceived to be unilateral and nonreciprocal. If religion is unique with respect to other cultural activities, it is rarely conceded that, therefore, these activities are unique with respect to religion. If Israel is unique with respect to Canaan, it is required that Canaan be held to be unique with respect to Israel. Uniqueness is an *ordinary* presupposition of definition and classification—it is not some odd point of pride. To the degree that it has become the latter, in circles of religious scholarship, it must be set aside. As William James reminds us:

> The first thing the intellect does with an object is to class it along with something else. But any object that is infinitely important to us and awakens our devotion feels to us also as if it must be *sui generis* and unique. Probably a crab would be filled with a sense of personal outrage if it could hear us class it without ado or apology as a crustacean, and thus dispose of it. "I am no such thing," it would say, "I am *myself, myself* alone."[19]

In the classification of religions, a dichotomous agenda of division has been most frequently employed.[20] However, unlike the biological system, there are usually normative implications or the assignment of positive or negative valences which render the classification useless. The most frequent of these illicit divisions may be listed, each of which may be further subdivided:

true/false
natural/revealed
with books/without books
natural/ethical
collective/individual
ethnic/universal
cosmic/historical
free/dependent
healthy/sick
affirming/denying
magical/religious
habitual/spontaneous

with the perceived positive pole identified with "us" and the negative with "them."

It might be possible to formulate properly the most common division in the following manner:

Are there gods or not?

If gods, are they personal or not?
If personal, are they in nature or above nature?
If above nature, is there one or more than one?

and so on through the history of the study of religion in the past two centuries. But the results will be ambiguous.

An alleged alternative, represented by long lists in "phenomenological" works, gives a taxonomy for particular religious traditions by identifying a single trait which is held to reveal the "essence" of that tradition. But the results are arbitrary and poorly defined, being determined by extrinsic apologetics. For example, combining the lists in G. van der Leeuw and G. Mensching:[21]

Primitive: religion(s) of "magical coherence."
China: religion of "restlessness and flight" or religion of "cosmic harmony."
Shinto: religion of the "sacral state and family community."
Greece: religion of "stress [or impulse] and form."
Rome: religion of "expediency."
Teutonic: religion of the "numinous tribe."
India: religion(s) of "infinity and asceticism" or of "peaceful unity and unifying peace."
Ancient Near East: religion(s) of "astral relationships."
Egypt: religion of "immortalized life."
Israel: religion of "will and obedience."
Zoroastrianism: religion of "ethical struggle."
Buddhism: religion of "nothingness and compassion" or religion of the "annulment of suffering."
Islam: religion of "majesty and humility" or religion of "perfect submission."
Christianity: religion of "love."

None of the above could lay claim to being correctly drawn differentia. They are merely slogans. But already, at this crude and jingoistic level, we encounter those distinctions which will be claimed to be definitive of the taxon, Judaism. It is a "true," "revealed" religion "with books," "ethical," "collective," "ethnic," "historical," "free," "healthy," and "affirming" with its decisive and unique differentium, "obedience to the Law" as opposed to "love." Or, to give the apologetic pedigree of this taxonomy, Jewish "Law" as opposed to Christian "Gospel."

I find no value in continuing the effort to make such lists of improperly constructed, impressionistic divisions. It would be possible, in principle, to construct a proper taxonomy. But this would require abandoning the inappropriate notion of "essence."

It would be possible as well, in principle, to construct a satisfying evolutionary classification of religions. But this would have to eschew the impossible presupposition of a common ancestor, replacing it by a model of multilinear evolution. But I know of no such attempt. What have been proposed as evolutionary classifications by students of religion are, in fact, the ordering of the previously cited "essential" characteristics by some sequential scheme—in effect, a quasi-temporal ranking of slogans.

I know of no examples of attempts at the polythetic classification of religions or religious phenomena.[22] It is in this area that the most fruitful future work will be done.

We have reached our detour's end. It seemed, at the outset, to be of some value to discern in a general fashion how those professionally concerned with classification approach their enterprise. For, if we cannot determine how to classify a walnut, *qal ve ḥomer,* how much more so Judaism! There is much about method that can be learned from colleagues in the biological sciences, more indeed than can be appropriated from the more usual physical model for the sciences.[23]

It is premature to propose a proper polythetic classification of Judaism, but it is possible to be clear about what it would entail. We would identify a set of characteristics and begin to trace their configurations. Biologists use from fifty to one hundred such characteristics—the possession of any one of which is sufficient for admission to the taxon. We would need to do the same. There is no necessity to integrate the characteristics in such a list; indeed, there is an imperative against reducing it monothetically. Because the notion of strict division has been abandoned, and with it the notion of the unique and sufficient cause, it will not matter if many of the characteristics of Judaism are found to be equally characteristic of other religious taxa. If we could generate such a list for early Judaism, Philo might possess a large number of such characteristics; his nephew, Tiberius Julius Alexander, might possess only one or two; Philo's brother might have as many characteristics as Philo, but a significant proportion of them might differ from Philo's.

Classification is but a stage in natural history; it is not yet science. For that, explanation is required. But classification is a necessary prerequisite. As F. Max Müller insisted, more than a century ago, "all real science rests on classification, and only in case we cannot succeed in classifying the various dialects of faith, shall we have to confess that a science of religion is really an impossibility."[24]

III

As a beginning, I propose two operations which might serve to free students of religion from the usual preoccupations with political and literary history and the temptation to reduce phenomena to "essences." I understand these to be propaedeutic to the later task of constructing a polythetic classification of early Judaism.

The first operation would be to select a single taxic indicator that appears to function within the tradition as an internal agent of discrimination and map it through a variety of the materials of early Judaism in order to gain some appreciation of the range of its application. For the purposes of this exercise, I have chosen circumcision. The second operation would be to take a limited body of material from early Judaism and map out all of its taxonomic indicators. These would later be compared with other, different sets of early Jewish data. For the purposes of this exercise, I have chosen a set of funerary inscriptions. In neither case is the intention of the exercise a monothetic one. We are not seeking integration and definition; rather we are attempting to take an initial step toward the listing of all of the characteristics of early Judaism. The final results would be in the form of a ranked but diverse and motley catalog of traits. At some later date, and with comparative materials, they would have to be grouped according to some quantitative technique of multidimensional scaling in the service of some theory.

One of the most important and persistent indicators for the taxon, Jew, is the practice of male circumcision. It appears to play the same sort of definitive role for both the birthright and converted Jew that the absence of a corolla but the possession of a four-toothed calyx with petals did for the walnut. Spinoza's frequently cited dictum is representative, "so great is the importance that I attach to the sign of circumcision . . . that I am persuaded that it is sufficient *by itself* to maintain the separate existence of the [Jewish] nation forever."[25]

Within the bulk of the Hebrew Scriptures, as in the Qur'an where it is nowhere mentioned, circumcision is assumed to be the characteristic of the Israelite rather than enjoined. There is no injunction concerning circumcision in the biblical legal codes or in Deuteronomy. What early narratives we possess reflect some concern with the uncircumcised outsider (Gen. 34:13–29; 1 Sam. 18:20–27; in both of these a ploy is the generative element of the plot and circumcision is scarcely the issue) or with the phenomenon of the uncircumcised Israelite (Josh. 5:2–9 and the murky narrative in Exod. 4:24–26; in each case the problem is "solved" by circumcision).

It is not until the Priestly tradition, itself one of the earliest witnesses to early Judaism, that we find most of the mentions of circumcision. The central text, Gen. 17:9–14, establishes circumcision as the definitive characteristic of the Israelitic male. Understood as a covenant in the flesh, it is required of every male Israelite and bondsman. The failure to circumcise means being cut off from the people, being excluded from the taxon. This establishes a dichotomous, definitive division within the horizon of this tradition.

Is he male?
If male, is he circumcised?

An affirmative answer to both these questions is a necessary and, in some interpretations, a sufficient reason to classify the individual as an Israelite or Jew (compare the late addition to P in Exod. 12:43–49).

Within Israelitic tradition, circumcision and the lack of circumcision can serve as general ethnic classifiers. For example, in early narrative, the Philistines are consistently referred to as "uncircumcised"; *ʿrl* becomes the term for gentile from its massive use in Ezekiel through the later materials. But there is a well-known problem with this taxic indicator. Circumcision *was not* a distinctive mark of the Israelite within the wider Near Eastern and Mediterranean world. For example, Herodotus, in the second book of his *Histories,* chapter 104, gives a catalog of seven peoples who practice circumcision and offers his usual explanation that each of them, with the possible exception of the Ethiopians, borrowed the custom from the Egyptians.[26] The question of borrowing and diffusion of the practice was raised often in the ancient world, returned to in the eighteenth century Deist debates, and became a major plank in Freud's reconstruction of the "Egyptian Moses." Indeed, from a broader comparative perspective, circumcision is widely distributed. It is the most common form of male initiation in nonliterate societies.[27]

Although there are few signs of an Israelitic ethnographic tradition analogous to the Ionian (although Deut. 2:9–3:11 and Gen. 10 are sufficient to demonstrate that such traditions did exist), it is inconceivable that this problem would not have been raised in learned Hebrew circles. Jeremiah 9:25–26 gives both an ethnographic catalog and attempts a solution: "I will punish all those who are circumcised but yet uncircumcised—Egypt, Judah, Edom, the sons of Ammon, Moab and all who dwell in the desert." In later centuries, the same polemic, "circumcised but yet uncircumcised," will be applied by the Samaritans and the Christians against the Jews.[28]

In the Greco-Roman period, circumcision, along with sabbath observance and abstinence from pork, serves as the common indicator employed by outsiders in classifying an individual as Jewish. This is particularly prominent in the Latin literary tradition. The Greek tradition, in addition to using circumcision as a taxic indicator, appears fascinated by the Maccabean practice of forced circumcision, particularly in the case of the Idumeneans. Circumcision was understood by these outsiders to be the *sine qua non* of Judaism—at times, regardless of beliefs. If polemicized against, it was because it was perceived as an act of bodily mutilation which takes its place in a series of such acts, from tattooing and branding to loss of limb and castration—a series seen as shameful operations performed on the body, most frequently on the body of a criminal or slave. The frequently cited interdiction by Hadrian derives from this perception. Hadrian's law was an extension of the prohibitions of Sulla, Domitian, and Nerva against castration to include circumcision. It was not limited to prohibiting the practice by Jews. A similar perception animates the bitter invective by Paul in Gal. 5:12 and Phil. 3:2b, and is the major charge in the Mandaean critique of Jewish circumcision.

The strongest and most persistent use of circumcision as a taxic indicator is found in Paul and the deutero-Pauline literature. Paul's self-description is framed in terms of the two most fundamental halakic definitions of the Jewish male: circumcision and birth from a Jewish mother.

> circumcised on the eighth day [by virtue of which I am] of the people of Israel / of the tribe of Benjamin, a Hebrew born of Hebrews . . . . [Phil. 3:5]

"Circumcised" is consistently used in the Pauline literature as a technical term for the Jew, "uncircumcised," for the gentile.

However, Paul is preeminently a boundary-crossing figure. He is one of the circumcised, preaching the gospel of Christ, "the servant of the circumcised" (Rom. 15:8) to the uncircumcised. What is at issue, both in Paul and the later literature of the Paulinists, is the attempt to establish a new taxon: "where there cannot be Greek and Jew, circumcised and uncircumcised, barbarian and Scythian" (Col. 3:11), "for neither circumcision counts for anything nor uncircumcision, but a *new creation*" (Gal. 6:15). Taking this last phrase in a taxonomic sense, the Christian is no longer to be classified by the old divisions. In contemporary Greek taxonomic terminology, he is a member of a "third race" *(triton genos)*, a term developed in Pythagorean circles to describe the unique position of Pythagoras and other kings and sages as neither gods nor men. This description of the Christian is shouted by Roman opponents (e.g., Tertullian *Scorpiace,* 10) and affirmed by early Christians. The best witness is the *Epistle to Diognetus,* where Christianity is described as neither Hellenic nor Jewish, it is a "new race" which, in order to understand, one must become a "new man" and listen to a "new story." The fifth chapter of *Diognetus,* with considerable rhetorical skill, heaps paradox upon paradox in an ethnography of this "new race." Christianity is neither this nor that, it is some "third thing."

Paul's theological arguments with respect to circumcision have their own internal logic and situation: that, in the case of Abraham, it was posterior to faith (Rom. 4:9–12); that spiritual things are superior to physical things (Col. 3:11–14); that the Christian is the "true circumcision" as opposed to the Jew (Phil.3:3); that the time is short, and therefore "every man must remain in the state in which he was called," the circumcised and the uncircumcised (1 Cor. 7:18–24). But these appear secondary to the fundamental taxonomic premise, the Christian is a member of a new taxon. The "circumcision party" (Gal. 2:11) fails to perceive this and seeks to enforce the old Jewish taxonomy rather than recognize the new taxon whose characteristic principles of division are described by the key words of Pauline theology, and into which baptism, the new rite of initiation, later called "the circumcision that belongs to Christ" (Col. 2:11b), provides entry.

In contradistinction to the situation faced by Paul in Galatia, the events of 175–167 B.C. raised the possibility of a Jewish "uncircumcision party" (but see 1 Cor. 7:18). One of the few significant mentions of circumcision in that collection of early Jewish writings, unfortunately lumped together by modern editors under the artificial title pseudepigrapha, is the expansion of the P narrative of Gen. 17:9–14 in Jubilees 15:11–34. In Jubilees, the practice is given a cosmic setting. The ordinance to circumcise on the eighth day is "an eternal ordinance [fore]ordained and written on the heavenly tablets" (15:25). The angels of the presence and of the sanctification were created circumcised (15:27). The text concludes with the warning that there will be:

> children of Israel . . . [who] will not circumcise their children according to this law . . . they will omit this circumcision of their sons and all of them . . . will leave their sons uncircumcised as they are born . . . they have treated their genitals as gentiles. [15:33–34]

This post facto prophecy appears to refer to the same event that recurs in the Maccabean literature. In several widely discussed passages, the Maccabean tradition portrays what must be understood as two separate, although related, acts. The first is the reference in 1 Macc. 1:15 to the voluntary action by some Jews, who quite clearly perceive themselves to have remained Jews, perhaps even as being superior Jews, in removing the mark of circumcision. For this group, epispasm was a part of a positive political and religious program which required this taxonomic marker to be abandoned.[29]

The second act is portrayed, by the Maccabean tradition, as being at the initiative of Antiochus IV. In a decree, he forbade the practice of infant circumcision (1 Macc. 1:48, 60–61; 2 Macc. 6:10, cf. Josephus, *Ant.* 12.254).

There appear to be two borderline classes: the first, a group of Jews who considered themselves to be Jews who voluntarily reversed circumcision; the second, a group of Jews who were forced to leave their children uncircumcised. It may be that these two groups were the same, that the hellenistic reform party might voluntarily reverse their own circumcision as adults and leave their children uncircumcised when newly born. This understanding seems required by the difficult passage in 1 Macc. 2:46–47, that Mattathias and his companions "*forcibly* circumcised all the uncircumcised babies they found within the borders of Israel and drove out the men of arrogance" who "fled to the gentiles" (2:44b). Against whose objections was force necessary? The context precludes the Syrians. The opponents in the passage are all Jews whether they be labeled "sinners," "lawless men," or "men of arrogance." It would appear that, by forcible circumcision, the children of the reform party were reclaimed to one definition of the taxon Jew; the adults of the reform party were expelled from the taxon and forced to flee "to the gentiles," forever barred from reentry.[30] Whatever the understanding, the actions of the reform party are of importance to the taxonomist of early Judaism. It was possible for a group of Jews to define themselves as Jews without circumcision.

Josephus, although closely dependent upon Maccabean tradition in his account of the events of 175–167 B.C. is more complex in the range of instances and interpretations of circumcision that he displays.[31] Here, I can provide only a bald summary of the six, quite different sorts of statements that he makes. (1) Jews are circumcised as a part of their "ancestral ways" which are constitutive of being a Jew (e.g., *Ant.* 1.192, 214). (2) Jews remain classified as Jews if they are circumcised, regardless of their adherence to other "ancestral ways" (e.g., *Ant.* 20.200). (3) One may be considered a Jew, or a "half Jew," if one is forcibly circumcised (*Ant.* 14.403 and elsewhere), but no one ought to be forcibly circumcised (*Vita* 113). (4) A convert to Judaism need not be circumcised, but may elect to (*Ant.* 20.41, 46). (5) Egyptians and others are circumcised. Circumcision is not definitive of the taxon Jew (*Ant.* 1.214; *C. Apion* 2.14). (6) Circumcision can occur for strictly medical reasons (for example, in the case of an ulcer of the penis) with neither religious nor ethnic significance (*C. Apion* 2.14).

Josephus states, on two occasions, that he will treat the reasons for circumcision more extensively in a later work. Perhaps the reference is to *Customs and Causes,* which is alluded to throughout *Antiquities,* but appears never to have been written. If it had, it would probably have closely resembled Philo's treatment of the subject in which the fifth and sixth understandings of circumcision in Josephus appear surprisingly dominant.

Philo, writing in Egypt, where circumcision remained an elaborate and officially sanctioned procedure for male members of Egyptian priestly families well into the second century,[32] might be supposed to be the one who would be most concerned with taxic understanding of circumcision and a desire to differentiate Egyptian from Jewish praxis. Not in the least! He appears to be preoccupied with refuting the charge by unidentified antagonists that the practice is foolish. In answering this charge, he deliberately disturbs the careful order of his treatise *Special Laws* in order to insert a preface dealing with circumcision. He offers three arguments of his own. The first, and most extensive, is an appeal to the Egyptian precedent. They are "a race regarded as preeminent for . . . its antiquity and its dedication to philosophy" (*Spec. Leg.* 1.2–3)—a unique passage in the Philonic corpus for its praise of Egypt in terms usually reserved for Israel. Therefore, Philo's argument runs, if the Egyptians circumcise, the Jewish practice is legitimated. It cannot, if Egyptian, be foolish. The second and third arguments are extremely compressed allegories to the effect that the removal of the foreskin is symbolic of the excision of pleasure or conceit.

What is of more interest is that the bulk of the preface to *Special Laws* is an anthology of the defenses made by his predecessors at Alexandria, "from the ancient studies of divinely gifted men who made deep researches into the writings of Moses" (*Spec. Leg.* 1.8). Four reasons are given. Circumcision prevents an ulcerated penis. It promotes cleanliness; indeed the Egyptians go farther and shave the pubic hair as well. It increases fertility by enabling the semen to travel in a straight line. Finally, and of a different order, the genitals are related, symbolically, to the heart and an allegory is constructed which alludes to the phrase "circumcised heart" as it appears in Scripture (Deut. 10:16 and 30:6; Jer. 4:4 as well as the phrase "uncircumcised heart" in Lev. 26:41 cited in his extensive commentary on Gen. 17 in *Quest. in Gen.* 3.46–47). Philo rejects none of these reasons, although each appears dependent upon exegetical traditions that he criticizes elsewhere. Neither in *Special Laws* nor in the more extensive parallel passage in *Questions in Genesis* 3.46–52 is there any taxonomic interpretation. For Philo, the practice seems to have little to do with either ethnic or religious identity. Circumcision is understood as practiced by intelligent peoples for hygienic reasons.

Although other passages can be added from other strata of early Jewish literature, they will not alter the conclusions that can be drawn from this brief survey. The wide range of uses and interpretations of circumcision as a taxic indicator in early Judaism suggests that, even with respect to this most fundamental division, we cannot sustain the impossible construct of a normative Judaism. We must conceive of a variety of early Judaisms, clustered in varying configurations.[33]

As the second operation, I have adopted the stratagem of describing systems of Jewish identity as gleaned from a set of funerary inscriptions. This body of data was chosen for several reasons. It is possible to gain a significant sample from widely scattered locales. There is an excellent body of scholarship on these remains. Of greater importance to the mapping enterprise is the fact that funerary inscriptions, by their very nature, are labels. They not only identify the name of the deceased, but also how the individual, or his relatives, wished to have him remembered. It is the only major collection of sources from early Judaism that is rarely argumentative or proscriptive. For all of their stylized elements, I have more confidence in the concreteness of the communities and personalities that lie behind these inscriptions than I could have in most of the other literary remains.[34]

For the present experiment, I have chosen three collections: a group of 584 inscriptions from Rome,[35] 318 inscriptions from Beth She'arim in Galilee,[36] and 92 inscriptions from Egypt.[37] This yields a total collection of 944 inscriptions, more than three-quarters of which are in Greek. The vast majority of names in all three groups, the most fundamental form of self-identification, are of Greek or Latin derivation.

Taking the total collection of 944 inscriptions, and noting only *explicit* taxic indicators, the following distribution occurs:

> 111 inscriptions identify the deceased by one or more of fourteen titles, each designating an office in the synagogue.
> 26 name the synagogue of which the deceased was a member.
> 25 call the deceased "pious."
> 23 name the individual as a rabbi (restricted to Beth She'arim).
> 11 make mention of priestly descent.
> 11 refer to the deity.
> 11 refer to the Law.
> 9 term the deceased a "Hebrew."
> 7 term the deceased a "Jew."
> 1 terms the deceased an "Israelite."
> 1 makes reference to "Judaism."

In addition, a number of unique descriptions occur, for example, "lover of his people" (*CIJ* 203), "lover of truth" (*CIJ* 481), "one who plucked the fruits of *sophia*" (*BS* 127).

As E. R. Goodenough, in his *Jewish Symbols in the Greco-Roman Period,* has led us to expect, the iconography found on these inscriptions exhibits an extremely limited vocabulary.

> 111 instances of a menorah.
> 41 instances of a lulab.
> 30 instances of an ethrog.
> 27 instances of a "flask" (restricted to Rome).
> 18 instances of a shofar.
> 6 representations of the Ark (restricted to Rome).

While there is little doubt that these various iconographic figures, especially the menorah, functioned as Jewish emblems, as may be demonstrated from Jewish coins, all of these symbols, in contradistinction to other symbols found on coins (e.g., the palm tree), are associated with the Temple or synagogue cult. If these be added to the preponderance of textual references to the synagogue in the inscriptions (12 percent of the total collection), the most basic self-identification of these Jews is in terms of relationship to and membership in the synagogue. I know of no other body of early Jewish evidence that would yield such a configuration.

If one were to use this collection of inscriptions as an index of characteristics, the two most frequent are the use of Greek and identification with the synagogue. But if the data were to be separated out by provenance and scaled by these two characteristics, they would cluster quite differently. All three areas would score high on the use of Greek—70 percent of the inscriptions from Rome, 60 percent from Beth She'arim, 97 percent from Egypt. If the areas were further subdivided by catacomb or family, another set of clusters would emerge. For example, at Beth She'arim catacombs 6, 8, and 20 are predominantly Semitic as opposed to catacombs 1–4, 7, and 11, which are largely Greek. In Rome, the catacombs at Appia and Monteverde appear most Romanized; the catacombs at Nomentana, least. In Rome, some 54 percent of the inscriptions are related to the synagogue; Beth She'arim has few such inscriptions; Egypt, none. In Beth She'arim, the title *rabbi* recurs with some frequency; it is absent from the other two areas. All three collections praise "piety." Rome and Beth She'arim make mention of priestly descent for both males and females; no such reference occurs in Egypt. There are few references to the deity in any of the collections. Both the Law and the self-designation Jew occur in Rome and Beth She'arim. Egypt appears to have neither distinctive Jewish titles nor institutions.

The most common epithet is "pious" (*hosios* or *ḥsyd*). It occurs most frequently as a virtuous attribute of the deceased (*CIJ* 1, 72, 93, 100, 103, 111, 145, 154, 158, 321, 363; *BS* 34, 35, 38, 157, 158, 163, 193). At times it occurs in conjunction with, or is apparently synonymous with, a set of closely related terms such as righteous (*dikeōn* or *ṣdyq, CIJ* 78, 110, 118, 150, 193, 201, 321, 363; *BSa* 25, 26), irreproachable (*amemptos, CIJ* 100, 154, 193), and, perhaps, "holy ones" (*hqdwšym, BSa* 17), as well as with terms suggesting innocence and purity (e.g., *CIJ* 233, *filiae sanctissimae;* 466, *anima innox*; cf. 210, *anima bona*). Four times, only at Beth She'arim, it appears as an element in a titular name (Rabbi N, the Pious—*BS* 41, 43, 44, 126). Twice it appears to be an individual's name (*BS* 157; *CPJ* 1536). There is also the collective use in the formula, "with the righteous, his sleep" (*CIJ* 55, 340).

The problem confronting the interpreter of these inscriptions is what meaning to assign to these designations. There are several excellent studies of both the Hebrew and Greek words for piety,[38] but none take the epigraphic evidence into account. The only brief study with which I am familiar, the few pages in Saul Lieberman's *Greek in Jewish Palestine,* concludes on an ironic note, "the epithet [pious] was readily and easily conferred on a person who more or less deserved it."[39]

It was an epigraphic convention, as would be expected, throughout the Greek and Roman world to enumerate the virtues of the deceased. Piety appears prominently in such lists. Some laudations were bare catalogs; others wove the elements into a rich, usually domestic, narrative description.[40] In light of this convention, but mindful of the synagogal context of the majority of the Jewish inscriptions, it is tempting to interpret the epithet as piety in relation to the Law, Jewish practice, and the synagogue. In its nominal forms, I do not doubt that such a case might be made. Likewise, in the very few instances where the content of the piety is made explicit, such as the Roman inscription, "pious observor of the Law" (*CIJ* 72). But other cases will not fit such an understanding. For example, among the Roman inscriptions which give the individual's age at the time of death, three have the epithet "pious" for young children. One, a boy, lived only two years, two months, and five days (*CIJ* 1). What might piety mean here? In other instances, "pious" seems interchangeable with other virtues such as "sweet" (*CIJ* 1, 84, 96, 119, 126, 141, 155, 169, 222, 225, 267, 273, 457) or with the unique Egyptian epithet, *chrēstē* which recurs forty-four times.[41] It does not seem possible to give further content to the term on the basis of the available evidence. The matter deserves further research.

The survey of the inscriptional materials may be concluded with some brief observations on the most explicit taxic indicators, the use of the terms "Hebrew," "Jew," and "Israelite." "Hebrew" does not occur in the Egyptian or Beth She'arim inscriptions. It is found as a self-designation five times on Roman Jewish inscriptions, in each case for a male (*CIJ* 354, 370, 379, 502, 505) and four times in the title, "Synagogue of the Hebrews" (*CIJ* 291, 317, 510, 535). Although there has been much discussion of this designation in the scholarly literature, I would suggest that *CIJ* 370, "Macedonius, the Hebrew, a Caesarean of Palestine," delimits the term. "Hebrew" is not a linguistic designation, but rather an ethnogeographical one. It indicates that the individual's place of birth was in Syro-Palestine from which he emigrated to Rome.[42]

The term, "Jew," occurs six times in the Roman inscriptions (*CIJ* 21, 41, 68, 202, 250, 296, and possibly 367 as well), and once from Beth She'arim (*BS* 158): four times on women's tombs, three times on proselytes'. To this list, the Roman inscription of the daughter of Menophilus should be added, "she lived a good life in Judaism" (*CIJ* 537). In none of these is there a suggestion of the older ethnogeographical sense of Judaean. The term is entirely reserved for the religious sphere into which one can be born and to which one can convert. There is a unique compound formula on one of the Roman inscriptions, "Irene, foster child, proselyte, her father and mother Jewish, an Israelite, lived three years, seven months, and one day" (*CIJ* 21). "Jew" in this text would appear to refer to the foster parents' status as birthright Jews. What meaning "Israelite" has for a proselyte cannot be determined, in part because this is the only occurrence of the designation in the entire corpus. "Israel" occurs several times, although never as a designation (e.g., *CIJ* 349, 526 as well as the formula *šlwm ʿl yśr'l*).

The data considered in this survey are skewed to some degree by the nature and conventions of sepulchral inscriptions, by socioeconomic factors of who gets buried, by whom and in what manner, and by the accidents of preservation and discovery. But this ought not to be allowed to become an excuse for jettisoning these materials. The same limitations obtain for every other form of evidence for early Judaism.

The picture that has emerged is not neat, and there remain specific problems of interpretation. Nevertheless, it has been possible to rough out a preliminary map, a set of characteristics centered largely on the synagogue which may be used as one cluster toward the eventual poly-thetic classification of Judaism. What has animated these reflections and explorations is the conviction that students of religion need to abandon the notion of "essence," of a unique differentium for early Judaism as well as the socially impossible correlative of a community constituted by a systematic set of beliefs. The cartography appears far messier. We need to map the variety of Judaisms, each of which appears as a shifting cluster of characteristics which vary over time.

As the anthropologist has begun to abandon a functionalist view of culture as a well-articulated, highly integrated mechanism and has slowly turned to accepting the sort of image set forth by F. E. Williams of culture as a "heap of rubbish," a "tangle," a "hotch-potch,"[43] only partially organized, so we in religious studies must set about an analogous dismantling of the old theological and imperialistic impulses toward totalization, unification, and integration. The labor at achieving the goal of a polythetic classification of Judaisms, rather than a monothetic definition of early Judaism, is but a preliminary step toward this end.

2 *In Comparison a Magic Dwells*

If I read a myth, select certain elements from it, and arrange them in a pattern, that "structure" is bound to be in the material unless I have misread the text or demonstrably misrendered it. The fact of its being there does not, however, indicate that my arrangement is anything more than my personal whim. . . . A myth is therefore bound to have a number of possible "structures" that are both in the material and in the eye of the beholder. The problem is to decide between them and to determine the significance of any of them.
David Maybury-Lewis

We stand at a quite self-conscious moment in the history of the study of Judaism. There are a variety of ways of articulating this self-consciousness, perhaps the most relevant formulation being our awareness that our scholarly inquiries find their setting (indeed, their legitimacy) within the academy. This provides not only the context for our endeavors, but their raison d'être. This is to say, no matter how intrinsically interesting and worthwhile the study of the complex histories and varieties of the several Judaisms may be, they gain academic significance primarily by their capacity to illuminate the work of other scholars of other religious traditions, and by the concomitant desire of students of Judaism to be illuminated by the labors of these other scholars. Judaism, for the academy, serves as exempli gratia. In the words of Jacob Neusner:

> I believe that section meetings in the history of Judaism [at the American Academy of Religion] should be so planned as to interest scholars in diverse areas of religious studies. If these [section] meetings do not win the attention and participation of a fair cross section of scholars in the field as a whole, then they will not materially contribute to the study of religion in this country. There is no reason for the study of

Judaism to be treated as a set of special cases and of matters so technical that only initiates can follow discussions—or would even want to.

This, I would submit, is a new voice and a new confidence. It is that of the study of Judaism come of age!

To accomplish such an agendum, it is axiomatic that careful attention must be given to matters of description and comparison—even more, that description be framed in light of comparative interests in such a way as to further comparison.

I

For a student of religion such as myself to accept willingly the designation "historian of religion" is to submit to a lifelong sentence of ambiguity. I cannot think of two more difficult terms than "history" and "religion." Their conjunction, as may be witnessed by every programmatic statement from this putative discipline that I am familiar with, serves only to further the confusion. It is necessary to stress this at the outset. If Judaism may assert no special privilege, neither can the historian of religion. The reflections embodied in this essay make no claim to be the result of clear vision from the "head of Pisgah." It is not the case that there is a model "out there" that needs only to be applied to the study of Judaism. There is no consensual format into which the scholar of Judaism needs only to feed his data. To the contrary, I intend this essay to be an exercise in collaboration. We need to think together about the issues presented to us by the assignment to be attentive to description and comparison. For me, this implies some attempt to map out the options in order to clarify what is at issue. The issues might as well be discussed in terms of Judaism.

I take my point of departure from the observation that each scholar of religion, in his way, is concerned with phenomena that are historical in the simple, grammatical sense of the term, that is to say, with events and expressions from the past, reconceived vividly. The scholar of religion is, therefore, concerned with dimensions of memory and remembrance— whether they be the collective labor of society or the work of the individual historian's craft.

The earliest full theory of memory (setting aside the Platonic notion of *anamnesis*) is in Aristotle's *De memoria et reminiscentia* 451b which describes memory as an experience of "something either similar or contrary to what we seek or else from that which is contiguous to it." Within discourse on memory, this triad remains more or less intact through a succession of writers as distinct in character but as similar in excellence as Augustine (*Confessions* 10.19) and Samuel Taylor Coleridge (*Biographia Literaria,* chap. 5–7). In the complex literature on mnemotechnics, it led to the elaborate Late Antique through Renaissance handbooks on visualization and *topoi*,[1] while, shorn of its specific context in memory, it was developed into the notion of the Laws of Association which so preoccupied the philosophical generations of Locke, Berkeley, Hume, Hartley, and Mill, receiving its definitive history in the famous appendix, "Note D**," in William Hamilton's edition of the *Works* of Thomas Reid.

As many will recognize, the formulation of the Laws of Association has played a seminal role in the development of theory in the study of religion. E. B. Tylor, in his first comparative work, *Researches into the Early History of Mankind* (first edition, 1865), postulated that a "principle of association" supplied the underlying logic for magical praxis: "any association of ideas in a man's mind, the vaguest similarity of form or position, even a mere coincidence in time, is sufficient to enable the magician to work from association in his own mind, to association in the material world."[2] J. G. Frazer, building explicitly on Tylor, developed a typology of magic:

> If my analysis of the magician's logic is correct, its two great principles turn out to be merely two different misapplications of the association of ideas. Homoeopathic magic is founded on the association of ideas by similarity; contagious magic is founded on the association of ideas by contiguity.

And Frazer repeats Tylor's charge that magic is a confusion of a subjective relationship with an objective one. Where this confusion is not present, the Laws of Association "yield science; illegitimately applied they yield magic."[3]

It requires but a small leap to relate these considerations of the Laws of Association in memory and magic to the enterprise of comparison in the human sciences.[4] For, as practiced by scholarship, *comparison has been chiefly an affair of the recollection of similarity. The chief explanation for the significance of comparison has been contiguity.* The procedure is homeopathic. The theory is built on contagion. The issue of difference has been all but forgotten.

Regardless of the individual scholar's theoretical framework, regardless of the necessary fiction of the scientific mode of presentation, most comparison has not been the result of discovery. Borrowing Edmundo O'Gorman's historiographic distinction between discovery as the finding of something one has set out to look for and invention as the subsequent realization of novelty one has not intended to find, we must label comparison an invention.[5] In no literature on comparison that I am familiar with has there been any presentation of rules for the production of comparisons; what few rules have been proposed pertain to their post facto evaluation.

Perhaps this is the case because, for the most part, the scholar has not set out to make comparisons. Indeed, he has been most frequently attracted to a particular datum by a sense of its uniqueness. But often, at some point along the way, as if unbidden, as a sort of déjà vu, the scholar remembers that he has seen "it" or "something like it" before; he experiences what Coleridge described in an early essay in *The Friend* as the result of "the hooks-and-eyes of the memory."[6] This experience, this unintended consequence of research, must then be accorded significance and provided with an explanation. In the vast majority of instances in the history of comparison, this subjective experience is projected as an objective connection through some theory of influence, diffusion, borrowing, or the like. It is a process of working from a psychological association to an historical one; it is to assert that similarity and contiguity have causal effect. But this, to revert to the language of Victorian anthropology, is not science but magic. To quote from a masterful study of this issue from a representative of one of the more lively and unembarrassed of the comparative disciplines, comparative literature:

> When we say that *A* has influenced *B,* we mean that after . . . analysis we can discern a number of significant similarities between the works of *A* and *B*. . . . So far we have established no influence; we have only documented what I call affinity. For influence presupposes some manner of causality.[7]

We are left with a dilemma that can be stated in stark form: *is comparison an enterprise of magic or science?* Thus far, comparison appears to be more a matter of memory than a project for inquiry; it is more impressionistic than methodical. It depends on what Henri Bergson, in his study of memory, termed:

> an intermediate knowledge, [derived] from a confused sense of the *striking quality* or resemblance: this sense [is] equally remote from generality fully conceived and from individuality clearly perceived.[8]

This may be tested against a review of the major modes of comparison.

In an essay written some years ago (and rather sarcastically entitled, to translate the tag from Horace, "When you add a little to a little, the result will be a great heap"), I tried to map out a paradigm for comparison, based on a survey of some 2500 years of the literature of anthropological comparison.[9] Four basic modes or styles of comparison were isolated: the ethnographic, the encyclopaedic, the morphological, and the evolutionary.

The *ethnographic* is based essentially on travelers' impressions. Something "other" has been encountered and perceived as surprising either in its similarity or dissimilarity to what is familiar "back home." Features are compared which strike the eye of the traveler; comparison functions primarily as a means for overcoming strangeness. As such, ethnographic comparisons are frequently idiosyncratic, depending on intuition, a chance association, or the knowledge one happens to have. There is nothing systematic in such comparisons, they lack any basis, and so, in the end, they strike us as uninteresting, petty, and unrevealing. In Lévi-Strauss's critique of Malinowski, such comparison loses "the means of distinguishing between the general truths to which it aspires and the trivialities with which it must be satisfied."[10]

The *encyclopaedic* tradition was not limited by the external circumstances of travel or contact. Rather than presenting items from a single culture that had been encountered by the author, as the ethnographic mode characteristically did, the encyclopaedic style offered a topical arrangement of cross-cultural material culled, most usually, from reading. The data are seldom either explicitly compared or explained. They simply cohabit within some category, inviting comparison by their coexistence, but providing no clues as to how this comparison might be undertaken. The encyclopaedic mode consists of contextless lists held together by mere surface associations in which the overwhelming sense is that of the exotic. Malinowski's description remains apt when he wrote of "the piece-meal items of information, of customs, beliefs and rules of conduct floating in the air" joined together in "lengthy litanies of threaded statement which make us anthropologists feel silly and the savage look ridiculous."[11]

The *morphological* approach is more complex with regard to the theoretical assumptions that are entailed (largely derived from Romantic *Naturphilosophie*). For the purposes of this essay, we can largely abstain from a consideration of these matters. Fundamentally, morphology allows the arrangement of individual items in a hierarchical series of increased organization and complexity. It is a logical, formal progression which ignores categories of space (habitat) and time. It has as its necessary presupposition an a priori notion of economy in which there are relatively few "original elements" from which complex systems are generated: the "all-in-all" and the "all-in-every-part." Both internal and external forces operate on these "original elements" to produce variety and differentiation in a manner which allows the morphologist to compare individuals in a morphological series using rubrics such as "representative/aberrant," "progressive/degraded," "synthetic/isolated," "persistent/prophetic," and to compare the individual with the generative "original element" (the archetype), either through direct comparison or as "recapitulation" or "repetition." The discovery of the archetype, as represented in the literature, has a visionary quality; it appears to be the result of a sudden, intuitive leap to simplicity. Characteristic of morphological presentations will be a dated account of the vision—Goethe gazing at a palmetto while strolling in an Italian botanical garden on 17 April 1787; Lorenz Oken accidentally stumbling over a deer's skull while walking in the Harz Forest in the spring of 1806. Nevertheless, in both the biological and the human sciences, morphology has produced major comparisons that have stood the test of time.

The *evolutionary* approach, which factors in the dynamics of change and persistence over time in response to adaptation to a given environment, has produced useful theory and comparisons in the biological sciences. I know of nothing in principle that would prevent fruitful application to the human sciences as well.[12] However, what is usually known as the evolutionary approach within the human sciences, related inextricably to what the late nineteenth century termed "The Comparative Method," is not fruitful, nor does it represent a responsible use of evolutionary theory. Evolution, as represented by the nineteenth- and early twentieth-century practitioners of anthropology and comparative religions, was an illegitimate combination of the morphological, ahistorical approach to comparison and the new temporal framework of the evolutionists. This impossible and contradictory combination allowed the comparativist to draw his data without regard to time or place and, then, locate them in a series from the simplest to the more complex, adding the assumption that the former was chronologically as well as logically prior. While such approaches to cultural materials are still practiced, albeit on a more modest scale, such attempts came quickly under the sort of criticisms leveled by F. Boas:

> Historical inquiry must be considered the critical test that science must require before admitting facts as evidence. By means of it, the comparability of the collected material must be tested and uniformity of processes must be demanded as proof of comparability . . . comparisons [must] be restricted to those phenomena which have been proven to be the effects of the same cause.[13]

I suspect that the majority of my readers would agree with this statement as well as with its concomitant stricture that comparison be limited to cultural artifacts contiguous in space and time—the method of "limited" or "controlled" comparison.[14] Unfortunately, these statements and strictures have also been used as the smug excuse for jettisoning the comparative enterprise and for purging scholarship of all but the most limited comparisons. As the Stranger from Elea reminds us, "A cautious man should above all be on his guard against resemblances; they are a very slippery sort of thing" (*Sophist* 231a).

We stand before a considerable embarrassment. Of the four chief modes of comparison in the human sciences, two, the ethnographic and the encyclopaedic, are in principle inadequate as comparative activities, although both have other important and legitimate functions. The evolutionary would be capable in principle of being formulated in a satisfactory manner, but I know of no instances of its thorough application to cultural phenomena. What is often understood to be the evolutionary method of comparison embodies a deep contradiction which necessitates its abandonment. This leaves only the morphological, carried over with marked success from the biological to the cultural by O. Spengler, and which has a massive exemplar in religious studies in the work of M. Eliade, whose endeavor is thoroughly morphological in both presuppositions and technical vocabulary, even though, in specific instances, its principles of comparison remain unnecessarily obscure. Yet, few students of religion would be attracted by this alternative. Because of the Romantic, Neoplatonic Idealism of its philosophical presuppositions, because for methodologically rigorous and internally defensible reasons, it is designed to exclude the historical. The only option appears to be no option at all.

In the past two decades, three other proposals have been made: the statistical (especially as embodied in the HRAF model), the structural, and "systematic description and comparison."

The statistical methods proposed are, without doubt, essential for evaluating comparisons in any mode, but they provide little, in themselves, by way of rules for the generation of comparisons. The only programmatic proposition, the HRAF project, is essentially a refinement of the encyclopaedic mode and is subject, with appropriate qualifications, to the strictures recited above.[15] However, the various discussions generated by this approach have yielded, as an urgent item on any comparativist's agenda, the question of the isolation of a unit for comparison with an invariant frame of reference. At present, the answers are too easily divided into those that resemble the ethnographic and those that resemble the encyclopaedic.

Structuralist comparison is more complex, and I shall be exceedingly brusque lest I distract from my theme. In terms of the descriptions presented above, I would classify structuralism as a subset of morphology, although with Marxist rather than Idealist presuppositions. The formal, comparative procedures of structural analysis appear to me to be identical with those in morphology. While I welcome the shift to Marx, who seems to me to be the necessary base for any responsible anthropological approach to culture, I do not find, as yet, that the structuralist program has come to clarity on the historical. To the degree that it is comparative, it falls prey to the strictures on morphology already presented; to the degree that it has been interestingly historical (e.g., M. Foucault), the comparative has been largely eschewed.

This leaves the proposal for systematic description and comparison which will be the subject of the third portion of this essay. To anticipate, although this is the least developed of the recent proposals, it is my suspicion that this may be but an elegant form of the ethnographic to the degree that the descriptive is emphasized, and the comparisons thus far proposed remain contiguous.

The new proposals have not allowed us to escape our dilemma. Each appears to be but a variant of one of the four modes of comparison. The embarrassment remains. The only mode to survive scrutiny, the morphological, is the one which is most offensive to us by its refusal to support a thoroughly historical method and a set of theoretical presuppositions which grant sufficient gravity to the historical encapsulation of culture. Therefore, I turn briefly to a consideration of an historical proposal from within the morphological mode.

II

Perhaps the most difficult literature from the past history of the human sciences for the modern reader to appreciate is the vast library that might be assembled on the hoary question of diffusion versus parallel or independent invention. It is a matter which has preoccupied comparativists from Herodotus to the present, and it is one of the few places where the validity of comparative evidence has been explicitly and continuously debated. From the perspective of our endeavor, this debate becomes of interest to the degree that it can be seen as a tension between a concession to the centrality of historical processes over against ahistorical constructs such as the "psychic unity of mankind."

It is to be regretted that much of this debate is so arid. Where there has been color and interest, it is usually the product of a long line of distinguished monomaniacs from G. Elliot Smith and W. J. Perry through Thor Heyerdahl. But there is one group among this number that I would want to argue deserves further attention, not so much for accomplishment as for endeavor. I refer to the Pan-Babylonian school, whose name is sufficient to drive usually calm scholars to a frenzy of vituperation. "Pan-babylonianism!—the word awakens the idea of an extreme generalization . . . of fantastic audacities."[16] From our perspective, their prime "audacity" was the daring attempt to historicize morphology from within.

To put the matter as succinctly as possible, what the Pan-Babylonian school introduced was the notion of a total system, to use their favorite word, a *Weltanschauung*. The importance of this cannot be overstated. Culture was removed from the biological to the realm of human artifact. It is man's intellectual and spiritual creation.[17] Concomitantly, the object of religion, for them the most total expression of "world view," is man's cultural and intellectual world, not the world of nature.[18] It is the inner relationships of the "elements," their system, their internal logic and coherence, that validates a "world view," not conformity to nature. Therefore, the "world view" may be articulated in a rigorously systematic

manner. Hence the "audacity" of the founder of the school, Hugo Winckler:

> I claim to have established a formula which explains every conception
> of Babylonian theology. In mathematics, a formula is a general expres-
> sion for the reciprocal connection of isolated facts, which, when it has
> been stated once for all, explains the phenomenon and settles the ques-
> tion. One may prove the truth of a formula by countless examples,
> illustrate it and show its practical utility, but when once the root prin-
> ciple has been found, there is nothing further to discover.[19]

The school—and in what follows I will summarize the work of Alfred
Jeremias as a typical and eloquent example—takes its departure from the
fact that, while anthropology brings ever new evidence for the contemporary "Stone Age" man (the "savage"), the then newly recovered and
deciphered literature of ancient Near Eastern civilizations reveals a cul-
tured, urban, rational, and spiritual man. Jeremias argued that we find,
"not hordes of barbarians, but an established government under priestly
control" in which "the whole thought and conduct of the people were
governed by a uniform intellectual conception . . . a scientific and, at the
same time, a religious system." This "system" had, as its chief aim, "to
discover and explain the first causes of visible things," these being dis-
cerned as a "microcosmic image of the celestial world."[20]

Jeremias concludes that the evolutionists are factually wrong, for there
is no sign of nature worship and the like in the Near Eastern materials,
no sign of slow development. Of more gravity, the evolutionary approach
failed to account for the "inner unity of the cults"[21] or, when they did,
turned to notions of independent or parallel development based on a
presupposition, which lacks all basis in fact, of the "psycho-mental unity"
of mankind.

Common to both these critiques, is the Pan-Babylonian notion of a
complex, well-integrated, primordial system at the base of culture. The
incremental hypothesis of evolution can be rejected because it cannot
yield this whole, but rather only a series of parts; the thesis of independent
or parallel development can be rejected because it cannot account for
systematic similarity (i.e., it can point only to highly general resemblances
or parallel single motifs, not to their similar formal combination). Hence
the school's preoccupation with diffusion.

> The ancient Oriental conception of the universe entirely precludes the
> possibility of independent origin in different places by the exact rep-
> etition of certain distinctly marked features that only migration and
> diffusion can satisfactorily explain.[22]

In his argument, Jeremias breaks with a set of explanations which have
hitherto characterized most comparative endeavors: single trait compar-

isons which fail to show how they are integrated into similar systems; "mental unity" which yields general similarities but cannot account for agreement of details or structures; borrowing, which will not allow the "specific character" of a nation to be expressed. He does so by postulating a rich model of cultural tradition that has three levels: (1) that of "world view," which is characterized by "imposing uniformity"; (2) that of "culture complex," the particular *Weltbild* or *Gestalt* of a given people; and (3) the linguistic manifestation of the interaction of these two. It is the "world view" which is diffused, modified by a particular "culture complex" and linguistically particularized in a text with its own quite specific context.

To put this model in a more contemporary translation. The "world view" is expressed by the unconscious syntactics of intellectual thought when applied to first principles. The "culture complex" provides the semantics—in Jeremias's view, a lexicon self-consciously transmitted by elites. The particular text is pragmatics, an individual expression reflecting, both consciously and unconsciously, the conjunction of syntax and semantics within a personal and historical environment. Or, to translate into yet more recent terminology, the "world view" is the unconscious deep structure, the "culture complex" is *langue,* the text is *parole*.

While the details of the various interpretations and patterns generated by this approach are fascinating, especially as many of them have been taken over in wholesale fashion, without acknowledgment, in the works of subsequent historians of religion, I give only one concrete example of their most imitated pattern.

Given the basic law of correspondence between the celestial world and the terrestrial, Jeremias postulates two ideal types which he designates the "Babylonian" and the "Canaanite" (he insists that the names be written with sanitary pips). The "Babylonian" is "original," it is a "purely astronomical theory," a cosmological pattern, which maintains the general correspondence of microcosm/macrocosm and traces world history as a cycle leading from chaos to creation to redemption by a savior sent by the creative deity to overcome the forces of chaos. The "Canaanite" is a secondary, "corrupt" system. (Corruption is a technical term in morphology). Here a seasonal, naturalistic interpretation has been given to the "Babylonian" cosmic cycle: the god of sun and spring who, after his victory over winter, built (or rebuilt) the world and took charge of its destiny. These two patterns, representing dual aspects of a "single, intellectual system," "spread throughout the world and, exerting a different intellectual influence over every civilization according to the peculiar character of each, developed many new forms." But each remains based on "die gleichen Grundlagen des Geisteslebens."[23]

Of course, the Pan-Babylonian school was wrong. At the factual level, its exponents placed too great a reliance on the high antiquity of Near Eastern astrological texts, dating them almost two thousand years too early. On the theoretical level, they placed too great a reliance on diffusion. Yet, in many ways they were right. They saw clearly the need to ground comparison and patterns in a historical process, saw clearly the need to develop a complex model of tradition and the mechanisms for its transmission, saw clearly the need to balance generalities and particularities in a structure which integrated both, saw clearly the priority of comparative systematics over the continued cataloging of isolated comparative exempla, saw clearly the power of pattern (and hence, of comparison) as a device for interpretation. They bequeathed to us this rich heritage of possibilities—and they bequeathed to us the problems as well. The two chief options followed by students of religion since then have has been either to continue its diffusionist program shorn of its systematic and theoretical depth (e.g., the Myth-Ritual school) or to cut loose the pattern and the systematics from history (e.g., Eliade). We have yet to develop the responsible alternative: the integration of a complex notion of pattern and system with an equally complex notion of history.

As will be detected, with my evocation of the ghost of the Pan-Babylonian school, I have been slowly moving closer to the matter of systematics and to the particularized portion of this essay, that of description and comparison in the history of Judaism. Not that the preceding has been remote. For example, I know of no idea so influential on biblical scholars, students of Judaism and of religion than the groundless distinction, first generated by the Pan-Babylonian school, between cyclical and linear time, the former associated by them with the Near East and myth, the latter, with Israel and history.[24]

III

It is most likely an accident, but it is also a fact, that three of the most distinguished, creative, native-born American historians of religion should have devoted substantial portions of their academic careers to undertaking systematic descriptions and comparisons of early Judaism: George F. Moore, Erwin R. Goodenough, and Jacob Neusner.

It is the task of the third part of this essay to review their work from the limited perspective of the considerations on comparison already advanced.

Considering its date of publication (1927) in the midst of the controversies over the *Religionsgeschichtliche Schule* and his own considerable comparative labors as the holder of one of the first endowed chairs in history of religions in this country, George Foot Moore's *Judaism in the First Centuries of the Christian Era: The Age of the Tannaim* is remark-

ably, in fact deliberately, free from explicit comparisons. Indeed, one of
Moore's central theses (against Bousset and other members of the
school)[25] is that Judaism is incomparable as a religious system. An examination of his work with an eye toward comparison reveals a consistent
pattern. (1) "Normative Judaism" is autochthonous. Any comparisons
which imply significant borrowing are to be denied.[26] (2) Therefore, the
largest class of comparisons to normative Judaism are negative. They are
used to assert the difference, the incomparability of the tradition.[27] (3)
The second largest group of comparisons are internal, to other forms of
Judaism: the biblical, the Alexandrian or hellenistic, the Samaritan. These
comparisons are occasionally used to measure the distance from the normative, but are more usually employed to assert the overall unity of the
system.[28] (4) Where non-Jewish parallels can be adduced, where borrowing may be proposed, is always in the area of "nonnormative" Judaism,
in those materials "ignored" or rejected by the normative tradition.
Hence, the greatest concentration of comparisons will be found in the
seventh part of Moore's work, devoted to "the hereafter," which focused
on apocalyptic and pseudepigraphic literature.[29] In other rare instances,
when borrowing or imitation is postulated, Moore emphasizes that it occurs in "late" post-Tannaitic texts, materials presumably "leaking" out
from under control.[30] (5) A final class of comparisons may be called pedagogic. These result from Moore's presumption that he is writing for a
largely Christian audience. Thus, while he is usually at pains to deny
Jewish precedents for Christian doctrine (especially those associated with
elements in Roman Catholic dogma),[31] he is prepared to offer analogies
to Protestant religious doctrines, presumably to help his reader understand.[32]

I can find only two interesting theoretical statements on comparison
within the three volumes of *Judaism*. Both raise the question of the systematic, although in quite different ways. The first is the last paragraph
of the work, the conclusion of the section on the nonnormative "hereafter":

> Borrowings in religion, however, at least in the field of ideas [in a note
> Moore writes, "the adoption of foreign rites and the adaptation of
> myths are another matter"] are usually in the nature of the appropri-
> ation of things in the possession of another which the borrower rec-
> ognizes in all good faith as belonging to himself, ideas which, when
> once they become known to him, are seen to be the necessary impli-
> cations or compliments of his own . . . [for example] the Persian scheme
> must have been most strongly commended by the fact that it seemed
> to be the logical culmination of conceptions of retribution which were
> deeply rooted in Judaism itself.[33]

While I do not quarrel necessarily with the notion in this passage (it reminds me of the exciting work of scholars such as Robin Horton),[34] Moore nowhere clarifies the meaning of terms such as "necessary implication" or "logical culmination," which hint at a generative, systematic logic. Rather, one feels when reading this paragraph as if one is in the presence of that remarkable figure in Borges's narrative, "Pierre Menard, Author of Don Quixote," who labored for years to produce a manuscript which repeated, word-for-word, Cervantes's masterpiece.[35] Jews did not borrow, for what they "borrowed" turned out to be already their own.

The second passage is the closest Moore comes to the articulation of an indigenous system—alas, it concerns the Levitical Code and not Tannaitic materials:

> They were ancient customs, the origin and reason of which had long since been forgotten. Some of them are found among other Semites, or more widely; some were, so far as we know, peculiar to Israel; but *as a whole, or, we may say as a system,* they were distinctive customs which the Jews had inherited from their ancestors with a religious sanction in the two categories of holy and polluted. Other peoples had their own [systems] . . . and *these systems also were distinctive.*[36]

But the thought remains undeveloped. We are left with only the atomism: each religion has one or more systems; they are each distinctive; they are each incomparable.

Neither of these statements is developed further in Moore. They remain as hints of the possibility of describing systems with generative logics of their own.

What Moore did accomplish in *Judaism* in an explicit fashion requires no rehearsal. Despite his statement that he has "avoided imposing on the matter a systematic disposition which is foreign to it and to the Jewish thought of the times,"[37] Moore applied to the Tannaitic documents a traditional Christian dogmatic outline ("Revealed Religion," "Idea of God," and the like), arranging his materials in a synthetic sketch in which the discrete items, despite his historical introduction and his catalog of sources, are treated ahistorically without individuality. Moore's *Judaism,* although confined to a single tradition, is clearly in the encyclopaedic mode. What he produced, in a most elegant and thoughtful form, was, essentially, an expanded chapter on Judaism from his two-volume textbook, *History of Religions.*[38] The suppressed member of the comparison throughout Moore's work is Protestant Christianity; it is this comparison that provides the categories for description and the occasions for exegesis. But, as it is suppressed, we are left with a dogmatic formulation of incomparability and an equally dogmatic description. Moore's work is unfortunately typical of most Jewish and Christian handbooks on Judaism.

It is the supreme achievement of this genre, but it provides no model for our inquiry.

The work of Erwin R. Goodenough richly deserves a monograph that has yet to be written. From our limited perspective, he presents himself as, perhaps, the most interesting single author. For, unlike Moore, from whom he self-consciously distances himself, comparisons abound, between Judaism and other Mediterranean cults, between "hellenistic" and "normative" Judaisms, between iconographic and literary materials. The comparisons are in the service of both a complex (and largely psychological) general theory of religion and of an equally complex historical reconstruction of Judaism. "I have not spent thirty years as a mere collector; I was trying to make a point."[39]

Fortunately for the reader's patience, it is not necessary to produce such a monograph at this time. From the various methodological statements Goodenough issued in the course of his long career, a consistent set of assumptions may be gleaned. He was successful in making his "point"![40] Baldly stated, Goodenough sought to establish several points: (1) Any given symbol (and it was crucial to Goodenough that one was dealing with an exceedingly economical group of symbols) had wide currency in the Mediterranean world; that is to say, it was part of a Mediterranean "lingua franca." The fact of currency could be established by the enumeration of examples drawn from the ancient Near East, Egypt, Greece, Rome, the Iranian empire, and the religious traditions of Judaism and Christianity. (2) The same symbol possessed a "common meaning," and this meaning was singular. He insisted that this meaning could be recovered by the (usually cultic) setting of the iconic symbol, as well as by its occurrence in texts (especially ritual materials). On occasion, a meaning may be explicitly given a symbol in literary materials (here, "theological" statements were given priority). Goodenough also held that symbols were effective primarily through "emotional impact," that they retained this capacity for the modern interpreter as well as for the ancient religionist, and thus could directly "give" their meaning to the modern student "attuned" to their "language." The contemporary scholar "must let the lingua franca speak to him . . . directly. . . . If this be subjectivism, let my critics make the most of it."[41] And so we should! (3) The symbols have been taken over in "living form" from the general milieu by Judaism. (4) They have retained the same "value" in Judaism when borrowed. (5) Although they retain this common "value," they have been subjected to a specifically Jewish "interpretation" (here, Philo and the rabbinic materials have priority). (6) In addition, there are a few specifically Jewish symbols, but these participate in the same general system of value and the same framework of meaning as those symbols which are part of the lingua franca. Around this skeleton, the vast exegetical and comparative labors of Goodenough on text and symbol are articulated.

I would hope that, in this summary, the reader would have anticipated my judgment. Shorn of his idiosyncratic psychologism (itself a powerful ahistorical presupposition), Goodenough's work is a variant of what has been previously described as the attempt to historicize morphology as exemplified by the Pan-Babylonian school. The system of "life" and "mysticism" at the level of the lingua franca functions as an analogue to "world view." Judaism and other national and religious systems which stamp their own peculiar understanding on this "common language" function as analogues to "culture complexes." The particular expressions, be they the writings of Philo or the murals at Dura Europos, function as analogues to the "linguistic" formulations.

I intend no criticism of Goodenough by labeling him a morphologist or by comparing him to the Pan-Babylonian school. He has opted for the most promising, but most unattractive, of the modes of comparison. In the same way that the structuralists have attempted to modernize the presuppositions of morphology by turning to Marx, Goodenough turned to his own understanding of Freud and Jung. This allowed him to affirm a generally ahistoric point of view, while asserting a modified diffusionism in specific instances (as when he described "syncretism" or the "Orphic reform"). However, he stands under the same strictures already articulated for both classical morphology and the Pan-Babylonian variant.

The last proposal to be passed under review is that by Jacob Neusner. While much that he has written is of direct relevance, he has summarized his program in an important essay, "Comparing Judaisms," which is also a review of E. P. Sanders's massive work, *Paul and Palestinian Judaism: A Comparison of Patterns of Religion.*[42]

Neusner takes as his starting point Sanders's introduction, where, after criticizing the frequent comparativist tactic of reducing the various world religions to "essences" which are then compared and the alternative comparativist device of comparing single, isolated motifs between religions, Sanders ventures a proposal for what he terms the "holistic comparison of patterns of religion."[43] This is to be the comparison of:

> an entire religion, parts and all, with an entire religion, parts and all; to use the analogy of a building, to compare two buildings, not leaving out of account their individual bricks. The problem is how to discover two wholes, both of which are considered and defined on their own merits and in their own terms, to be compared with one another. I believe that the concept of a "pattern of religion" makes this possible.[44]

Allowing, for the moment, the language of "entire" and "wholes" to stand unquestioned, and setting aside the difficulty, indeed the impossibility, of comparing two different objects, each "considered" and "defined in their own terms"—a statement which he cannot mean literally, but which he gives no indication as to how he would modify—Sanders compounds confusion by further defining the notion of pattern. It is not a total, historical entity (e.g., Judaism, Christianity, Islam), but "only a given more or less homogenous entity." How much "more," how much "less" is needed to posit homogeneity and, hence, a pattern is left unclear. It is a matter of seeing "how one moves from the logical starting point to the logical conclusion of the religion." But the notion of "logic" is nowhere clarified. Indeed, it seems thrown aside by Sanders's exclusion of what he terms "speculative matters" of methodology and by his strange insistence that the logic is one of "function."[45] Given these restrictions, I am baffled by what "entire religion, parts and all" could possibly mean for Sanders. I find no methodological hints on how such entities are to be discovered, let alone compared. His results give me no grounds for confidence.

It is at this point that Neusner joins the discussion. He affirms the enterprise of comparing "an entire religion, parts and all, with other such *entire* religions"[46] and goes on to state as a prerequisite for such "systematic comparison" (the term Neusner substitutes for Sanders's "holistic comparison") "systematic description." Who could disagree? We must describe what we are comparing before we compare. But much hinges on the meaning of the term "systematic." In Neusner's generous, initial proposal:

> Systematic description must begin with the system to be described. Comparative description follows. And to describe a system, we start with the principal documents. . . . Our task then is to uncover the exegetical processes, the dynamics of the system, through which those documents serve to shape a conception, and to make sense of reality. We must then locate the critical tensions and inner problematic of the system thereby revealed: What is it about?[47]

Here the difficulties begin. Despite the bow to the notion of the social construction of reality, for Neusner, a system is a document, located at a quite specific point in space and time, a system is the generative logic (in Neusner's term, the "agendum") of a quite particular document, its "issues." The more one goes on with Neusner, the more it becomes clear that each important document may well be a system in itself. How, then, is each documentary system to be compared with each other? Let alone, with "an entire religion, parts and all"? I can find no answer to these questions in Neusner. Rather I find an elegant ethnography of Mishnah, and, to some degree, of Tosefta and Sifra. As I have argued above, comparison in such an ethnographic mode is necessarily accidental.

It would appear that Neusner has proposed what might be taken for an effort in historicizing atomism, a proposal for comparing "Judaisms,"[48] an enterprise seen as problematic by Neusner. He appears to eschew wider comparison which he views as that which often "compares nothing and is an exercise in the juxtaposition of incomparables."[49] If this be an exaggeration, and there is much in Neusner's recent writings that suggests that it is, what in method and theory prevent it? We are left with the dilemma shrewdly stated by Wittgenstein:

> But isn't *the same* at least the same? We seem to have an infallible paradigm of identity in the identity of a thing with itself. . . . Then are two things the same when they are what one thing is? And how am I to apply what the one thing shows me to the case of two things?[50]

Wittgenstein's last question remains haunting. It reminds us that comparison is, at base, never identity. Comparison requires the postulation of difference as the grounds of its being interesting (rather than tautological) and a methodical manipulation of difference, a playing across the "gap" in the service of some useful end.

We must conclude this exercise in our own academic history in a most unsatisfactory manner. Each of the modes of comparison has been found problematic. Each new proposal has been found to be a variant of an older mode: Moore, of the encyclopaedic; Goodenough, of the morphological; Neusner, of the ethnographic. We know better how to evaluate comparisons, but we have gained little over our predecessors in either the method for making comparisons or the reasons for its practice. There is nothing easier than the making of patterns; from planaria to babies, it is done with little apparent difficulty. But the "how" and the "why" and, above all, the "so what" remain most refractory. These matters will not be resolved by new or increased data. In many respects, we already have too much. It is a problem to be solved by theories and reasons, of which we have had too little. So we are left with the question, "How am I to apply what the one thing shows me to the case of two things?" The possibility of the study of religion depends on its answer.

3 *Sacred Persistence: Toward a Redescription of Canon*

In 1968, in a pioneering article entitled, "Judaism in the History of Religions," Jacob Neusner argued not only that the issues and methods of history of religions must be applied to Judaism, but also that "the particular, Jewish data might modulate the categories characteristically employed by the historian of religions."[1] That is to say, Neusner laid down a challenge to achieve reciprocity. Judaism should look different when interpreted from the perspective of the history of religions; the history of religions should be altered by the act of interpreting Jewish data. Some modest progress has been made with respect to the first item on Neusner's agenda. There are an increasing number of historians of religion turning their attention to the study of Judaism and other western religious traditions; there are a significant number of scholars working with these materials from other perspectives who are familiar with, and at times employ, the kinds of categories and methods associated with various understandings of the history of religions. But little progress can be reported on Neusner's second item—which is for me, as an historian of religion, by far the most important. The characteristic categories remain more or less intact. The old ones have not been "modulated," new ones have not been proposed. In this essay, I should like to attempt a modest beginning at accepting Neusner's challenge.

I

In the prolonged discussions in recent times on the nature and status of models in the sciences, a most important contribution has been made by Max Black and Mary Hesse with their notion that models bear close structural similarities to metaphors, that both invite us to construe one thing in terms of another (most usually, that which is problematic in terms of that which is relatively better understood) so that we may see things in a new, and frequently unexpected, light. A model, in short, is a "redescription."[2] I should like to propose that an historian of religion is in a splendid position to offer a redescription of certain categories of religious experience and expression which we associate primarily with the West.

In this essay, I should like to address a topic which has often been held to be a major difference between western religious traditions and other religions—the canon and its authority—and subject it to a preliminary redescription.

My attention was drawn to the particular tack I wish to take by being invited to give yet another lecture on "The Persistence of the Sacred." This is a commonplace, a phrase that often recurs in the writings of historians of religion, sociologists, and anthropologists of various persuasions. Yet a few moments of reflection should drive one to the same conclusion I reached: it is really no topic at all. If the sacred, the holy, the divine, or what have you, is all that it is alleged to be, one of its more frequent characterizations is that it is eternal, enduring, or timeless. That the sacred persists is no novel thesis, it is all but a tautology. Even if one assumes that the phrase implies the other, at times pejorative, sense of persistence, the history of religions testifies to a belief that the sacred stubbornly persists in having traffic with man and the cosmos, even at the risk of becoming somewhat bothersome.

But such uses are not what those who employ such a phrase appear to have in mind. They appeal to an anthropological or quasi-biological notion—though one whose cogency I equally doubt—that the sacred, now understood anthropologically as religion (or, in less fortunate though more contemporary terms, as religious response, perspective, dimension, or world view) is one of the enduring, species-specific definitions of man. Man is (or, is among other things) *Homo religiosus*. For example, the eminent British anthropologist, Raymond Firth: "religion is universal in human societies. This is an empirical generalization, an aggregate of a multitude of specific observations."[3] Such a formulation is widespread, and often serves as a kind of demonstration of the "truth" of religion in a manner reminiscent of earlier attempts to establish "Natural Religion," but it is no more successful. Any enumeration of the persistent features of man (from opposed thumbs to erect posture), or even of the persistent and allegedly unique features of man (e.g., use of symbols, speech, laughter, religion) must record a set of traits so numerous and diverse as to result in a motley list rather than a persuasive demonstration of "truth" or of an "essence." Such an approach has proven incapable of supplying a satisfactory definition of either man or religion. Nor have there been any satisfying criteria established to enable us to isolate any one of these "persistences" as being more revealing of human nature than another. We need to recall Karl Popper's caution against using historical, enumerative arguments to establish certainty.

It is far from obvious, from a logical point of view, that we are justified in inferring universal statements from singular ones, no matter how

numerous: for any conclusion drawn in this manner may always turn
out to be false: no matter how many instances of white swans we have
observed this does not justify the conclusion that *all* swans are white.[4]

To translate this into our terms: no matter how many instances of human
religiosity we have observed, this does not justify the conclusion that man
is religious. Besides, to quote Melford Spiro, "Does the study of religion
become any the less significant or fascinating if, in terms of a consensual,
ostensive definition it was discovered that one or six or sixteen societies
did not possess religion?"[5]

Nor can the notion of persistence be rescued by turning to another
anthropological or quasi-biological commonplace: the propensity of religion to "survive," to persist in what is, at times, perceived as a hostile
or indifferent environment. That "it" (whatever "it" is) persists in a
"modern" or "secular" age (whatever that is) says nothing in itself. I
know of no *heilsgeschichtliche* hymn to the vermiform appendix!

But thinking through this issue has one positive result. If we invert the
topic and think about "sacred persistence," we touch a theme that seems
quite pervasive, but little explored. I take some assurance in this stratagem
from the fact that one of the oldest classical definitions of religion (Cicero)
and one of the most persuasive modern interpretations (Freud) both take
their starting point from the observation of the phenomenon of sacred
persistence.

In his dialogue, *De natura deorum,* written about 45 B.C., Cicero placed
in the mouth of the Stoic Balbo an etymology of the adjective *religious*
as being derived from *relegere* meaning to gather together, to collect, to
go over again, to review mentally, to repeat. Balbo proposes that, "those
who carefully reviewed and went over again all that pertained to the rituals
of the gods were called religious from *relegere*."[6] His argument requires
that this exegetical activity be understood as a constant preoccupation.
Although the etymology is most likely false,[7] it remains a shrewd insight,
based on observation, of a significant (perhaps, even distinctive) characteristic of religious thought.

Almost 2000 years later, in 1907, working from a similar grounding in
observation but from radically different presuppositions, Freud, in his
brief essay "Obsessive Acts and Religious Practices," proposed an analogy between "what are called obsessive acts in neurotics and those of
religious observances by means of which the faithful give expression to
their piety." While there is much in Freud's subsequent genetic account
that is problematic, his original description of the obsessiveness common
to both neurosis and religion as:

> *little* preoccupations, performances, restrictions and arrangements in
> certain activities of everyday life . . . elaborated by *petty* modifications

. . . [and] *little* details . . . [the] tendency to displacement . . . [which] turns apparently *trivial* matters into those of great and urgent importance[8]

remains, for me, the most telling description of a significant (perhaps, even distinctive) characteristic of religious activity that I know.

II

I should like to focus on the issue of sacred persistence: the rethinking of each little detail in a text (Cicero), the obsession with the significance and perfection of each little action (Freud).[9] But I shall take a somewhat roundabout route to my topic.

Almost the first thing observed by any traveler, be he professional or amateur, is the wide diversity between peoples as to food, both with respect to things they will eat and things they will not eat. From Herodotus to the present day, anecdotal instances of variation in diet have provided one of the immediate, all but intuitive, demonstrations of the notion of cultural relativism. One need only think of the instinctive horror aroused in us by the grisly enumeration of the ingredients which make up the witches' brew in *Macbeth* and then reflect on the fact that, deprived of imaginary substances ("scale of dragon"), indigestible condiments ("tooth of wolf"), and cannibalistic tidbits ("liver of blaspheming Jew . . . nose of Turk and Tartar's lips") all of the other items—from toads to baboons—are part of some other peoples' quite ordinary diet! And even the sorts of items just excised are eaten, or believed of others to be eaten, on extraordinary occasions.

Despite the ingenuity that has been brought to the subject by scholars of every persuasion, the old tag, quoted by Herodotus from Pindar, "custom is king over all," remains the most common, relativistic explanation.[10] This or that food or avoidance of food can be accounted for, but, aside from the obvious rule that it ought not to be poisonous (and even that is sometimes violated), no general principles have been found.

On the one hand, there appear to be virtually no limits to what people can and do eat if looked at globally. On the other hand, there appear to be the most stringent limits on what any particular group of people can, and will, eat, and a most intense reluctance to alter these boundaries. Only rarely, and under unusual circumstances, has a culture adopted a new food as its staple diet (Ireland and the potato is the most familiar, but highly specialized, exception). New foods have been the hallmark of the countercultural individual or group—a means of expressing distance from, hostility to, or transcendence of one's culture.

A rehearsal of these well known facts obscures what is a more important observation. Granted that food is best understood as a cultural rather than a natural category, the dynamics of its limitation and variation are more complex than a simple relativism would suggest.

A given foodstuff represents a radical, almost arbitrary, selection out of the incredible number of potential sources of nutriment that are at hand. But, once the selection is made, the most extraordinary attention is given to the variety of its preparation. That is to say, *if food is a phenomenon characterized by limitation, cuisine is a phenomenon characterized by variegation.* This most important and suggestive rule may be simply tested. Make a list of the basic foodstuffs regularly eaten. It will be a short one. Then make a list of the modes of preparation, the names of specific dishes that you know. Whether you are thinking of bread, pasta, wine, cheese, beef, potatoes, or chicken, your list will stagger the ingenuity of a Linnaeus!

To take but one example. We think almost exclusively of wine as being made from a single species of grape *(Vitis vinifera)* despite what we may know of the "quaint" British dedication to dandelions or rhubarb, or the equally "quaint" passion of some of our grandparents for elderberries. But, having so sharply limited the almost infinite potential of the vegetable kingdom (almost any fruit, flower, or root can be made into wine), we culturally vary, again almost infinitely, the grape. Most of us could, with a little thought, reproduce the "classification designed for the average consumer" in the new edition of the *Encyclopaedia Britannica* which contains over one hundred generic and varietal names,[11] not to speak of the other systems which are simultaneously employed: that of the vintage years and rules of etiquette (to whom, when, how, at what temperature, in what, with what to serve the various kinds of wines). In addition to these systems which are in common use, there are also the more specialized systems employed by the connoisseur, the sommelier, and vintner: the classifications by châteaux and growths, the laws of the appelations d'origine, and so forth.

The same sort of process may be observed with respect to every important human phenomenon and has received growing attention in recent studies of language, law, and taxonomy. An almost limitless horizon of possibilities that are at hand (in nature) is arbitrarily reduced (by culture) to a set of basic elements (in terms of the example—food). This initial arbitrariness is, at times, overcome by secondary explanations which attempt to account for the reduction (e.g., pork causes trichinosis). Then a most intense ingenuity is exercised to overcome the reduction (in terms of the example—cuisine), to introduce interest and variety. This ingenuity is usually accompanied by a complex set of rules.

Without attempting a full discussion, I note that in cognate fields where such processes have been studied, much of the recent debate has focused on the status of the reduction and, especially, on the status of the exercise of ingenuity. For some, the emphasis has been on the "givenness" of the basic elements as primordial and the secondary (indeed, at times, the degenerative) character of the ingenuity. For others, the basic elements are fundamentally arbitrary (although scholars usually prescind from questions of origin and truth with respect to the reduction) and ingenuity is understood as either work (world construction or the like) or play.

It is at this point in these reflections, as one thinks of the possibilities for applying this general model of cultural activity to religious phenomena, that one finds oneself both assisted and left unsatisfied by the studies of historians of religion. It has been the special contribution of the historian of religion to insist on the all but infinite nature of the plenum which confronts man in his religiousness while, at the same time, pointing to the reduction of this plenum by the various historical and cultural units they study. That is to say, to return to the previous analogy, historians of religion have pointed to the innumerable species of plants and animals that are at hand and have focused some attention on the reduction of these "natural" possibilities to food. For example, the revolutionary words of Mircea Eliade in the introduction to his major morphological treatise:

> We must get used to the idea of recognizing hierophanies absolutely everywhere. . . . Indeed we cannot be sure that there is *anything* . . . that has not at some time in human history been somewhere transformed into a hierophany . . . it is quite certain that anything man has ever handled, come in contact with or loved *can* become a hierophany. . . . It is unlikely that there is any animal or any important species of plant in the world that has *never* had a place in religion. In the same way too, every trade, art, industry, and technical skill either began as something holy, or has, over the years, been invested with religious value. This list could be carried on to include man's everyday movements (getting up, walking, running), his various employments (hunting, fishing, agriculture), all his physiological activities (nutrition, sexual life, etc.). . . . But somewhere, at a given time, each human society chose for itself a certain number of things, animals, plants, gestures, and so on and turned them into hierophanies; and, as this has been going on for tens of thousands of years of religious life, it seems improbable that there remains anything that has not at some time been so transfigured.[12]

At the same time, the historian of religion has been less convincing in explicating the second moment in our model: that of ingenuity, of cuisine. In part this is because historians of religion have traditionally resisted the anthropological as the cost of preserving the theological, preserving what they believe (I think wrongly) to be the "irreducible, sui generis" nature of religious phenomena. They have therefore tended to opt for what I have described as the first interpretation of our model, that which has insisted on the "givenness" of the basic elements as primordial and the secondary, degenerative character of ingenuity. Thus ingenuity is often displaced as mere routinization or swallowed up by postulating some ontic primordium which manifests itself in a variety of forms, apparently independent of human agency. Both degrade the anthropological dimension in a way I find inexcusable, the former by robbing it of significance, the latter by denying its existence.

To take but one example—the characteristic and influential argument of Adolf Jensen, building on the work of Leo Frobenius and the Frankfort *Paideuma Schule*. All truth, meaning, and value are located in what Jensen describes as a primal, creative moment of ontic "seizure," a "revelation," a "direct cognition of the essence of living reality." Myth, he argues, "always begins with a condition antecedent to concretization, when the creative idea is already in existence and finally manifests itself through the mythic event." The first "concretization," the first "formulation," is an "intuitive spontaneous experiencing" which Jensen terms "expression." Expression is, for Jensen, an essentially passive experience equivalent to the religious term "inspiration." All subsequent "formulations" and "concretizations" are reinterpretations of this primal experience and are termed by Jensen, "applications"—a pejorative word in his lexicon. "Application" over time leads to "mere survivals" of the original, authentic "seizure" and "first expression." All "application" for Jensen is under the sway of the iron "law of degeneration," or "semantic depletion" and results in the original "spontaneity" becoming a "fixed but no longer understood routine"—a statement, on Jensen's part, of the traditional Protestant bugaboos of "habit," "dogma," and "magic" which has resulted in the vast majority of religious phenomena remaining unintelligible to most western scholarship. Jensen insists that:

> According to the inescapable law, anything that culture has created must grow more distant from the [original] content of the creative idea; finally it will only be a pale reflection of its original expression . . . [according to] the process of gradual semantic depletion along the way from "expression" to "application."

Or, need it be translated, from authentic prophecy to Pharisaism or Catholic casuistry! Jensen claims that the history of religions is littered with examples

> of the transformation from meaningful belief to absurdity, where the nuclear thought has been lost in historical changes, but the externals are reverently preserved and brought into harmony with new concepts.

Even though such applications and reinterpretations might be judged, from some perspectives, to have been "successful elaborations," Jensen sharply disagrees; "weighed ideologically, the 'successful developments' constitute pauperization and semantic depletion."[13]

I find Jensen's argument extremely dubious in many respects, not the least of which is the fact that, as has been characteristic of many historians of religion, he has attempted a theological apologetic without a theology— if by the latter term one understands, at the very least, a community's self-reflection. Shorn of this necessary communal, and hence, traditional dimension, one is left with the impossible generic abstraction of *Homo religiosus* responding to religion in general and, paradoxically, religion becomes, as it does in Jensen and many historians of religion, an essentially inhuman activity.

I have come to believe that a prime object of study for the historian of religion ought to be theological tradition, taking the term in its widest sense, in particular, those elements of the theological endeavor that are concerned with canon and its exegesis. That is to say, bracketing any presuppositions as to its character as revelation (and from this question, the historian of religion must abstain), the radical and arbitrary reduction represented by the notion of canon and the ingenuity represented by the rule-governed exegetical enterprise of applying the canon to every dimension of human life is that most characteristic, persistent, and obsessive religious activity. It is, at the same time, the most profoundly cultural, and hence, the most illuminating for what ought to be the essentially anthropological view point of the historian of religion and a conception of religion as human labor. The task of application as well as the judgment of the relative adequacy of particular applications to a community's life situation remains the indigenous theologian's task, but the study of the process, particularly the study of comparative systematics and exegesis, ought to become a major preoccupation of the historian of religion.

This has a number of consequences. It would mean that students of religion might find as their most congenial colleagues those concerned with biblical and legal studies rather than their present romantic preoccupation with the "primitive" or the "archaic"—terms which have largely meant simple or primordial in the sense of uninterpreted, and which have given historians of religion license for ultimate acts of imperialism, the removal of all rights to interpretation from the native, and the arrogation of all such rights to themselves. It would mean that historians of religion might redirect their attention from their present equally romantic fixation on multivalent and condensed phenomena, such as symbols, which have more often served as eloquent testimony to the exegetical ingenuity of the researcher than of the community that has bound itself to them, and should rather become concerned with prosaic, expository discourse. It implies that historians of religion will not lose their freedom to study the all but limitless horizon of human religious experience and expression and objects of religious concern, but that they will take as a prime interpretative and comparative task the understanding of the surrender of that freedom by the communities they study and the rediscovery of that freedom through the community's exercise of ingenuity within their self-imposed limits.

I do not want, in this essay, to dwell on the implications for history of religions. Rather I should like to reflect further on the notion of canon as a way of exploring the proposition that sacrality persists insofar as there are communities which are persistent in applying their limited body of tradition; that sacred persistence, in terms that are congruent with both Cicero and Freud, is primarily exegesis; that, if there is anything that is distinctive about religion as a human activity, it is a matter of degree rather than kind, what might be described as the extremity of its enterprise for exegetical totalization. To do so I must undertake a redescription of the category canon.

III

I know of no comparative study of canon and, therefore, I must invite the reader into the historian of religion's workroom in order that he may observe and evaluate some of the preliminary typologies that might be developed and a sample of the kinds of data such a study might employ. I have drawn many of my examples from nonliterate peoples in order to further the enterprise of redescription. Such societies would seem, at first glance, to be those for whom the category of canon would be most difficult to establish, as the notion of canon, in ordinary use, is primarily associated with the western "Peoples of the Book" (Judaism, Christianity, Islam, and Manichaeism and other Iranian traditions). It appears to be a relatively rare phenomenon within the history of religions, even among literate groups. With the possible exception of Islam, it occurs only at a secondary or tertiary stage of the tradition. But, I want to insist that canon, broadly understood as the arbitrary fixing of a limited number of "texts" as immutable and authoritative, is far from unusual. At the same time, I want to give full due to the necessary concomitant of exegetical ingenuity which ought to prevent our applying terms such as "closed," "static," or "cool" to societies which possess canons—even those which we classify as nonliterate.

To begin the task of redescription. Canon is a subtype of the genre *list*. The list is, perhaps, the most archaic and pervasive of genres.[14] It has received surprisingly little scholarly attention. Most lists, whether in simple enumerative or nominal form, or in more complex forms such as lexica and encyclopaedia, are open-ended. That is to say, they have neither a necessary beginning nor end save that provided by the duration of the attention of their compiler or the use to which the list is to be put. There is no necessary order. Everything may appear to be quite arbitrary. Hugh Kenner has argued that lists are characterized by the notion of the "isolated fact," the "fragmentation of reality," the "nearly surrealistic discontinuity of the final product." He maintains that "nothing, except where a cross-reference is provided, connects with anything else . . . or affords perspective on anything else."[15] Indeed, not even the cross-reference guarantees much. One is reminded of the fact that in the French Enlightenment *Encyclopédie,* more than half of the cross-references are to nonexistent articles![16] This "discontinuity" may be illustrated by an ancient list, the Middle Kingdom Ramesseum Onomasticon (P. Berlin 10495) as edited by A. H. Gardiner. The text begins with a list of plant names and liquids (largely undecipherable), then birds, fishes, a second list of birds, a list of quadrupeds, a list of fortresses in the south, a list of twenty-nine towns, a list of types of baked goods, a list of grains, a list of forty-nine parts of an ox, a list of fruits and spices, and, finally, a list of twenty names for cattle. A scribal note (lines 324–25) reports that there should have been a total set of 343 items, but in fact there are only 323. A count of the items in the text reveals that, in reality, 321 are listed.[17] The same "discontinuity" is characteristic of the medieval encyclopaedia tradition.[18] For example, in the popular *De proprietatibus rerum* by Bartholomaeus Anglicus (composed between 1220 and 1240), the original printed edition of 1470 begins with God *(De deo)* and concludes, twelve hundred and thirty chapters later, with an alphabetical list of thirty-six eggs (from *De ouis aspidum* to *De ouis vulturis*). In the 1574 edition of the French translation by Jehan Corbichon, a treatise on bees has been added. In the English translation by John Trevisa (c. 1400), the text concludes with an alphabetical listing of musical instruments.[19]

When lists exhibit relatively clear principles of order, we may begin to term them *catalogs,* a subtype of the list whose major function is that of information retrieval. It makes little difference whether we are dealing with oral or literary materials. Both possess mnemonic devices and codes of classification. The items in a catalog remain heterogeneous. The catalog, in principle, is open. But an account of why the items have been brought together can be given, transmitted, and learned.

For example, it is one thing to find in history of religion's manuals the principle that the beginning or first time is pristine or precious and requires celebration; it is quite another thing to encounter a list of first times from an Iatmul informant in New Guinea and attempt to appreciate the application of this principle in native practice and exegesis. The same ceremony *(naven)*, undertaken by mother's brother, will be performed for the male:

the first time a boy kills an enemy or foreigner or victim bought for this purpose . . . the [first] killing of any of the following animals: birds, fish, eel, tortoise, flying fox; [the first] planting of any of the following plants: yams, tobacco, coconut, areca, betel, sago, sugar cane; [the first] spotting of an opossum in the bush; the [first] felling of a sago palm, opening or beating sago; [the first] using of a spear thrower; [the first] using a throwing stick to kill a bird; [the first] using an axe; [the first] sharpening of a fish spear; [the first] cutting a paddle; [the first] making a canoe; [the first] making a digging stick; [the first] making a spear thrower; [the first] incising patterns on a lime gourd; [the first] plaiting of an arm band; [the first] making of a shell girdle; [the first] beating a hand drum, beating a slit drum, blowing a trumpet, playing a flute, beating the secret slit gongs; [the first) travelling to another village and returning; [the first] acquiring of shell valuables; [the first] buying of an axe, knife, mirror or other trade goods; [the first] buying of an areca nut; [the first] killing of a pig and sponsoring of a feast.[20]

Note that these last items are an excellent example of native exegetical labor. Traditional articles of value and exchange (shells, areca nuts, pigs) have been extended by analogy and the application of principle to the postcolonial purchase of foreign, manufactured items (axe, knife, mirror). This is the only portion of the catalog left open in an explicit fashion—''or other trade goods''—to allow for further novelty and innovation not under native control.

The Iatmul enumeration is a simple catalog which organizes a heterogeneous group of materials around the single principle: the first performance of a cultural activity is to be celebrated. However, the schema according to which the various items are listed and grouped is more complex. It does not testify merely to the centrality of the notion of ''first time,'' but represents a map of a particular culture's selection, out of the multitude of elements which make up their common life, those which are capable of bearing obsession, those which are understood as significant. Properly interpreted, it is a diagram of the characteristic preoccupations (as well as the occupations) of the Iatmul. I do not intend a full analysis of this catalog, or, what would be of more importance, a correlation of such an analysis with other elements in the ethnography of the Iatmul, but I would note that the catalog is organized around the rubric: relations with strangers. The catalog has two sections: the first begins with killing an enemy, foreigner, or victim; the second, with journeying to another village and returning (safely). The rest of the catalog is generated by association:

killing humans
killing animals for food
preparation of plant foods

use and manufacture of tools for killing and for agriculture
by analogy, use and manufacture of ceremonial objects
use of ceremonial instruments

And the second series:

travelling to foreign places
acquiring foreign goods
inviting others to feast

Note that, in this case, I have supplied some of the explicit rubrics, principles, and rules by which the catalog was generated. In many societies, there is a native meditation of these principles which may be called, to use Albrecht Alt's useful term, *Listenwissenschaft*.[21] This is a science which takes as its prime intellectual activity the production and reflection on lists, catalogs, and classifications, which progresses by establishing precedents, by observing patterns, similarities, and conjunctions, by noting repetitions. Such a science is particularly noticeable in omen and legal materials. It is prevalent in Near Eastern literature from the extensive Babylonian omen series to the quite parallel Talmudic enterprise. But *Listenwissenschaft* is an all but universal phenomenon.

To provide but one complex example, taken from Claude Lévi-Strauss, *The Elementary Structures of Kinship:*

> For several very primitive peoples of the Malay Archipelago, the supreme sin, unleashing storm and tempest, comprises a series of superficially incongruous acts which informants list higgledy-piggledy as follows: marriage with a near kin; father and daughter or mother and son sleeping too close to one another; incorrect speech between kin; ill-considered conversation; for children, noisy play; for adults, demonstrative happiness shown at social reunions; imitating the calls of certain insects or birds [particularly the cicada]; laughing at one's own face in the mirror; and, finally, teasing animals and, in particular, dressing a monkey as a man and making fun of him.

Lévi-Strauss goes on to ask the obvious question:

> What possible connection could there be between such a bizarre collection of acts? . . . Why does native thought group them under one heading? Either native thought must be accused of being incoherent or . . . [there must be] a common characteristic which . . . makes these apparently heterogenous acts express an identical situation. A native remark puts us on the track. The Pygmies of the Malay Peninsula consider it a sin to laugh at one's own face in the mirror, but they add that it is not a sin to ridicule a real human being [to his face] since he can defend himself. This interpretation obviously also applies to the dressed up monkey which is treated as a human being when it is teased and looks like a human being (just as does the face in the mirror),

although it is really not one. This interpretation can be extended to the imitation of certain insects or birds. . . . By imitating them, one is treating an emission of sound which "sounds" like a word as a human manifestation when it is not. Thus we find [in the list] two categories of acts definable as an immoderate use of language: the first, from a quantitative point of view, to play noisily, to laugh too loudly or to make an excessive show of one's feelings; the second, from a qualitative point of view, to answer sounds which are not words, or to converse with something (mirror or monkey) which is human only in appearance. These prohibitions are all thus reduced to a single denominator: they all constitute a misuse of language.

I shall break off the quotation at this point and not follow the relationship that is posited between "misuse of language" and the incestuous acts in the catalog, nor the extension of these principles to the complex set of actions forbidden by the Malaysian Dyaks under the rubric that it is forbidden to give "a man or animal a name that is not his or its . . . or to say something about him [or it] that is contrary to his nature."[22] I have dwelt on this example at some length because it is revelatory not only of the intellectual activities of *Listenwissenschaft,* but also of its "science." A number of processes are involved in generating such a catalog. First, the empirical collection of data—in the Malay example, what happened in a village at the same time as a "storm and tempest" occurred; the remembering or recording of such cooccurrences over a period of time; then, the discovery of a pattern to the synchronisms; and, finally, the determination of a common principle that underlies the pattern, one that may be used predictively (omen) or generalized either in a proscriptive manner (law or taboo) or in a retrospective mode (history).

The only formal element that is lacking to transform a catalog into a *canon* is the element of closure: that the list be held to be complete. This formal requirement generates a corollary. Where there is a canon, it is possible to predict the *necessary* occurrence of a hermeneute, of an interpreter whose task it is continually to extend the domain of the closed canon over everything that is known or everything that exists *without* altering the canon in the process. It is with the canon and its hermeneute that we encounter the necessary obsession with exegetical totalization.

It would be difficult to demonstrate the notion of canon in nonliterate societies so long as we think of canon as a corpus of written texts. It is clear from the presence of multiple, everchanging versions as well as from the evidence for native debate over what version is to be "authoritative" for a particular recitation,[23] that one may not simply turn to oral material such as myth. Regardless of the mnemonics, a corpus of myth is rarely held to be closed.

One possibility is to examine the widespread evidence for the use of a totalistic and complete system of signs or icons which serve as functional equivalents to a written canon.

At its simplest level, such a canon may be illustrated from the Walbiri of Central Australia as reported by Nancy Munn.[24] A set of less than two hundred and fifty designs, capable of being reduced to a small set of basic elements which are extended through combination, is used to accompany and encapsulate every narrative from a story of everyday activity to the report of a novel dream, or to the transmission of esoteric ancestral traditions. Each element bears a wide range of meanings (quite arbitrary with respect to its visual form), but is unambiguous in context. It may be drawn in the sand as a woman tells a story, taught to children as a "language system," or painted on the body of a male during initiation. But in each case, although the lexicon is complete and public, there is no hermeneute—although his role is to some degree substituted for by the narrator. That is to say, in this most simple system, we find no clear evidence for the processes of interpretation, but rather a process of translation of the verbal into the visual, or, more accurately, of the simultaneous and parallel expression of both. The designs are not mere illustrations of the narrative; they are the result of ratiocination. When a given design can synonymously (although not simultaneously) denote a variety of things, there is a principle by which these referents are perceived both as similar and as reducible to the geometric form that calls them to mind. At the same time, the system appears closed. It is capable of extension, so as to include novelties, without the need for adding any new designs. The process of the public acceptance of such extension would seem to presuppose some hermeneutic activity which requires further research.

Similar systems, though more complex, show forth the interpreter's role with clarity. For example, the Senufo set of 58 figurines of human and animal forms presented to novices in a "fixed order" with oral interpretation during initiation rites as described by Bochet, which correspond to the basic classes of cosmic, human, and social relations: an "inventory," according to Bochet, that "constitutes a sort of lexicon of symbols and different possible ways of using them."[25] Or the even more complex, totalistic, theosophical system of 266 signs, capable of being "read" in four different ways depending upon one's stage of initiation, among the Dogon, which is still being deciphered by the French anthropological team associated with Marcel Griaule.[26]

There is a double value in examining this sort of corpus of nonliterate canonical materials. First, it reveals that a canon cannot exist without a tradition and an interpreter. That is to say, without the public lexicon *(langue)* and the explicit engagement in application *(parole)*, the closure of canon would be impossible. Second, in each instance the strategy seems the same. The process of arbitrary limitation and of overcoming limitation through ingenuity recurs. As the pressure is intensified through extension and through novelty, because of the presupposition of canonical completeness, it will be the task of the hermeneute to develop exegetical procedures that will allow the canon to be applied without alteration or, at least, without admitting to alteration—what Henry Maine analyzed as the process of "legal fiction."[27] Indeed, in some complex situations, there may be a further need to develop parallel, secondary traditions that will recover the essentially open character of the list or catalog.

A preliminary comparative survey of a wide range of materials reveals that the canonical-interpretative enterprise is most prevalent in five situations: divination, law, legitimation, classification, and speculation. Cross-cultural study has convinced me that the primary *Sitz im Leben* of canon is divination. At the very least, it is in divinatory procedures that we may observe with particular clarity the relationship between canon and hermeneute. Therefore, I will draw my final examples from reports of African divination, from Victor Turner's study of the Ndembu and William Bascom's study of the Yoruba.

Among the Ndembu, there are two features of the divinatory situation that are crucial to our concern: the diviner's basket and the diviner's process of interrogating his client.

The chief mode of Ndembu divination consists of shaking a basket in which some 24 fixed objects are deposited (e.g., a cock's claw, a piece of hoof, a bit of grooved wood, a black withered fruit). These are shaken in order to winnow out "truth from falsehood" in such a way that a few of the objects end up on top of the heap. These are "read" by the diviner with respect to both their individual meanings and their combinations with other objects and the configurations that result. The client's situation is also taken into account in arriving at an interpretation. Thus, to invoke the categories of classical linguistics, there is a semantic, syntactic, and pragmatic dimension to the "reading." Each object in the basket is publicly known and has a fixed range of meanings. Although some debate about this or that possibility of interpretation is possible among diviners, the broad semantic field is never violated. The total collection of 24 objects is held to be complete and capable of illuminating every situation. Nothing new may be added to the basket, although the objects themselves may be subjected to a variety of manipulations.[28]

What enables the fixed canon of divinatory objects in the diviner's basket to be applied to every possible situation or question is not the number of objects (as in all canons, the number is relatively small) nor the breadth of their range of meanings. Rather it is that, prior to performing the divination, the diviner has rigorously questioned his client in order to determine the latter's situation with precision. The diviner functions with respect to his client much as the successful preacher functions with respect to his congregation. Application, here, is not a generalized systematic process, but a homiletic endeavor, a quite specific attempt to make the "text" speak to a quite particular situation. If, at one level, the lists of divinatory objects and their general public meanings, as printed in Turner, serve as a lexicon to the language of divination, at another level, the objects as applied after the interrogation quite clearly function as speech, as unique and individualized sentences addressed to an unduplicatible audience. It is the genius of the diviner in his role as hermeneute to match a public set of meanings with a commonly known set of facts (so-and-so is sick; so-and-so's relative died) in order to produce a quite particular plausibility structure which speaks directly to his client's condition, which mediates between that which is public knowledge and the client's private perception of his unique situation.

The opposite divinatory situation is represented by the Yoruba procedure. Here the central rule is that the diviner knows nothing of his client's situation, not even his question. Rather the diviner serves as a mediator, making available the canonical resources to the client, but leaving the application entirely in the latter's hands.

> The basis of Yoruba divination (Ifa) is a large repertoire of poems. These are correlated with a set of 256 divination figures. . . The diviner selects one of these figures by a simple process. While shaking sixteen palm nuts in his loosely clasped hands . . . he abruptly tries to lift all of the nuts out of his left hand with his right. Because of the size of the nuts, it is virtually impossible to hold all sixteen of them in one hand; thus, one or two will remain in the left hand. If one nut remains, the diviner draws two parallel lines in the powder in his divination tray. If two nuts remain, he draws one line. He makes repeated casts and records his results until he completes a figure consisting of two parallel columns of four marks each. . . . This arrangement of marks forms one divination figure. . . . Since each column has 4×4, or 16 possible combinations of marks, the two columns combined have a total of 16×16, or 256, possible combinations.

Once the figure is drawn and named, the diviner recites a set of poems that are associated with it. A novice diviner knows four poems for each figure (a total of 1024 poems, five to fifty lines each); an experienced diviner knows as many as eight.

> After hearing the full set of poems, the client chooses the one that seems most relevant to his problem. Not knowing the client's case, the diviner has no way of manipulating his client's interpretation or choice of verse. What is at stake is something not open to the public view. . . . It is rather a purely private relationship between an individual and his own destiny.[29]

In the Yoruba instance, strikingly similar to the Chinese *I Ching,* it is not so much the text of the poems that constitutes the canon, but rather the mathematically fixed number of possible divination figures. These give access to a possible set of interpretations (the poems) which vary in number according to the skill and training of the tradent. But it is the individual who must decide which one is the most plausible. It is the individual who serves as his own hermeneute.

As one examines the great variety of such canons and divinatory situations, he will be struck by the differences in exegetical techniques and skills, by the variety of presuppositions. But the essential structure of limitation and closure along with exegetical ingenuity remains constant. It is this which provides a suggestive base for a redescription of canon.

Other work remains to be done: an examination of the rules that govern the sharp debates between rival exegetes and exegetical systems in their efforts to manipulate the closed canon. There is need for a careful study of individuals who may be termed tribal theologians, who raise the endeavors of exegetical ingenuity to the level of a comprehensive system. I look forward to the day when courses and monographs will exist in both comparative exegesis and comparative theology, comparing not so much conclusions as strategies through which the exegete seeks to interpret and translate his received tradition to his contemporaries.

I have attempted a redescription of canon from the perspective of an historian of religion. I have argued that canon is best seen as one form of a basic cultural process of limitation and of overcoming that limitation through ingenuity. I have proposed some basic distinctions between list, catalog and canon. I have suggested that for nonliterate peoples, canon is most clearly to be perceived in divinatory situations and have described the range of the roles interpretation and application play in such procedures. By such a redescription, I hope to have suggested how the categories used by historians of religion might be "modulated" by taking seriously structures characteristic of western religious traditions, and vice versa. It is only by such mutual modulation, within the context of comparison, that progress in the study of religion will be possible.

4 The Bare Facts of Ritual

I may be doing wrong, but I'm doing it in the proper and customary manner.

George Bernard Shaw

I

There is one aspect of scholarship that has remained constant from the earliest Near Eastern scribes and omen interpreters to contemporary academicians: the thrill of encountering a coincidence. The discovery that two events, symbols, thoughts, or texts, while so utterly separated by time and space that they could not "really" be connected, seem, nevertheless, to be the same or to be speaking directly to one another raises the possibility of a secret interconnection of things that is the scholar's most cherished article of faith. The thought that the patterns and interrelationships that he has patiently and laboriously teased out of his data might, in fact, exist is the claim he makes when his work is completed as well as the claim that appears to be denied by the fact that he has had to labor so long. The scholar lives in the world that the poet Borges has described. And this is why coincidence is, at one and the same time, so exhilarating and so stunning. It is as if, unbidden and unearned by work and interpretation, a connection simply "chose" to make itself manifest, to display its presence on our conceptual wall with a clear round hand.

I should like to begin this essay with one such coincidence and juxtapose two texts separated in time by some eighteen centuries. The one is from Kafka, the other from Plutarch.

Leopards break into the temple and drink the sacrificial chalices dry; this occurs repeatedly, again and again: finally it can be reckoned on beforehand and becomes a part of the ceremony.[1]

At Athens, Lysimache, the priestess of Athene Polias, when asked for a drink by the mule drivers who had transported the sacred vessels, replied, "No, for I fear it will get into the ritual."[2]

These two texts illustrate the sovereign power of one of the basic building blocks of religion: ritual and its capacity for routinization.

Both fragmentary stories take their starting point in what we would most probably call an accident. Both give eloquent testimony, in quite different ways, to the imperialistic eagerness with which ritual takes advantage of an accident and, by projecting on it both significance and regularity, annihilates its original character as accident.[3] But our two texts, while remarkably similar in structure, differ quite sharply in how they see and evaluate this process. They seem to suggest, at least by implication, two differing theories about the origin of religion.

Both texts set the action they describe within a temple. In Kafka, the locale is apparently some jungle shrine; in Plutarch it is a sacred place within the heart of a cosmopolitan city—the dwelling place, north of the Parthenon, of the ancient wooden statue of Athene Polias, "the holiest thing" within all Athens.[4] This temple setting is more than mere scenery. It serves to frame all that follows.

When one enters a temple, one enters marked-off space in which, at least in principle, nothing is accidental; everything, at least potentially, is of significance. The temple serves as a *focusing lens,* marking and revealing significance. For example, in Jewish tradition gossip in the temple and in the Land of Israel (which they understood to be an extended temple) is Torah.[5] If an accident occurred within its precincts, either it must be understood as a miracle, a sign that must be routinized through repetition, or it will be interpreted as impurity, as blasphemy. Thus the lamp in the temple that unexpectedly burned for eight days according to a late rabbinic legend was retrojected as having given rise to the festival of Hannukah, the first feast to enter the Jewish liturgical calendar without scriptural warrant, claiming only human decree rather than divine command, and hence, itself, potentially blasphemy.[6] In the case of the oil lamp, the interpretation was one of miracle. On the other hand, when the high priest in Jerusalem spilled a basin of sacred water on his feet rather than on the altar the accident was understood as blasphemy and he was pelted by the crowd.[7]

A sacred place is a place of clarification (a focusing lens) where men and gods are held to be transparent to one another. It is a place where, as in all forms of communication, static and noise (i.e., the accidental) are decreased so that the exchange of information can be increased. In communication, the device by which this is accomplished is redundancy; in our examples, through ritual repetition and routinization. In Kafka's story, the leopards were received as a message (a miracle, a sign) and incorporated, through routinization and repetition, into the ritual. In Plutarch's story, this potential was refused by the priestess, who saw the possibility of blasphemy.

There is a vast difference between the actors in the two stories. But we are in danger of dwelling on this difference in such a way as to mislead ourselves badly. There appears to us to be something mysterious, awesome, and awful about the leopards, but there is nothing at all extraordinary about the mule drivers. Therefore the first may appear to us as being inherently religious, the latter, quite commonplace and secular. From the vantage of such an understanding, Kafka would appear to be drawing on romantic theories of religion as the epiphantic. That may well be what he had in mind, but I would opt for a different understanding. For leopards in a jungle seem as commonplace as mule drivers in an ancient city. The leopards in Kafka's story do nothing mysterious; in fact, they do what the mule drivers desire to do. They are thirsty, and they drink. That they drink from a "sacrificial chalice" is what the readers and celebrants know. The leopards presumably do not. They simply see a bowl of liquid, as the pigeons that sometimes make their way into Catholic churches do not know that the stand of holy water at the entrance was not put there for their relief as a bird bath.

Indeed this is necessarily so if we take seriously the notion of a temple, a sacred place, as a focusing lens. The ordinary (which remains, to the observer's eye, wholly ordinary) becomes significant, becomes sacred, simply by *being there*. It becomes sacred by having our attention directed to it in a special way. This is a most important point, one that is only recently gaining acceptance among historians of religion although it was already brilliantly described by A. van Gennep in *Les Rites de passage* (1909) as the "pivoting of the sacred."[8] That is, there is nothing that is inherently sacred or profane. These are not substantive categories, but rather situational or relational categories, mobile boundaries which shift according to the map being employed. There is nothing that is sacred in itself, only things sacred in relation.

To digress from Kafka and Plutarch to another set of ancient stories about ritual. In the extensive Egyptian *logos* in book 2 of his *Histories,* Herodotus tells that Amasis, "a mere private person" who was elevated to king but despised because of his "ordinary" origins, had a golden foot pan in which he and his guests used to wash their feet. This was melted down and remolded into the statue of a god which was reverenced by the people. Amasis called an assembly and drew the parallel as to "how the image had been made of the foot pan, in which they formerly had been used to washing their feet and to deposit all manner of dirt, yet now it was greatly reverenced. And truly it has gone with me as with the foot pan. If I were formerly a private citizen, I have now come to be your king, and therefore I bid you to do honor and reverence to me."[9] This is a sophisticated story which foreshadows the kinds of subtle distinctions later political thought made between the king as divine with respect to office and human with respect to person. Divine and human, sacred and profane, are maps and labels not substances; they are distinctions, of "office." This is almost always misunderstood by later apologetic writers who used the Amasis story to ridicule idolatry.[10] Likewise the analogous *topos* found independently in both Israelitic[11] and Latin[12] tradition of the carpenter who fashions a sacred object or image out of one part of a log and a common household utensil out of the other.[13] Similar too is the opposite theme to the Amasis story, that a statue of a deity would be melted down and used to fashion a commonplace vessel: "Saturn into a cooking pot; Minerva into a washbasin."[14] The *sacra* are sacred solely because they are used in a sacred place; there is no inherent difference between a sacred vessel and an ordinary one. By being used in a sacred place, they are held to be open to the possibility of significance, to be seen as agents of meaning as well as of utility.

To return to Kafka and Plutarch. Neither the leopards nor the mule drivers can be presumed to know what they do or ask. The determination of meaning, of the potentiality for sacrality in their actions, lies wholly with the cult. The cult in Kafka's story perceives significance in the leopards' intrusion and, therefore, converts it from an accident into a ritual. The leopards no longer appear whenever they "happen" to be thirsty: "It can be reckoned on beforehand and becomes a part of the ceremony." In the Plutarch story, the priestess rebuffs the potential for significance. Whether the mule drivers will ever thirst again, whether or not they wished to drink from the sacred vessels they had just transported or from some "ordinary" cup makes no difference. If done in the temple, with the authority of the priestess, their act is potentially a ritual.

Why does the priestess refuse? What should we understand her answer, "No, for I fear it will get into the ritual," to mean? There is a thin line, as Freud most persuasively argued, between the neurotic act and religious ritual, for both are equally "obsessed" by the potentiality for significance in the commonplace.[15] But this presents a dilemma for the ritualist. If everything signifies, the result will be either insanity or banality. Understood from such a perspective, *ritual is an exercise in the strategy of choice*. What to include? What to hear as a message? What to see as a sign? What to perceive as having double meaning? What to exclude? What to allow to remain as background noise? What to understand as simply "happening"? The priestess is exercising her sense of the *economy of signification*. To permit something as apparently trivial as a drink of water to occur in the temple runs the risk of blurring the focus, of extending the domain of meaning to an impossible degree. It is to run the risk of other ritual acts being perceived as banal, as signifying nothing. We do not know whether, in this particular instance, she was right. But we can affirm that, as priestess, she has acted responsibly.

II

I invoked, earlier, the name of Jorge Luis Borges as the mythographer of scholarship. I shall take my clue for the latter part of this essay from this gifted Argentinian writer. In his short story, "Death and the Compass," Borges has his police commissioner, Lönnrot, declare to a colleague, "Reality may avoid the obligation to be interesting, but hypotheses may not. . . . In the hypothesis you have postulated [to solve the murder] chance intervenes largely. . . . I should prefer a purely rabbinical explanation."[16] Let me raise a "rabbinical" question. What if the leopards do not return? What if the mule drivers had taken their drink without asking anyone and then were discovered? What then? Here we begin to sense the presence of one of the fundamental building blocks of religion: its capacity for rationalization, especially as it concerns that ideological issue of relating that which we do to that which we say or think we do.

This is not an unimportant matter in relationship to the notion of ritual as a difficult strategy of choice. It requires us to perceive ritual as a human labor, struggling with matters of incongruity. It requires us to question theories which emphasize the "fit" of ritual with some other human system.

For the remainder of this essay, I should like to offer a concrete example which not only will illustrate the problematics and rationalizing capacities of religious ritual and discourse but also allows us to reflect on the dilemmas created for historians of religion by these capacities. I should like to direct attention to a set of bear-hunting rituals as reported, especially, from paleo-Siberian peoples. I have chosen this example because it is well documented in ethnography and has been of great importance in a number of theoretical discussions of ritual.

We need, at the outset, to fix on a traditional cultural dichotomy: agriculturalist and hunter. Within urban, agricultural societies, hunting is a special activity, remote from the ordinary rhythms of life, in which man steps outside of his cultural world and rediscovers the world of nature and the realm of the animal, frequently perceived as a threat. The hunter tests his courage in an extraordinary situation. It is this fortitude in confronting the dangerously "other" that has been celebrated in the novels of authors such as Hemingway, or in the compelling *Meditations on Hunting* by the Spanish philosopher Ortega y Gasset. Within agricultural, urban societies, the religious symbolism of hunting is that of overcoming the beast who frequently represents either chaos or death. The hunt is perceived, depending on the symbolic system, as a battle between creation and chaos, good and evil, life and death, man and nature, the civil and the uncivil. The paradigm of such a symbolic understanding is the royal hunt which persists from ancient Sumer and Egypt to the contemporary queen of England, mythologized in legends of heroic combats with dragons, and partially secularized in the relatively recent ceremony of the Spanish bullfight. The king, as representative of both the ruling god and the people, slays the beast.[17]

In contrast, among hunting societies, hunting is perceived as an everyday activity. It is not understood as an act of overcoming but as a participation in the normal course of things. The hunter and the hunted play out their roles according to a predetermined system of relationships. This system is mediated, according to the traditions of many hunting peoples, by a "Master of the Animals," a "Supernatural Owner of the Game," who controls the game or their spirits, in northern traditions most frequently by penning them. He releases a certain number to man each year as food. Only the allotted number may be slain in a manner governed by strict rules. Each corpse must be treated with respect. The meat must be divided, distributed, and eaten according to strict rules of etiquette, and the soul of the animal must be returned to its "Supernatural Owner" by ritual means. If the system is violated, game will be withheld and complex ceremonies, frequently involving the mediation of a shaman, are required to remove the offense and placate the "Master."[18]

Beyond this mythology underlying the hunt, it has long been clear that the hunt itself can be described as a ritual having several more or less clearly demarcated parts. In what follows, I am largely dependent on the outlines provided by A. I. Hallowell's classic study, *Bear Ceremonialism in the Northern Hemisphere,* as well as Evelyn Lot-Falck's more recent monograph, *Les Rites de chasse chez les peuples sibériens,* supplementing them, where appropriate, with details from other ethnographies.[19]

The first group of rituals may be brought together under the heading "preparation for the hunt."[20] One set of rituals Lot-Falck interprets as ceremonies designed to "insure the success of the hunt" under which she includes various forms of "divination" (oracles from bones and flight of arrows predominate) and rites which she terms "magical ceremonies employing sympathetic magic"—a theme to which I shall return. These may be of several types: mimetic dances "prefiguring" the hunt, the stabbing of an "effigy" of the animal, and the like. There are also invocations to the "Master of the Animals" or to the individual hunter's "guardian spirit," or attempts, through ritual, to "capture the game animal's soul." The bulk of the rituals of preparation are concerned with the purification of the hunter, purification by smoke being the most widespread. A variety of avoidances are observed, particularly of women and sexual intercourse and of contact with the dead. Finally, almost universally, there is a ceremonial hunt language.[21] The animals are believed to understand human speech, and it would be a gross violation of etiquette to announce that one is coming to kill them. A variety of euphemisms and circumlocutions are employed.

The rituals surrounding the second important moment of the hunt, "leaving the camp," appear to express the hunter's consciousness of crossing a boundary from the human social world into a forest realm of animals and spirits.[22] Leaving in a rigidly prescribed order, as if to carry human social structures into another's domain, the chief rituals focus on gaining permission from the forest to enter, with the key image being that of guest. Thus the earliest extant Finnish bear rune addresses the forest as "lovely woman—hostess good and bountiful" and requests entrance.[23] I would argue that the complex of host/guest/visitor/gift comprises the articulated understanding of the hunt. The forest serves as a host to the hunter, who must comport himself as a proper guest. The hunter is a host inviting the animal to feast on the gift of its own meat. The animal is host to the hunters as they feed on its flesh. The animal is a gift from the "Master of the Animals," as well as being a visitor from the spirit world. The animal gives itself to the hunter. The hunter, by killing the animal, enables it to return to its "Supernatural Owner" and to its home, from which it has come to earth as a visitor.[24]

The third moment in the hunt seen as ritual is the "kill," which is likewise governed by strict rules of etiquette.[25] Most of the regulations seem designed to insure that the animal is killed in hand-to-hand, face-to-face combat. For example, in some groups, the animal may be killed only while running toward the hunter or (when a bear) only while standing on its hind legs facing the hunter. It may never be killed while sleeping in its den. In addition, it may only be wounded in certain spots (the most frequent interdiction is against wounding it in the eye) and the wound is to be bloodless. The controlling idea is that the animal is not killed by the hunter's initiative, rather the animal freely offers itself to the hunter's weapon. Therefore, the animal is talked to before the kill; it is requested to wake up and come out of its den or to turn around and be killed. To quote one example, from D. Zelenin:

> The Yakuts say that if one kills a bear in his hibernation den, without taking care to awake or warn him, other bears will attack the hunter while he sleeps. A Nanay hunter, upon encountering a bear in the open, does not kill him at once, but begins by addressing dithyrambic praise poems to him and then prays that the bear will not claw him. Finally he addresses the bear: "You have come to me, Lord Bear, you wish me to kill you. . . . Come here, come. Your death is at hand, but I will not chase after you."[26]

Among almost all of these northern hunting groups, there is a disclaimer of responsibility recited over the animal's corpse immediately after it has been killed.[27] "Let us clasp paws in handshake. . . . It was not I that threw you down, nor my companion over there. You, yourself, slipped and burst your belly."[28] Even responsibility for the weapons will be disclaimed: "Not by me was the knife fashioned, nor by any of my countrymen. It was made in Estonia from iron bought in Stockholm."[29]

The conclusion of the hunt proper, the "return to camp," has been described by Lot-Falck as a "strategic retreat."[30] The hunters leave the world of the forest and return to that of the human, bearing the corpse of the slain animal. There is continued need for etiquette in the treatment of the corpse, in the reintegration of the hunters into human society, in the eating of the flesh, and in insuring that the animal's soul will return to its "Supernatural Owner." The corpse may be adorned and carried in solemn procession. The hunters continue to disclaim responsibility, reminding the animal that now its soul is free to return to its spiritual domicile and assuring it that its body will be treated with respect. "You died first, rather than us, greatest of all animals. We will respect you and treat you accordingly. No woman shall eat your flesh. No dog shall insult your corpse."[31] Ceremonies of purification are performed by and for the hunters on their arriving at camp; women play a prominent role in ritually greeting the men, reintegrating them into the domestic world.

The animal's corpse is butchered and divided according to strict rules of rank and prestige so that its body becomes a social map of the camp. Certain parts are set aside, in particular the head and bones. Among northern hunters, bones play an analogous role to that of seeds in agrarian societies. Bones endure; they are the source of rebirth after death. The bones are a reservoir of life; they require only to be refleshed.[32] The meal is governed by rules, as the animal is an invited guest at a banquet held in his honor and consisting of his meat. Each piece of meat, as it is consumed, is wedded, in some traditions, to the life of the one who eats. The animal's "generic" life endures in the bones; its "individuality" is preserved by its consumer.[33] The majority of these return elements are joined together in the series of ancient texts which were collected by Elias Lönnrot as the forty-sixth rune of the Finnish *Kalevala*.[34]

Having followed the standard reports and interpretations to this point, we must, at this time, ask some blunt questions. In particular, can we believe what I have summarized above on good authority? This is a question which cannot be avoided. The historian of religion cannot suspend his critical faculties, his capacity for disbelief, simply because the materials are "primitive" or religious.

First, some general questions. Can we believe that a group which depends on hunting for its food would kill an animal only if it is in a certain posture? Can we believe that any animal, once spotted, would stand still while the hunter recited "dithyrambs" and ceremonial addresses? Or, according to one report, sang it love songs![35] Can we believe that, even if they wanted to, they could kill an animal bloodlessly and would abandon a corpse if blood was shed or the eye damaged? Can we believe that any group could or would promise that neither dogs nor women would eat the meat, and mean it? Is it humanly plausible that a hunter who has killed by skill and stealth views his act solely as an unfortunate accident and will not boast of his prowess? These, and other such questions, can be answered from the "armchair." They do not depend on fieldwork but upon our sense of incredulity, our estimate of plausibility. Our answers will have serious consequences. For if we answer "yes" to these questions, if we accept all we have been told on good authority, we will have accepted a "cuckoo-land" where our ordinary, commonplace, common-sense understandings of reality no longer apply. We will have declared the hunter or the "primitive" to be some other sort of mind, some other sort of human being, with the necessary consequence that their interpretation becomes impossible. We will have aligned religion with some cultural "death wish," for surely no society that hunted in the manner described would long survive. And we will be required, if society is held to have any sanity at all, to explain it away.

If our sense of incredulity is aroused, we need, as historians of religion, to get up from the armchair and into the library long enough to check the sources. For example, despite the description of the hunt I have given, most of the groups from which this information was collected do not, in fact, hunt bears face-to-face but make extensive use of traps, pitfalls, self-triggering bows, and snares. In more recent times, the shotgun has been added to their arsenal.[36] This precludes most of the elements of ritual etiquette I have described: no hand-to-hand combat, no addressing of the bear, no control over where it is wounded. The Koryak and Chukchi are characteristic of those who actually encounter a bear. When attacking the bear in winter, while it is in its den, they block the entrance to the den with a log, "break in the roof and stab the beast to death or shoot it." When bears are encountered outside their den, in spring or autumn, they set packs of dogs on it to "worry the animal."[37] No sign of ritual etiquette here! Of even greater interest is the following. The Nivkhi *say* that "in order not to excite the bear's posthumous revenge, do not surprise him but rather have a fair stand-up fight," but the same report goes on to describe how they *actually* kill bears: "a spear, the head of which is covered with spikes, is laid on the ground, a cord is attached to it and, as the bear approaches [the ambush] the hunter [by pulling up on the cord] raises the weapon and the animal becomes impaled on it."[38] As this last suggests, not only ought we not to believe many of the elements in the description of the hunt as usually presented, but we ought not to believe that the hunters, from whom these descriptions were collected, believe it either.

There appears to be a gap, an incongruity between the hunters' ideological statements of how they *ought* to hunt and their actual behavior while hunting. For me, it is far more important and interesting that they say this is the way they hunt than that they actually do so. For now one is obligated to find out how *they* resolve this discrepancy rather than to repeat, uncritically, what one has read. It is here, as they face the gap, that any society's genius and creativity, as well as its ordinary and understandable humanity, is to be located. It is its skill at rationalization, accommodation, and adjustment.

I first became aware of this particular set of issues when reading the account of pygmy elephant-hunting in R. P. Trilles's massive study, *Les Pygmées de la forêt équatoriale*. Let there be no misunderstanding. A pygmy who kills an elephant by means other than a deadfall does so by an extraordinary combination of skill and nerve. After shooting it with poisoned arrows, an individual, possessing what Trilles terms an *audace singulière* runs under the elephant—what one of their songs describes as "this huge mass of meat, the meat that walks like a hill"—and stabs upward with a poisoned spear.[39] The corpse is then addressed in songs. Combining two of these, one hears an extraordinary set of rationalizations.

1. Our spear has gone astray, O Father Elephant.
   We did not wish to kill you.
   We did not wish to kill you, O Father Elephant.
2. It is not the warrior who has taken away your life—
   Your hour had come.
   Do not return to trample our huts, O Father Elephant.
3. Do not make us fear your wrath.
   Henceforth your life will be better.
   You go to the country of the spirits.

   . . . .
   We have taken you away, but we have given you back
   a different sort of life.
   Against your children, Father Elephant, do not be angry.
   You begin a better life.

This is immediately followed by the ecstatic cry:

   O honor to you, my spear!
   My spear of sharpened iron, O honor to you![40]

The progression is clear. (1) We did not mean to kill you; it was an accident. (2) We did not kill you; you died a natural death. (3) We killed you in your own best interests. You may now return to your ancestral world to begin a better life. The final ejaculation may be paraphrased: "Never mind all of that. Wow! I did it!"

Once we have heard this last prideful cry, and remember the details of the poisoned arrows and spears, we are in danger of dismissing the rest as hypocrisy. The hunter does not hunt as he says he hunts; he does not think about his hunting as he says he thinks. But, unless we are to suppose that, as a "primitive," he is incapable of thought, we must presume that *he* is aware of this discrepancy, that he works with it, that he has some means of overcoming this contradiction between word and deed. This work, I believe, is one of the major functions of ritual.

I would suggest that, among other things, *ritual represents the creation of a controlled environment* where the variables (i.e., the accidents) of ordinary life may be displaced *precisely* because they are felt to be so overwhelmingly present and powerful. *Ritual is a means of performing the way things ought to be in conscious tension to the way things are in such a way that this ritualized perfection is recollected in the ordinary, uncontrolled, course of things.* Ritual relies for its power on the fact that it is concerned with quite ordinary activities, that what it describes and displays is, in principle, possible for every occurrence of these acts. But it relies, as well, for its power on the perceived fact that, in actuality, such possibilities cannot be realized.

There is a "gnostic" dimension to ritual. It provides the means for demonstrating that we know what ought to have been done, what ought to have taken place. But, by the fact that it is ritual action rather than everyday action, it demonstrates that we know "what is the case." Ritual provides an occasion for reflection and rationalization on the fact that what ought to have been done was not done, what ought to have taken place did not occur. From such a perspective, ritual is not best understood as congruent with something else—a magical imitation of desired ends, a translation of emotions, a symbolic acting out of ideas, a dramatization of a text, or the like. Ritual gains force where incongruency is perceived and thought about.

Two instances may be provided from the northern hunters by way of illustrating the implications of such an understanding of ritual.

As is well known, a number of these circumpolar peoples have a bear festival in which a bear is ritually slain.[41] To give a brief, highly generalized description. A young, wild bear cub is taken alive, brought to a village, and caged. It is treated as an honored guest, with high courtesy and displays of affection, at times being adopted by a human family. After two or three years, the festival is held. The bear is roped and taken on a farewell walk through the village. It is made to dance and play and to walk on its hind legs. Then it is carefully tied down in a given position and ceremonially addressed. It is slain, usually by being shot in the heart at close range; sometimes, afterward, it is strangled. The body is then divided and eaten with ceremonial etiquette (the same rules that pertain to the consumption of game). Its soul is enjoined to return to its "Owner" and report how well it has been treated.

Many valuable interpretations of these festivals have been proposed, each illuminating important elements of the ritual. I should like to suggest another aspect: that *the bear festival represents a perfect hunt.*[42] The etiquette of the hunt—the complex structures of host/guest/visitor/gift—presupposes a reciprocity that cannot be achieved in the actual hunt because, at the very least, one of the parties, the bear, will more than likely *not* play its appointed role. In the actual hunt, the hunter might attempt to play his part; the animal will not reciprocate, nor will it respond in the required manner. And the bear's failure to reciprocate will prevent the hunter from making his attempt if the hunt is to be successful qua hunt (i.e., the gaining of meat without injury or loss of life to the hunter). But in the bear festival all of the variables have been controlled. The animal has been compelled to play its part. The bear was treated correctly as a guest. It was constrained to rejoice in its fate, to walk to its death rather than run away, to assume the correct posture for its slaughter, to have the proper words addressed to it (regardless of length) before it is killed, to be slain face-to-face, and to be killed in the proper all-but-bloodless manner.[43] It is conceivable that the northern hunter, while hunting, might hold the image of this perfect hunt in his mind.[44] I would assume that, at some point, he reflects on the difference between his actual modes of killing and the perfection represented by the ceremonial killing.

I would advance a similar proposal for interpretation of what is usually termed "mimetic" or "sympathetic hunting magic."[45] The basic idea of such magic, according to most scholars, is that of "like producing like," with the notion that when the hunter has made a representation of the animal and then acted out killing it, there is an "expectation that the hunter will be able to inflict a corresponding injury to the real animal . . . [and] what was done to an accurate portrayal of the animal would, sooner or later, happen to the animal itself."[46] I would insist, on the contrary, that "sympathetic hunting magic" is not based on the principle that "like produces like," but rather on the principle that the *ritual is unlike the hunt*. Such "magic" is, once more, *a perfect hunt with all the variables controlled*. The figure, the representation of the animal, is immobile because it is inanimate. The proper words may be spoken, the animal may be placed in the proper position, it may be wounded in the proper place, and it surely will not bleed. Such a ceremony performed before undertaking an actual hunt demonstrates that the hunter knows full well what ought to transpire if he were in control; the fact that the ceremony is held is eloquent testimony that the hunter knows full well that it will not transpire, that he is not in control.

There is, I believe, an essential truth to the old interpretation of "sympathetic magic" as an "offensive against the objective world"[47] but that the wrong consequences were deduced. It is not that "magical" rituals compel the world through representation and manipulation; rather they express a realistic assessment of the fact that the world cannot be compelled. The ritual is incongruent with the way things are or are likely to be, for contingency, variability, and accidentality have been factored out. The ritual displays a dimension of the hunt that can be thought about and remembered in the course of things. It provides a focusing lens on the ordinary hunt which allows its full significance to be perceived, a significance which the rules express but are powerless to effectuate. It is in ritual space that the hunter can relate himself properly to animals which are both "good to eat" and "good to think."

5　The Unknown God: Myth in History

Men of Athens, I perceive that in every way you are religious. For as I passed along and observed the objects of your worship, I found also an altar with this inscription on it: To an unknown god. What therefore you worship as unknown, this I proclaim to you.

Acts 17:23–24

Like the Greeks, they [the Maori] have given a place to the unknown [Christian] God among their other divinities.

Taranaki Herald, 20 September 1862

I

I intend to reflect on the problem of myth and history—not as usually put, as a distinction between repetition and uniqueness, circularity and linearity. For so stated, it is an uninteresting discussion, one more influenced by biblical apologetics and the frustrated attempt to locate the Bible as unique than by the proper concerns of the historian of religion.[1] Rather I should like to reflect on the historicity of myth, not in the sense of recovering historical realia from myths—the sort of patient, critical enterprise carried out with notable success by the Africanists[2]— but rather on the historical context of myth and the question of the utility of concern for such context in the interpretation of texts by historians of religion. This grows out of an increasing preoccupation with making clear and explicit the *preinterpretative decisions and operations* undertaken prior to exegesis by the historian of religion. Such public clarity is a necessary step in the formation of a discipline, and too often refused by historians of religion.

In chapter 6, I will seek to set the well-known Ceramese myth of Hainuwele within the context of a post-European "cargo situation" rather than interpreting it as an archaic, tuber cultivator text, and the Babylonian Akitu festival within a hellenistic postconquest situation rather than viewing it as reflecting archaic, second millennium New Year rituals involving the humiliation and/or death of the king (or deity). This allows me to develop the theme of "rectification," obscured by previous interpreters who held both these texts to be archaic and, hence, both the myths and rituals to be concerned with repetition.[3] In this essay, I should like to attempt the same sort of analysis for a Maori cosmogony, the creation of the world by Io.[4]

I have not chosen this Maori text at random. It has played an important role in the development of the history of religions. A succession of major scholars have devoted articles to it.[5] It has attained all but canonical status within the discipline. Indeed, this status has been imputed to its native context as well. Thus Eliade terms it "the Polynesian cosmogonic myth," one that stands "high in the estimation of the Polynesians."[6]

In their use of the text, scholars of religion have focused on three topics: (1) the "High God" and the question of *Urmonotheismus,* using this text to extend the range of this religious form to Oceania; (2) the question of the relationship of the "High God" to "secondary deities"; and (3) the notion that in archaic religion, the cosmogony provides the model for all creative human activity (a portion of this text has been used, especially by Eliade, as *the* proof text for this point).

A "High God" text was chosen as well because the problem with which this essay is concerned was raised with respect to this sort of data at an early date, albeit in a somewhat unrefined form. I need not rehearse the dramatic discovery of the figure of "All Father" among the Australian aborigines, especially as set forth in the writings of A. W. Howitt in the *Journal of the Royal Anthropological Institute* between 1882 and 1887,[7] and the use of this material, along with comparative data, to develop a theory of the origin of religion by Andrew Lang in *The Making of Religion,* especially in two chapters entitled, "The High Gods of Low Races," and "More Savage Supreme Beings."[8] Nor do I need to rehearse the extension of the Australian materials to other cultures in the massive works of Father Wilhelm Schmidt and Raffaele Pettazzoni.[9] It may, as well, be recalled that in an article entitled, "The Limits of Savage Religion," E. B. Tylor, largely in response to Lang, forcefully argued that the "High Gods" were the result of direct or indirect influence from missionary activities by European Christians.[10] Although such influence could often be questioned in the specific examples Tylor adduced,[11] Tylor's point has always seemed to me persuasive, at least to deserve more attention than the slighting references often given to it in the works of historians of religion. Important reformulations of Tylor's model, made with better evidence and more sophisticated theories, have been proposed, on somewhat different grounds, in the case of African traditions by Robin Horton and Jack Goody. Indigenous, latent "High Gods" become increasingly explicit in response to missionary activities and native theological speculation.[12] This is to reopen the question of the historicity of the "High God" myths in particular cultural settings in contrast to some postulation of their timeless and universal archaic presence.

II

To begin with an agendum for the preinterpretative study of the Maori text, we need, first, to establish *context,* both native context and our academic context. The latter is suggested by the debates over *Urmono- theismus.*

The first step must be the gathering of the most proximate contextual information, that conveyed in the text as published.[13] The cosmogony, according to a prefatory editorial note, was given in Maori by a native, Tiwai Paraone, of the Maru-tuahu (Ngati Maru) tribe of Hauraki, to a British colonial officer, Colonel Gudgeon, in the last quarter of the nine- teenth century. (The latter point is an inference. The note, published in 1907, states "some years ago.") Whether it was given in oral or written form is nowhere stated, but an oral recitation is strongly suggested by the style of parts II and III, by the reference in V to memory and in a footnote by the translator discussed below. The text was presented by Gudgeon to the Polynesian Society in New Zealand, under whose auspices it was translated by Hare Hongi. The Maori text with English translation was published in the *Journal of the Polynesian Society* for 1907 and was widely distributed as well by a separate offprint.

Gudgeon's original document is not available for study. One later scholar terms it "a mystery jealously guarded by the editors" of the *Journal.*[14] As neither I nor many other historians of religion who have written on this text read Maori, we must presume the text to be well translated. This presumption is supported by the fact that, save for one detail, there is little difference, apart from matters of style, between Hare Hongi's 1907 translation and a later translation of the text, by J. Prytz Johansen, published in 1958.[15]

As the editorial note makes clear, Io is being presented to the readers of the *Journal* as a hitherto secret deity. He is alleged to be the supreme creator god of the Maori, unknown to the majority of the Maori as well as to all Europeans. Knowledge of Io was reserved to the highest class of priesthood. His name could be uttered only in settings of extreme ritual purity.

To evaluate this claim, we must evaluate the sources. We are given three names for which information external to the text may be sought. (1) *Tiwai Paraone.* Nothing further is known for certain. His name does not recur in any other article on the Maori that I have seen. He is listed as a (native) corresponding member of the Polynesian Society from 1894 through 1913. There is, presumably, archival material concerning him.

(2) *Colonel Gudgeon*. Walter Edward Gudgeon (1842–1920) was a prominent British colonial and military figure. Distinguished during the Maori Wars, he served successively as captain of the native constabulary, under secretary of defense, commissioner of police for the dominion, and a judge of the Native Land Court. He was a founding member and first president of the Polynesian Society and wrote extensively on the Maori.[16]
(3) *Hare Hongi*. A Maori half-breed with the British name of H. M. Stowell. An exceedingly eccentric and often unreliable scholar, he played an important role in the early years of the society.[17] From such data, not much of importance may be concluded with any degree of assurance.

Staying with the text as published, we need next to attempt to describe it, fix its boundaries and form, and determine its setting. This is extremely difficult, for the text appears quite variegated.[18]

The opening section is a creation myth presented in poetic form. This is rare among collected Maori cosmogonies. Does this suggest that it was recited at a ritual? Again, this would be unusual. Section II describes I as "sayings" and records their recitation in a variety of cultic and noncultic settings.[19] Thus I appears unusual when compared with other Maori materials, a necessary step in preinterpretation in order to locate the particular text under discussion.

Section II contains what appear to be a poetic commentary and a prose one on the use of the myth in I. To whom is it addressed? Who are the "friends" referred to at the beginning of the prose commentary? Is this a part of the original text addressed by a Maori priest to the devotees of Io? Is it similar to a sermon preached on a sacred text? Or, are the "friends" the presumed western readers and the comments intended as testimony as to how the text was used in the cult by Tiwai Paraone or someone else?

Section III appears to be a personal aside. By Tiwai Paraone? By someone else? I do not know why the square brackets were inserted by the editors. Unlike the conventions in publishing ancient texts, there is no apparent consistency to the use of brackets and parentheses in the *Journal*.

Section IV appears to be a prose fragment of a cosmogony. It seems out of place in its present location, but connects well with the conclusion to I. Does this suggest some textual disarrangement? Is this a mark of oral composition?

Section V continues the myth of Io in a "recital." Was this originally a part of I? Is it another version? It is in more traditional Maori form and introduces a number of familiar Maori deities and cosmogonic motifs, especially the separation of Sky Father (Rangi) from Earth Mother (Papa). The second list in V is structured around the common Maori theogonic motif of sexual generation. But who are the "brethren" in the strange aside that begins this section? Are they devotees of Io? Is the question to be interpreted as catechetical? Are they the Maori ("many brethren") as distinct from the devotees of Io? Are they the Europeans?

The final section VI appears to be a set of learned glosses. By whom? They summarize traditional Maori lore, especially the legends of Maui, the Polynesian trickster. Io is mentioned only once, by way of an aside. What is this section's relationship to the Io tradition? Does it belong with this text?

We can answer none of our preinterpretative questions about this text with any security. The best we can conclude is that the text, at first glance, appears to be composite. This is recognized by Hare Hongi in a footnote to his translation:

> the text may be described as the fragment of a mosaic, some of the missing parts of which have been substituted [for] by slightly later material, which causes a confusion of the original pattern.

By whom was this "substitution" performed? On what basis does he conclude that there has been use of "slightly later material"? What does he mean by "the original pattern"? Does Gudgeon's original manuscript provide additional information that was available to him, but not to us? He continues:

> Had the reciter been asked to repeat it on many different occasions, each recital being separately written, slight variations would have enabled such a reconstruction of its parts as to more really accord with its antique and original setting. It is now apparently too late to do this and we are obliged to take it as we find it. In some important respects, the fragment is unique. It is informing in its introduction of new ideas.[20]

The preinterpretative questions raised thus far make the text difficult to interpret insofar as they raise fundamental issues as to the nature and extent of the text which is to be exegeted. Is the poetic myth (section I) the text, and all the rest native interpretation? This is how the majority of scholars have considered the text, and therefore they have dispensed with commenting on sections II through VI. Are I and II the text? So Eliade and Long.[21] Are I and V, the poetic "recitals," the text? So Johannes C. Andersen.[22] Or should we attempt to interpret the entire text as given, I through VI, while recognizing its apparently composite character? The latter task has not been undertaken.

If these preinterpretative questions about the extent of the text give rise to frustration, questions about the setting of the text result in further puzzlement. By whom was it said? To whom was it addressed? Is there a difference between its original setting and its presentation to Gudgeon? If we accept the statement that the cult of Io was a secret group which jealously guarded its traditions, here we find a possibly initiated native telling a certainly uninitiated foreigner its secret myths and rituals. In what sort of a setting might this occur? Why? Does this affect our understanding of the text?

If we assume that the persona of the text is Tiwai Paraone—an assumption I am not at all certain we are entitled to make—was he a priest of Io or a member of the cult? Was he fully initiated? Was he a learned, native outsider? As there are no certain clues external to the text, we must derive our information from the aside in III.

He does not seem to be a fully initiated member, most certainly not a priest, as he invites his listener to "seek out a skilled Maori" for details about the rituals he names. He knows something about the Io cult, but not much. He "knows not the details," his information is "fragmentary," he has "caught but fragments." But why should even these be revealed to an outsider? The text was given by a native informant to a British soldier in a period of military conflict between the Maori and the Whites, during a time of rejection, by the Maori, of European missionaries and culture. (Note the reference to the Waikato War and to the Maori hearts "which were torn from them by Christian doctrine and European law.") The person who speaks in section III expects to die soon. He believes that the rituals he describes are no longer efficacious. Even the war ritual was not used against the Whites.

The persona in III explicitly asks our question: "Why then need I withhold these sacred rituals?" But how do we interpret his answer? Are we receiving the traditions of a man in despair who is convinced that a cherished cult no longer has power? Does he believe that his culture is breaking apart, and that secrecy no longer matters? Is he resentful of the cult's apparent failure and seeking to damage it further by revealing its secrets? Does he believe that the teachings of the cult were false? Or does he believe that the Maori are doomed, and is he seeking to pass on to their conquerors their valued spiritual heritage? All of these reasons have been the motivation for revealing secret traditions in other societies (especially among the Amerindians). Which one of these, or what other one (e.g., he was paid), is operative here? We cannot know on the basis of the information given in the text. Yet our evaluation of the text, which is at the same time an evaluation of the informant, would be aided if we could. *The text is a transaction between two quite particular individuals at a quite particular time.* The attempt to clarify these particularities must be a leading item in the preinterpretative agendum.

III

Our text was first published in 1907. It is the *earliest* extensive source of information on Io and, as such, takes on peculiar importance.[23] The next moment of significance is 1913, which must be taken as *the* creative year in Io scholarship. Two scholars, Elsdon Best and S. Percy Smith, both associated with the Dominion Museum and the Polynesian Society, issued massive documents on the Io cult, derived from native informants, which present total, esoteric systems of Io mythology, theosophy, and cult. The material is varied. Lists of titles, invocations, and rituals predominate.[24] The source of these materials is alleged to be a secret Maori "college" of *tohungas* (priests skilled in ancient lore).

There is nothing inherently improbable in this. We know of many such esoteric tribal traditions and institutions. It has been one of the deficiencies of ethnography that such evidence—and, for that matter, both formal and informal native exegetical labors—have not been well collected. However, our evaluation of such materials must depend on our evaluation of the informants. (Carlos Castaneda's reports of the "teachings" of Juan Matus would be an obvious example of both the claim and the need for an evaluation of the claim.)

Smith and Best relied on a single informant for the bulk of their data. H. Te Whatahoro (J. M. Jury) was a baptized Christian half-breed who had lived most of his life in European style and whose skill in the Maori language appears to have been deficient. According to what can be pieced together from several sources, in the late 1850s a group of Maori from the Wairarapa District, meeting on political matters, agreed that ancient tribal traditions should be taught to a group of young men. Three priests, each a former convert to Christianity, agreed to undertake the task. Moihi Te Matorohanga served as the prime tradent, with Nepia Pohuhu and Paratene Te Okawhare supplementing his accounts. Whatahoro was to act as "scribe." The materials were dictated over the better part of a decade in a specially constructed ritual house. The manuscripts remained in Whatahoro's possession. In 1899, Tamanau Manupuku made a plea that a record be made of old Maori traditional learning before those who were knowledgeable died out. In 1905, there was an intertribal meeting which formed a committee (the Taane-nui-a-rangi komiti) and a number of old manuscript books and oral traditions were put "forward and the selection of the best of these made by a popular vote." In 1906–7, the committee agreed on the "authorization" of the materials recorded by Whatahoro from Matorohanga, Pohuhu, and Okawhare. These were transcribed into two volumes which the committee sealed. In 1910, these volumes were deposited in the Dominion Museum. They are now lost. But copies of them by Hare Hongi and Best survive, as well as a large collection of Whatahoro manuscripts. These, supplemented by questions asked of Whatahoro by Best and Smith, are alleged to provide the bulk of the Io traditions that they record.[25]

There is considerable evidence that Best mistrusted Whatahoro. Smith appears to have had no questions concerning his credibility.[26] Later scholars have treated the matter of Whatahoro's veracity with more severity.[27] The judgment by E. W. G. Craig is typical: "The information on Io certainly flowed freely, but how much of it stemmed from the original teachings of Te Matorohanga, and how much from Whatahoro's fertile imagination, it is impossible to say."[28] More recent study of the complex Whatahoro manuscripts has demonstrated that none of the Io materials are contained in documents that may be traced back to the traditions "approved" by the Taane-nui-a-rangi committee and, hence, to Matorohanga.

> Almost all of *Te Kauae Runga* ["Things Celestial"—the first part of the Whatahoro materials published by Smith as *The Lore of the Wharewānanga*] corresponds with the contents of Best's copies of the original Taane-nui-a-rangi manuscripts which are said to have been approved by a committee of tribal leaders from the Hawkes Bay and Wairarapa areas. If authentic tradition can be defined as that body of lore which is accepted as genuine by mature well-informed members of the group concerned, *Te Kauae Runga* (with the exception of Chapter 2 [i.e., the chapter containing almost all of the Io materials]) can be accepted as such.[29]

With the 1913 publications by Best and Smith, a period of intense discussions of Io began. Europeans tended to treat these reports with either excessive skepticism or credulity, both equally naive.[30] For the Maori, decisively defeated by the British, the "discovery" of Io was an occasion for intense national pride.[31] A number of books and articles, in Maori and English, most published in New Zealand, claimed to give further details. I find nothing in this literature after 1913 that cannot be accounted for as an extension or elaboration of the materials in Best and Smith which were available in both Maori and English.

During this period, two further tasks were attempted, although both were present in rudimentary form prior to 1913: the collection of evidence for the prehistory of the Io cult and the demonstration of its wide diffusion throughout Polynesia. Neither of these attempts can be judged successful, although they persist in the literature.[32]

In what might be termed a quest for prestigious origins, the literature on the Maori prior to the period 1907–13 was ransacked for possible references to Io. It is likely that none of the references that were uncovered would have seemed of great significance before the publications by Hare Hongi, Best, and Smith.

The first strategy was to collect reports of an alleged, unnamed Maori supreme being from the early period of European contact with the Maori, the assumption being that these were reports of Io, but without mention of his tabooed name. A handful were located. They are all vague and suggest the use of Christian vocabulary on the part of missionary writers rather than signs of the presence of a cult of Io. For example, "there is not a wind that blows but that they [the Maori] imagine it bears some message from the supreme being."[33] From such materials, nothing can be concluded with certainty.

The second strategy was to note mentions of Maori deities whose names were secret, the assumption being that this prohibition was a sufficient cause for assuming that the deity was Io. Perhaps the most influential example would be an anthology of such reports, undated and from un-identified informants, which appeared in 1904 in E. Tregear's widely quoted *The Maori Race:*

> Each initiate into the sacred mysteries considered his knowledge as a trust to be guarded against the outer world, and it is only under the most exceptional circumstances that information could be acquired. Some gods could only be named in the Whare Kura or Whare-wananga (temples) of the tribe. To utter "the ineffable name" (Io) under a roof of any kind was to blaspheme most frightfully, and would be a sacrilege that only an ignorant person (religiously ignorant) like a European would have the depravity to attempt. Even the names of ancestors, as god-descended, would not be regarded as treated with due respect if mentioned at certain times or in unsuitable localities. A European student of Maori lore once ventured to speak to an old priest whom he met in a country store (shop) and asked him some question about ancient history. The Maori turned round with a disgusted look and remarked, "This is no place in which to speak of solemn things."[34]

There appears to be nothing in this composite account that would suggest to anyone not already committed to the notion of Io, that the reference is to a supreme being, let alone that the deity be identified as Io. What is reported is a set of well-known cultic regulations concerning purity and secrecy of names. The plural "gods" and the fact that the same prohibitions are applied to ancestors and tribal traditions indicate that nothing like Io is being referred to. Rather this is a catalog of items which may not be mentioned except in a sacred precinct.[35] That Tregear, in 1904, draws the assumption that the reference is to Io indicates only that the deity was being discussed in the circle of European scholars associated with the Polynesian Society and with colonial activities prior to the 1907 publication of the Io cosmogony.

Finally, there was the attempt to recover explicit mentions of Io's name in materials prior to 1907–13. The earliest alleged reference to Io as a supreme deity occurs in a report, published in 1876, by C. O. Davis:

while travelling with a distinguished Maori chieftain some years ago, he inadvertently revealed the fact that the Maoris in olden times worshipped a Supreme Being whose name was held to be so sacred that none but a priest might utter it at certain times and places. The name was Io, perhaps an abbreviation of Io-uru. Witnessing my anxiety to obtain further information on the subject, he refused to disclose any more Maori secrets as he called them, and politely referred me to an old priest who resided about one hundred miles off.[36]

Here too, as in the case of Tregear, one must ask whether the identification with Io is not a gloss, rather than a direct statement from the informant. Perhaps Davis was influenced by his transcription and translation, later in the same volume, of what he claims to be "one of the oldest" Maori prayers—if accurate, the earliest reference to Io in direct Maori speech published by a European.

Move on, O Whakatau
Move to Hawaiki
Establish there thy house
As though it were [beneath] the *maru* [shadow, shelter or sacred leadership, or protecting care] of Io.[37]

However, as Buck has demonstrated, Davis misread the text. The fourth line, which he divided, *Me ko maru a Io,* ought to be read, *Me ko Te Maru-aio,* "your house, the Shelter-of-Peace." Buck dismisses Davis's reference as "pseudo-evidence."[38]

In a chapter entitled "The God Io," John White, in 1887, offered a single sentence from Ngati Hu tradition which is the first unambiguous claim concerning Io in direct native speech: "Io is really the god. He made the heaven and the earth."[39] Without context, it is impossible to evaluate this claim. The rest of White's chapter contains a yam-planting invocation in which "O Io" appears at the end of each unit—most probably to be understood as the refrain "i-o!"[40] rather than as the god's proper name—and a lengthier section which explains that Io means "twitch" and goes on to record a set of omens from the Ngati Ruani based on various spasms that serve as "signs of good and evil."[41] As one scholar caustically notes, "White supported a page of a god Io with three pages of twitches (io), but capitalization does not convert a muscular twitch into a god."[42]

Elsewhere in his multivolume work, White records a Ngati Tahu genealogy with Io at its head, followed by Io-nuko and Io-rangi. This genealogical cosmogony, with its implied notion of sexual generation, compares well with many other traditional Maori cosmogonies, but represents a different mythologem than that of Io as sole creator. It does demonstrate the ease with which Io could be inserted at the head of a traditional Maori cosmogony.[43]

The most curious tradition in White is one that reports, again from the Ngati Tahu, that a "heretical teacher" held that "Tiki made man, whilst the fathers had always maintained that it was Io."[44] The "heresy" is, of course, traditional Maori lore. If the text is not European (as Johansen conjectures), then it suggests a beginning, among the Ngati Tahu, of an attempt to substitute Io for a variety of traditional Maori deities and their functions, although the theme of anthropogony in this form does not reappear in later Io traditions.[45]

Of White's five traditions concerning Io, at most three (more probably, two) can claim to survive criticism. Nevertheless, we have for the first time clear evidence for the earliest European knowledge of Io and reports of the deity's presence in indigenous Maori speculation. The date of White's publication, 1887, accords with the general range of time in which Gudgeon must have received the cosmogony printed in 1907.

In 1891, Tregear's authoritative *Maori-Polynesian Comparative Dictionary* defined Io as, "God, the Supreme Being," citing Davis and White.[46] In an appendix, he printed a Moriori genealogy with Rangi and Papa as the primordial parents and Io and Io-rangi as the tenth and eleventh of their "heaven born" descendants. This text may be used as evidence for Io's name as a deity. But it directly contradicts any understanding of Io as supreme deity. It does witness to the ease with which Io could be inserted into a traditional genealogy.[47] In the same appendix, Tregear published a Maori genealogy from the Ngati Maniapoto collected by William Mair which is headed by "Te-Ahau-o-te-Rangi (Io)" who generates Rangi and Papa. The parenthetical identification of Io is, most likely, a gloss by Tregear and not part of the original report.[48]

Finally, in the same issue of the *Journal of the Polynesian Society* as Hare Hongi's translation, there is a long narrative poem on the ascent of Tane through the heavens to "the very home in Heaven, this of Io," the title, "Io-the-parentless" occurs, and there is a possible additional reference to Io as "the nameless one." This poem seems to derive from the Whatahoro collection, and, therefore, cannot be used as independent evidence. It is an early version of what will appear in 1913.[49]

This concludes a survey of all the known independent references to Io that appeared prior to 1907–13.[50] It may be significant that none of the texts which make explicit claims regarding Io and his status suggest secrecy or the presence of separate "Io colleges," major motifs in the later, more extensive, reports. However, in 1899, S. Percy Smith referred to this:

> On the subject of Io, as the Supreme God of the Maori, a good deal could be said by a very limited number of our members [of the Poly-

nesian Society]. But they, we think, with the deep sympathy the old Pakeha Maori had with his teachers, remain silent, feeling that there are certain subjects so extremely sacred to the Maori of old that it is in them a sacrilege to speak. But *taihoa* [presently, bye and bye].[51]

I suspect this is more eloquent witness to the existence of an "Io college" among the old British colonial hands clustered around the Polynesian Society, than it is to the presence of such a "college" among the Maori.

There is one additional text, only recently republished, which may be the earliest reference to Io. In a letter, most probably sent to a Christian missionary, which gives an account of the acknowledgment of Potatau I as king by various Maori tribes, published in the *Southern Cross* for 6 August 1858, one Te Tapihana, a teacher of the Ngati Hikairo, is depicted as stepping forth and saying, "Name the King, O Io, O Io." The correspondent, Wiremu Tamihana, explains, "He meant, 'Name the King, O William, O William,' " with apparent reference to William Thompson Tarapipipi, one of Potatau's chief supporters.[52] The setting would seem to be wrong for this to be a reference to the secret Io. It is a large public gathering, including at least one European Christian missionary (Rev. Robert Burrows).[53] Yet there is a connection posited, in the later Io traditions, between Io and the institution of kingship or chieftainship.[54] The strange interpretation given Tapihana's petition by Tamihana *might* be related to the well-documented practice of substituting another, often nonsensical name, for the tabooed name of a chief.[55] I shall return to this text, below.[56]

Eliminating those texts which are doubtful, a sparse but suggestive picture may be sketched. The name Io is known to Europeans as early as 1887 (possibly as early as 1858). He is stated to be the supreme god, the maker of heaven and earth (Ngati Hu tradition). His name is inserted in various genealogical traditions (Ngati Tahu, Ngati Maniapoto[?], Moriori), but only once in its expected position of primacy. The statement with which I began this survey may be affirmed—the text translated by Hare Hongi in 1907 is the earliest published extensive information on Io and, as such, takes on peculiar importance.

As might be anticipated, given the period in which Io came into scholarly prominence, there were some attempts to provide a diffusionist account of Io in the Victorian sense of the word.[57] I cite only some representative examples:

1. It would seem that the name of Io originated in the East, since we are told that among the ancient Egyptians Io was the lunar goddess and in the language of the Argives the moon itself.
2. Can there be any doubt that the Maori deity Io is the same as the circum-Levantine Iao? If the two are identical, another clue is furnished for the threading of the labyrinth built by the Polynesians in their wanderings.

3. The Maori people obtained the name for the chief god from the Assyrians.
4. The Phoenician god Io was the supreme god of the Maori, who still on occasions keep a *hakari,* or feast, also of Cushite origins.[58]

However, most attempts were made not to prove Old World diffusion, but rather to demonstrate a pan-Oceanic distribution of the deity.

The earliest example, consistently adduced by subsequent scholarship, is a fragment of a text from Tahiti, recorded by Edmond de Bovis in 1855 and first published by him in 1863.

> In the beginning there was nothing but the god Jhoiho; there was next an expanse of water which covered the abyss and the god Tino-ta'ata (human form) floated on the surface.[59]

This is palpably a native paraphrase of Genesis 1:1–2, and cannot be used as evidence for a cult of Iho in the Society Islands, which would be the ideological as well as the linguistic equivalent of the Maori Io.[60] De Bovis recognized the close parallel to Genesis, but assumed the Tahitian tradition was independent. In fact, the text represents native Christian tradition from an area that had knowledge of biblical stories some thirty years before the arrival of the first missionaries, and for more than eighty years before de Bovis collected his text.[61] The otherwise unknown Jhoiho appears to be a native attempt at reproducing the name Jehovah.[62]

After 1913, two additional "Io cults" have been claimed: Kiho (or Kiho-Tumu) in the Tuomotus and 'Io in Hawaii.[63] Both have been proven to have been directly influenced by knowledge of the Io materials published in 1913.[64] There is no evidence for Io as an archaic, pan-Oceanic supreme deity.[65]

On the basis of this survey of published Io materials, some tentative historical conclusions may be suggested. (1) Io, as a "High God," is a post-European phenomenon.[66] (2) If we set aside the Tamihane letter of 1858,[67] there is a small collection of contextless, brief references to Io in the literature from 1887 to 1907. Little can be determined from these. (3) The first extensive information on Io is the publication of Gudgeon's text in 1907. (4) The only other major source of information is from Te Whatahoro as translated and edited by E. Best and S. Percy Smith in 1911 and published in 1913. Whatahoro's reliability as a tradent is open to severe question, being a Christian half-breed of uncertain skill in Maori. While there is little doubt that much of Whatahoro's materials can be traced back to the teachings of three formerly Christian Maori priests during the period 1863–86, the materials on Io *do not* seem a part of this transmission. There is good reason to believe that Whatahoro added the Io materials during the period 1908–11, *after* the publication of Gudgeon's text.[68] The basis for the Io traditions in Best and Smith can neither be recovered nor evaluated. (5) With both the 1907 and 1913 Io texts available in English *and* Maori, it would appear that all subsequent Io traditions among the Maori are dependent on these texts. At least, the burden of proof would fall on those who would assert otherwise. (6) All evidence for Io outside of New Zealand is either dependent upon the publications of 1907 and 1913 or upon false inference from native attempts to transliterate Jehovah or paraphrase biblical traditions in native Christian discourse.

These preinterpretative conclusions appear exceedingly negative as to the trustworthiness of the Io traditions and place a great burden on the 1907 text. But further reflection suggests that they, and the data from which they were drawn, contain some important clues to a possible reconstruction and reconsideration of the Io tradition and, therefore, of the 1907 text.

The necessary quest by the historian of religion for context as a prior condition for the interpretation of any religious text, requires, in this instance, further inquiry.

IV

Examining the traditions surveyed in the previous section suggests some chronological convergence. Geographical convergence, while less apparent, seems also present.

Starting with the text translated by Hare Hongi, the prefatory note to the 1907 publication states that Gudgeon received the text "some years ago." Gudgeon refers to the text in 1905.[69] Taking this date as the *terminus ad quem,* the *terminus a quo* may be established as 1885. In that year, *The History and Doings of the Maori* was published under the name of Gudgeon's father, T. W. Gudgeon. However, the son, W. E. Gudgeon, "supplied and wrote most of the matter contained" in the book.[70] No mention of Io occurs. Therefore, it may be assumed that the text and information concerning Io became available to Gudgeon between 1885 and 1905. But, there is more. Gudgeon was away from New Zealand, serving as the British president at Rarotonga from 1899 to 1909, after which he retired to Auckland until his death in 1920. Therefore, it seems likely that both the text and knowledge of the traditions of Io became available to Gudgeon between 1885 and 1899. I am tempted to suggest a further refinement, the period 1894–99, when both Gudgeon and Tiwai Paraone were members of the Polynesian Society, the former as its first president (1892), the latter as an early native corresponding member—but this must remain sheer conjecture.

If these arguments be accepted, then the possible dates for Gudgeon's text, 1885–99, overlap with the dates for the earliest independent notices of Io surveyed above, 1887–1907. Furthermore, while I doubt the antiquity of the Whatahoro traditions concerning Io as being older than 1908, *if* they could be traced back in some form to the Matorohanga transmission, the dates on Whatahoro's manuscripts, 1863–86, likewise converge.

The geographical provenance of the various traditions appears more scattered. Plotted according to the location of the tribes to which they are attributed or to which their tradent belonged, a clear concentration appears in the Taranaki-Waikato region. Three of the six items may be mapped in this district.[71]

Taken together, chronology and geography seem to suggest that the Io traditions reached some measure of formulation in the 1880s in the Taranaki-Waikato region. I doubt that the creation of Io as a "High God" began elsewhere or much antedated this period.

There are thematic interrelationships as well. Both the earliest tradent (Tamihane) and the latest (Whatahoro) are identified as Christians. The persona in the 1907 text states in section III that, "the fragments" of the Io theosophy "may be placed side by side with the law to become a basis for the history following on after our own time."[72] Best, in 1913, reports that his informant (probably Whatahoro) had claimed:

> I think that if your missionaries had sympathy with our people and had patiently studied the cult of Io instead of despising and condemning our belief, that the cult [of Io] would have been incorporated into your Bible.[73]

There can be little doubt that one of the purposes of the meetings of the 1850s, sealed by the Taane-nui-a-rangi committee, was an effort by formerly Christian Maoris to produce a native counterpart to the Christian Bible.[74] Finally, there is the similarity of the various transliterations of the name Jehovah in Polynesian biblical translations and paraphrases (Ihowa in Maori, Jhoiho in Tahiti, Io-ora in Rarotonga), all of which preexist any certain knowledge of the Io cult.

These thematic elements appear to point to the following conclusions. (1) The Io cult was developed in the 1880s. It was most probably created earlier, perhaps as early as the late 1850s. The cult was centered in the Taranaki-Waikato region. (2) It was deliberately created as a Maori parallel to biblical tradition. Hence, the parallels often adduced between Io traditions (e.g., section III) and Genesis must be taken as deliberate imitations.[75] By this interpretation, *the Io cult is an instance of Maori syncretism.*

If this hypothesis be valid, historians of religion will have lost an allegedly archaic "High God" and an important proof text for the nature of primitive ritual, but they will have gained an interesting *new religion,* no less interesting in its modernity than it would be if it were truly "neolithic."[76]

The question that ought to occur to any historian of religion at this point in his preinterpretative labors is whether there is any historical situation that makes these conjectures plausible and that he can connect with the specific text at hand. The answer, I believe, is affirmative. The chronology and geography, the variety of former converts as important tradents, and the desire to find Maori equivalents for European institutions must instantly coalesce for even the most casual student of New Zealand history. The context is the period and the region of the Maori Wars, a complex set of political and religious rebellions against colonial authority which began in the 1840s, intensified during the decade 1860–70, and ended (with some exceptions) in Maori defeat by 1880.[77] A review of this history becomes a necessary part of the preinterpretative study of the Io cosmogony.

V

Captain Cook was the first European to have direct recorded contact with the Maori (1767–70).[78] In the nineteenth century, contact became more intense. The first Christian missionary arrived in 1814.[79] In 1838, New Zealand was annexed by Great Britain.

Three elements in the colonization of New Zealand were of special importance.[80] (1) The explosion of the White settler population resulted in the relative as well as the absolute decline of the Maori. The number of Maori stood between 150,000 and 200,000 in 1800; by the *Census Report* of 1861, their number had been reduced to 55,336. In 1840, there were no more than 2,000 Whites, chiefly from Australia. By 1858, the Whites outnumbered the Maori. Following the discovery of gold in 1860, there was a fivefold increase in the White population in less than a decade. By 1880, there were 546,000 Whites and no more than 46,000 Maori, including some 7,000 half-breeds.[81] (2) The introduction of the musket had a devastating effect on tribal warfare. Furthermore, needing cash to purchase weapons, together with the increased pressure from the increasing settler population, the Maoris sold off their land at a rapid rate. (3) Most serious of all, in a tribal culture whose ideology traced ownership of the land back to the "original canoes" of the fourteenth-century migration to New Zealand, was the insatiable settler appetite for land, primarily for agriculture and grazing. The forests were diminished at a rate of some 5 percent per year. Out of the twelve million acres that could be cultivated, about one fifth of the total land area of the two islands, more than one and a half million acres, had been cleared and planted by 1870. This would rise to seven million acres by 1880.[82]

The Crown, by treaty with some Maori tribes in 1840, had preemptive rights to purchase Maori land. This was exercised, often paying the Maori six pence per acre and selling it to settlers for twenty times that amount.

Not only were the ancestral traditions being violated and the Maori being cheated, but also land titles, in a nonliterate culture, were extremely vague from a European viewpoint. The Maori had to resort to Native Land Courts where administrators such as Col. Gudgeon served as judges. The decisions of these courts concerning disputed property often led to intense tribal conflicts.[83] Taken together, this ensemble of elements provided a well-known scenario for the rise of nativistic resistance movements.[84] Two such movements, the King Movement and the Hauhau (Pai Marire), provide a possible context for the development of the Io traditions.

From the early 1840s through the 1850s, a number of Maori land leagues were formed. These leagues, in one district or another, sought to prevent further Maori land sales to the White settlers. In 1857, these various initiatives came together in the first attempt at a postcolonial, pan-Maori political movement—the King Movement.[85]

In June 1858, drawing upon a mixture of traditional Maori and borrowed European models of political organization, a confederation of Central North Island tribes (the Waikato, Ngati Hau, Ngati Maniapoto, and Ngati Tuwharetoa) elected a Maori king, Potatau Te Wherowhero (Potatau I), to provide leadership for a united front against further land sales to the Europeans.[86] Based upon traditional ideas of the land being under the *mana* of chiefs, in the face of the capitulation of some chiefs to the pressure to sell off their lands to the Whites, the controlling notion of the King Movement was that of placing a confederation of tribal lands under the all-encompassing *mana* of a chief of chiefs, the king, who would not weaken.[87] The king was advised by a council, which closely resembled the traditional *runanga,* and it, in turn, monitored a countercolonial system of local courts, councils, and a hierarchy of officials, as well as publishing its own newspapers.[88] From the beginning, there seems to have been tension between the older, more traditional chiefs represented by Potatau I, who were legitimated by their *mana* and who spoke in terms of ancient lore, and the younger, mission-educated chiefs, represented preeminently by Wiremu Tamihana, the prime statesman of the King Movement, who was a Waikato Christian and who employed diplomatic and political skills and spoke in terms of biblical and liturgical rhetoric.[89]

At first, the White attitude toward the Maori king was one of bemused tolerance. But this was followed, in 1860, by a military response. The first Maori War (the Taranaki or Waitara campaign), ended inconclusively. In 1861, Wiremu Tamihana negotiated a truce on behalf of the new king, Tawhio (Potatau II), the old king having died.

The second Maori War, the Waikato War, was fought in the king's home territory. It ended in military defeat for the Maoris in April 1864. Tamihana and the Ngati Hau defected. The king fled into the northern forest tribal area of the Ngati Maniapoto, which became designated as "King Country." A military solution by the Maori to their problems had proven impossible.

I would suggest that *the King Movement provides the most proximate context for the development of the Io cult and for the understanding of the 1907 Maori cosmogony.* The earliest reference to Io that is known is in Wiremu Tamihana's account of the public acknowledgment of Potatau Te Wherowhero as king in 1858.[90] The majority of instances of mentions of Io in reports prior to the publication of the cosmogony in 1907 occur in "King Country," especially from among the Ngati Maniapoto (see p. 84).[91] Main events from the history of the King Movement are referred to in section III of the 1907 text: the Waikato War, the name of the Kingite statesman, Wiremu Tamihana,[92] the military defeat of the Maoris, the fact that European property law was destroying the Maori. The voice of the persona who speaks in III is most likely that of a member of the militaristic faction within the King Movement that suffered defeat in April 1864 and went into exile with the king.[93]

In 1864, a second movement intersected with the King Movement. Known popularly as Hauhau, but more accurately, especially in its formative stages, as Pai Marire (Good and Peaceful), it had its origins, in 1862, in a reported vision of the angel Gabriel seen by a Taranaki Maori, Te Ua Haumene Horopapera Tuwhakararo.[94]

Te Ua was born in the early 1820s. Taken captive at an early age by the Waikato, he lived in their territory, at Kawhia, and was baptized there by Wesleyan missionaries and given the Christian name of Horopapera (Zerubbabel). Although trained in mission schools and skilled in reading the Bible in Maori, he claimed to have had a traditional Maori education. Returned to Taranaki in 1840, he served as a church monitor and as a lay preacher known for his intensive study of Scripture. In 1860, he became active in the King Movement and fought in the Taranaki-Waitara War. Some nineteen months after Tamihana's truce, he had his vision.

"The circumstances of this visitation [from Gabriel] might have lent themselves to the formation of a cargo cult."[95] On 1 September 1862, the steamer *Lord Worsley* ran aground on the southwest coast of Taranaki carrying a rich cargo (including ammunition and 3,000 ounces of gold) and an equally rich complement of White passengers (including three members of the New Zealand House of Representatives, an infantry captain, and a nun). There was conflict between militaristic and pacifist factions, both within and without the King Movement, as to what to do with the cargo and passengers. In this setting, and in a state of intense agitation over the fate of the ship, Te Ua had his first vision on 5 September. The central element in the vision was that Te Ua "should reject the war-like practices."[96]

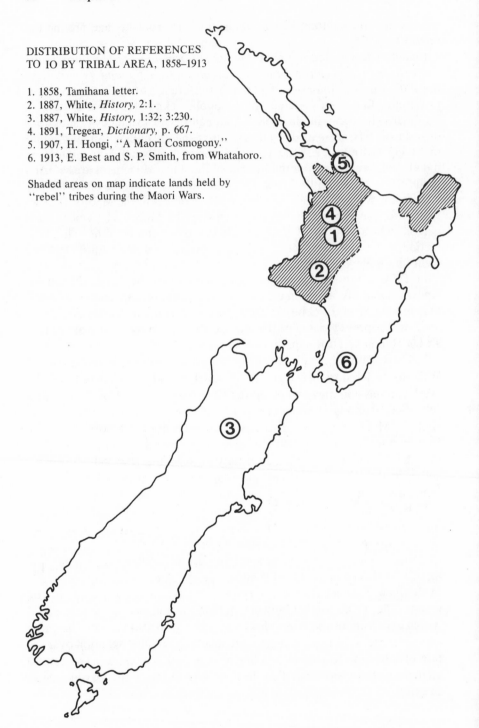

DISTRIBUTION OF REFERENCES
TO IO BY TRIBAL AREA, 1858–1913

1. 1858, Tamihana letter.
2. 1887, White, *History,* 2:1.
3. 1887, White, *History,* 1:32; 3:230.
4. 1891, Tregear, *Dictionary,* p. 667.
5. 1907, H. Hongi, "A Maori Cosmogony."
6. 1913, E. Best and S. P. Smith, from Whatahoro.

Shaded areas on map indicate lands held by
"rebel" tribes during the Maori Wars.

This vision provided the central core of Te Ua's message. During the period 1862–64, he preached peace among the Kingites. For example, in a speech to emissaries of the king, dated 13 January 1863, he declared:

It was time that begat the black and the white. Indeed, this is a concern of the Lord of Peace. Taunting and jeering is an evil. Therefore the white must not bait the black nor the black the white. . . . I became a minister in the past years when the sword was wielded. It was in the last year of the encounter [1861] that I began to speak out and argue, my chief concern being my love for this, my homeland, in the hope that the peoples of Taranaki and Ngatiruani would support the King movement. . . . [Now I ask you to] concede peacefully and seek that which is the God of Peace and help succor his people, his forsaken, naked, separated, and half-standing people. . . . Turn to that which concerns you, to the key of the land which is peace. Whatever your belief, be humble before the Lord of Peace and his followers.[97]

Following the defeat of the King Movement in April 1864, Te Ua's promise to teach "a new peaceful gospel" and "the things of the past which were hidden"[98] attracted increased attention. Potatau II, the second Maori king, adopted Pai Marire in August 1864, receiving from Te Ua his cult name of Tawhiao (To Hold the People Together). Yet, even by this time, it is apparent that Te Ua's influence within his own cult was on the wane. A militaristic solution to the Maori situation would, once more, be attempted. Te Ua died after only four years of cult activity (October 1866). His teachings remained influential on a variety of Maori prophets and cults to the present time.

Much can be written about the complex religious movement created by Te Ua; much would be familiar from the literature on cargo cults, and need not be rehearsed. What characterized Te Ua was his extraordinary and consistent emphasis on peace in a time of military conflict, on a complex religious solution to the Maori situation.

Te Ua declared the name of his god to be Ihowa (Jehovah). He recognized Christ, the Holy Spirit, Gabriel, and other Christian figures alongside a host of Maori deities. Two seem to have been his own creation—Riki, god of war, and Rura, god of peace. He identified himself with Rura as well as with the Israelites in their desire to retake Canaan, signing his letters, "the peaceable Jew." He placed great emphasis on ecstatic speech (probably the original meaning of "Hau") and gave new impetus to the Maori traditional, formal religious sayings *(karakia)*. Through this, Te Ua attempted to give the Maori the possibility of direct access to Ihowa without the written Bible and the Christian missionary as intermediaries.[99]

It *may* be possible to posit a connection between Pai Marire and the 1907 cosmogony, although I do so with extreme caution. I have quoted a portion of Te Ua's speech to emissaries from the Maori king, delivered in January 1863. Three of the king's representatives are named. One of them is Paraone. Was this the same individual who became Gudgeon's informant? I doubt it. It cannot be established on the basis of the available evidence, although the name is not common. If it were to be the case, then it would establish that the tradent of the 1907 cosmogony was not only a member of the King Movement, but also well placed in its hierarchy. Further it would establish direct connection with Te Ua and his message of the Ihowa of Peace, as well as his promise to teach "the things of the past that were hidden."

John White, then native magistrate at Wanganui, who took a deep interest in Pai Marire, the same who twelve years later would begin the work of translating the materials for his *Ancient History of the Maori,* records, in a note dated 2 May 1864, that this same Paraone, after the defeat of the King Movement in April, was one of those who withdrew to the forests of "King Country" to "await the millennium."[100]

Such a native figure might well have been attracted to the variety of Christian-Maori cults founded by members of the King Movement and influenced by Te Ua following the prophet's death: the Taikomako cult (founded 1886); the cult of Ti Whiti and Tohu (1867); Tawhiao's own cult, the Tariao (1877); Ringatu (1874); the cult of Te Mahuki (1880). Such a native may have joined, as well, in the later creation and elaboration of the Io cult which was centered in the same geographical region during the same span of years.

This is all speculation. It seems to me unlikely that an individual with such a history would have been invited to join the Polynesian Society and become associated with the core of the British colonial establishment.[101] But if this Paraone is not "our" Paraone, and if "our" Paraone is not the persona of the text, someone with a history very much like the one I have inferred does stand behind the 1907 cosmogony, especially as the persona of section III.

These various cults, all more or less distinguished by their pacifism, may be related to two enigmatic traditions that cannot be dated with certainty—both were published late—although Johansen speculates that they are early evidence for a more primitive form of Io, perhaps "another Io" which preexisted the traditions of Io as supreme being.

The first is a brief lexical reference to a deity named Ioio-whenua who "represents peace and all peaceful conditions and pursuits . . . in Matatua lore."[102]

The second was collected by S. Locke from the Ngati Kahungunu, the putative center of the Whatahoro traditions of Io.[103] It is a myth which records a conflict between Rongomaraeroa, "whose sphere is that of providing food, sending his people on travels, dancing and building homes," and Tumatauenga, whose "sphere is always war and fight."[104]

The conflict is mediated by Io, who builds "a fortified place with palisades, and a watch tower," for "Io's work is that of building fortified places with palisades" and by a female deity, Mohanuiterangi. Through her, "a permanent peace was concluded. It was a peace which woman had mediated, a consolidated peace in the sacred precinct."[105]

If Johansen is right, then the earliest stratum of Io tradition associates Io with peace. Is this some development from Te Ua's Ihowa of Peace or from his invention of Rura?

Drawing these various contextual elements together, I would suggest that *the cult of Io must be understood in direct relationship to the King and Pai Marire movements; that the cult of Io, rather than continuing these movements' attempts to supplant the missionaries' Bible with ecstatic speech, sought the longer and more speculative road of providing a Maori parallel to the Bible, utilizing the revitalized* karakia *and the more prosaic forms of traditional Maori mythological and genealogical lore.*[106] I would suggest that in the same way that the traditional Maori cosmology of ten heavens had two additional heavens superimposed in the Io traditions to "make room" for Io,[107] so too with the myth. The traditional Maori mythology and cosmology has not been disturbed in the 1907 text. It was merely prefaced by the newly created, allegedly esoteric, Io mythology.

VI

If the above be taken as a plausible account of our text's context, then we may proceed to the final element in the preinterpretative agendum, a speculative reconstruction of the 1907 text. Here the historian of religion must attempt to order what is perceived as a composite document.

The typical form of Maori cosmogony is genealogy, consisting of a set of proper names related to each other, sexually, by division.[108] This is what is given in sections V and VI—indeed, in the first summary in section V, Io's name has merely been inserted at the head of a traditional list.[109] These sections represent the indigenous, generative core of the text. There is nothing specific to the Io cult in them. They have been adapted and adopted by the cult. It is possible to invoke the Horton and Goody models. Io, in relation to these traditional materials, might be understood as an expression of an indigenous impulse to posit a primordial unity.[110]

For the specifically Io mythology in the text, a history of tradition reconstruction may be proposed. The brief invocation to the power of the *karakia* in II might well be considered a prologue. Careful reading of the prose commentary in II reveals that it is not the myth of creation which is being repeated—*pace* Eliade[111]—but rather the original *karakia*, the originating formulae. "There are three occasions on which the *karakia*s in these words are brought out."[112] The *karakia*s are the generators of the myth.

In the cosmogony, it is the words which Io speaks which function as *karakia*s. Four such formulae occur in I:

1. "Night, a day owning night."
2. [Cannot be translated.]
3. "Let one night be above/ and one night below.
   Night, the magician's night.
   Night, the priest's night/ a subjected night.
   Let one Day be above/ and one Day below.
   Day, the magician's day.
   Day, the priest's Day/ a resplendent Day, a bright Day."
4. "Te Wai-ki-Tai-tama, divide the waters,
   So that heaven will unfold itself.
   Heaven has been lifted up.
   Te Tupua-horo-nuku is born."[113]

Around the base of these four sayings, the deliberate attempt to parallel Genesis 1 in section I and IV was, most likely, constructed.

The ritual parallels that can be cited elsewhere in Maori practice suggest that II is a genuine reflection of a cult.[114]

Section III is a personal aside by the informant.

At this point the preinterpretative labors may cease. An historian may wish to take up the various connections proposed between text and context and, through archival research, may uncover other evidence either for Io or for more secure connections between the cult of Io and its historical setting. The historian may wish to pursue more definite identification of the tradent of the 1907 text and recover more precisely the manner of its transmission. The historian of religion has a different task. He may choose to refuse further interpretation (if, for example, his interest in the text required that it serve as witness to an archaic pre-European "High God"); or, he may choose to continue with the tasks of exegesis and the question of further relationships between this text and other forms of religious expression both within and without New Zealand.

I would draw only one set of conclusions for the historian of religion from these preinterpretative investigations. The 1907 Io cosmogony might be labeled a fraud. It most certainly is not "neolithic," it is not "the Polynesian creation myth," and it cannot be used as evidence for *Ur-monotheismus* or for the nature of archaic ritual, as has been done in previous scholarship. But it is a genuine, perhaps even an eloquent, expression of a more recent form of Maori religion, the interpretation of which may now be undertaken, but only after the necessary labors of preinterpretation have been completed.

The text gives witness to a people who have moved, in large numbers, through several forms of religion in a short period of time: native, Christian, repudiated Christian, nativistic, King, Pai Marire, Io, and various forms of active and passive resistance. Through the kind of careful preinterpretative investigation that is a necessary prerequisite for the historian of religion's investigation of any religious text, we have been led to an appreciation of *religious work* which will repay further study, here and elsewhere. This native work has been obscured by taking the text to be static, to be archaic, to be a myth. By placing it back within its context, the historian of religion may begin to perceive its labors, its strains, its achievements. Such a study may allow us to begin to interpret properly and appreciate *homo religiosus* as being, preeminently, *homo faber.*[115]

6 A Pearl of Great Price and a Cargo of Yams: A Study in Situational Incongruity

In recent years, a number of somewhat superficial comparisons have been proposed between early Jewish and Christian apocalyptic and messianic movements and the widespread, contemporary religious phenomena variously designated as cargo cults or nativistic revitalization movements.[1] This essay is an attempt at a more complex mode of analysis of this topic by means of a comparison of the ritual texts for the Babylonian New Year (Akitu) festival with the Ceramese myth of Hainuwele. Both of these texts are believed by scholars to be extremely "archaic" and have been employed as paradigms for the interpretation of other texts (the former, most prominently by the Myth-Ritual school; the latter, by the Frobenius *Schule*). Both have been subjected to intensive analysis and enjoy a consensus as to the broad outlines of their interpretation. I shall dissent from this consensus. Neither text has been previously identified as being related either to apocalyptic tradition or to a cargo cult. I shall insist on such a relationship. By taking so quixotic and experimental an approach to these texts and by invoking the notion of situational incongruity,[2] I hope to suggest to my colleagues in the history of religions, biblical studies, and anthropology some possibilities for fruitful collaboration.[3]

With respect to both of the texts to be discussed in this paper, I should like to employ a simple stratagem in order to gain a point of entry. I would hope that the reader will be seized by an element of incongruity in each text, that he will both trust his sense of incongruity and allow himself to suppose that the same element appeared incongruous to the originators of the text, and that, thereby, he will be led to presume that the text is, among other things, a working with this incongruity.

I

The portion of the Akitu festival to which I want to draw attention is that for which it is most justly famous—the so-called ritual humiliation of the king on the fifth day of Nisannu:

(415) When he [the king] reaches [the presence of the god], the *urigallu*-priest shall leave (the sanctuary) and take away the scepter, the circle and the sword [from the king]. He shall bring them [before the god Bel] and place them [on] a chair. He shall leave (the sanctuary) and strike the king's cheek. (420) He shall place the . . . behind him. He shall accompany him (the king) into the presence of the god Bel . . . he shall drag (him by) the ears and make him bow down to the ground. . . . The king shall speak the following words (only once): "I did [not] sin, lord of the countries. I was not neglectful (of the requirements) of your godship. [I did not] destroy Babylon. I did not command its overthrow. (425) [I did not] . . . the temple Esagil. I did not forget its rites. I did not rain blows on the cheeks of a protected citizen.[4] . . . I did not humiliate them. I watched out for Babylon. I did not smash its walls.

. . . .
(Response of the *urigallu*-priest)
Have no fear . . . (435) which the god Bel. . . . The god Bel [will listen to] your prayer . . . he will magnify your lordship . . . he will exalt your kingship. . . . On the day of the *eššešu*-festival, do . . . (440) in the festival of the Opening of the Gate, purify [your] hands . . . day and night. . . . [The god Bel], whose city is Babylon . . . whose temple is Esagil . . . whose dependents are the people of Babylon. . . . (445) The god Bel will bless you . . . forever. He will destroy your enemy, fell your adversary." After (the *urigallu*-priest) says (this), the scepter, circle and sword [shall be restored] to the king. He (the priest) shall strike the king's cheek, (450) if the tears flow, (it means that) the god Bel is friendly; if no tears appear, the god Bel is angry: the enemy will rise up and bring about his downfall.[5]

The central acts of the ritual—the startling portrait of a king being slapped and pulled about by his ears—have most usually been interpreted as symbolic of "dying-rising." I am convinced, especially by the researches of Lambrechts, that this is an illegitimate category for archaic Near Eastern religions. What evidence exists for a "dying-rising" pattern is from the Late Antique and Christian eras, with the possible exception of Dumuzi, whose alternation between earth and the underworld does not conform to the alleged pattern.[6] In other interpretations, the humiliation is understood to be a descent into chaos (or Saturnalian role reversal) characteristic of New Year celebrations, or as a ritual expiation by the king on behalf of his people (i.e., as a scapegoat pattern).[7] Certainly the sequence of actions appears incongruous and without parallel.[8]

But these actions, understood as the humiliation of the king, have deflected attention from the even more incongruous "negative confession."[9] What *native* king of Babylonia ever contemplated or was guilty of destroying or overthrowing his capital city, Babylon, smashing its walls, or neglecting or destroying its major temple, Esagila? These would be inconceivable actions for a native king. But these *were* the actions of *foreign* kings (Assyrian, Persian, and Seleucid) who gained the throne of Babylon by conquest: the best-known examples, among others, would be Sennacherib, Xerxes, and Antigonus. As with Cyrus among the Israelites (whose promise to rebuild Jerusalem and restore its national temple concludes the Jewish version of the Hebrew Scriptures as organized after the Roman destruction of the temple), so too for the Babylonians—foreign kings could be named who restored Babylon and its temple, Esagila: Tiglath-Pileser III, Sargon II, Ashurbanipal, Nebuchadnezzar, Cyrus, Alexander, Seleucus I, Antiochus I, and Antiochus IV. Read in this light, the ritual of the Akitu festival becomes, in part, a piece of nationalistic religious propaganda. If the present king acts as the evil foreign kings have acted, he will be stripped of his kingship by the gods; if he acts in the opposite manner and "grasps the hand of Marduk," his kingship will be established and protected by the gods.

This combination of elements is paralleled in the Seleucid era "copy" of the previously unknown Adad-shuma-usur Epic recently published by A. K. Grayson. It narrates the rebellion by a group of native Babylonians against a foreign (Kassite) king. "The cause of the rebellion was neglect [by the king] of Marduk and Babylon . . . after the rebellion, the penitent king confesses his sins to Marduk and thereafter carries out the restoration of the temple, Esagil." The relevant portion of the text (II.22–31) is fragmentary, but, like the Akitu festival, contains a royal confession and a reference to the *kidinnu*.[10]

Such an interpretation of the Akitu festival is rendered all the more plausible by the dating of the two surviving cuneiform texts of the ritual. Despite the assumption of most scholars, that the texts provide a witness to "the New Year Festival in the form it took at Babylon in the first millennium,"[11] both copies are, in fact, from the *Seleucid* period. The various earlier texts, which speak of Marduk being captured and imprisoned, which have often been homologized to the "ritual humiliation" of the king under the pattern "dying-rising," are, in fact, of Assyrian rather than Babylonian provenance and would appear to be parodies rather than accounts of actual rituals.[12] My own conjecture would be that, while there are clearly ancient references to *an* Akitu festival, the situation and ideology projected by the Seleucid ritual texts go back no earlier than the time of Sargon II (i.e., 709 B.C.)—the earliest conqueror of Babylon consciously to adopt the Babylonian pattern and etiquette of kingship[13]— under whose rule, for the first time, one encounters texts which speak of the pattern of Assyrian recognition of the rights and privileges of the "protected citizens" of Babylon.[14] The ritual would remain relevant through the reign of Antiochus IV, the founder of the *polis* of Babylon according to an inscription dated September 166 B.C.,[15] although with heightened tension, as a pattern designed to deal with more proximate Assyrian monarchs is *reapplied* to the more foreign Seleucid rulers.

It may be that the ritual text is a witness to a *reinterpretation* of a more archaic ritual. Note that the king is slapped twice: once in the "humiliation" scene and once, after his reenthronement, as an oracular action.

> The scepter, circle and sword [shall be restored] to the king. He (the priest) shall strike the king's cheek, if the tears flow, (it means that) the god Bel is friendly; if no tears appear, the god Bel is angry: the enemy will rise up and bring about his downfall.

It is this second slapping that may be the original element in the ritual. In its most archaic form, it was probably a ritual to insure rain for the New Year inasmuch as the association of tears and blessing makes little sense in any other context.[16] Such a rain ritual would be reinterpreted as a general oracle of political success and prosperity, and then, in the first slapping, reinterpreted and replicated as a piece of nationalistic propaganda. It may, in fact, be fruitful to consider the two slapping incidents in the same ritual program as a case of redundancy, with the second reinforcing the political context of the first. That is, if the king does not comport himself as a proper, native Babylonian king (first slapping), the gods will be angry and "the enemy will rise up and bring about his downfall" (second slapping). The first implies a direct divine sanction; the second, an indirect divine sanction.

If this interpretation of the "humiliation" episode is correct, then we may gain a new understanding of the central role of the so-called creation epic, Enuma elish, in the New Year's ritual. It is now a general consensus that a major presupposition of the Myth-Ritual school was in error. Contrary to what has been maintained, the Akitu festival was not a reenactment of the creation myth. But it has been rarely noted that, apart from an enigmatic commentary of Assyrian provenance,[17] our sole Babylonian witness to the connection of the Enuma elish with the Akitu festival is the same ritual text from the Seleucid era we have been considering.[18] I am tempted to adopt Pallis's suggestion that, in the ritual text, "Enuma eliš is no fixed concept. . . . Enuma eliš simply denotes a version of the creation story in general,"[19] and I will insist that, whatever text is being referred to, it is not necessarily the "epic" as reconstructed by modern scholarship under that title.

Nevertheless, the "humiliation" of the king on day five is preceded by the recitation of a cosmogonic text on day four—whatever that text may have been. I take this to be significant. If we may use the general form of the reconstructed "creation epic" to gain a point of bearing, then it becomes important to emphasize that Enuma elish is not simply, or even primarily, a cosmogony. It is preeminently the myth of the establishment of Marduk's kingship and the creation of his city (Babylon) and his central capital temple (Esagila). These are parallel creations. Originally redacted during the first period of Assyrian domination (and here I must accept Lambert's observation that "the *Epic of Creation* is not a norm of Babylonian or Sumerian cosmology. It is a sectarian and aberrant combination of mythological threads woven into an unparalleled compositum. . . . The various traditions it draws upon are often so perverted to such an extent that conclusions based on this text alone are suspect")[20] Enuma elish establishes clear parallels between Marduk's kingship in heaven and the kingship of Babylon, the creation of the world and the building of Esagila.[21] The opposite would be the case as well. Destroy Babylon or Esagila, neglect Marduk, pervert kingship, and the world will be destroyed.

Before introducing one additional set of Babylonian materials, it is necessary to pause and reflect on the implications of this analysis of the Akitu festival for the more general theme. I am not claiming that the ritual of the Akitu festival is an apocalyptic *text*. I am suggesting that it reflects on an apocalyptic *situation*. In the Near Eastern context, two elements are crucial: scribalism and kingship. The *situation* of apocalypticism seems to me to be the cessation of native kingship; the *literature* of apocalypticism appears to me to be the expression of archaic, scribal wisdom as it comes to lack a royal patron. Indeed, I would suggest further that the perception of the meaning of the *fact* of the cessation of native kingship moves from the *apocalyptic pattern* that the wrong king is on the throne, that the cosmos will be thereby destroyed, and that the right god will either restore proper native kingship (his terrestrial counterpart) or will assume kingship himself, to the *gnostic pattern* that if the wrong king is sitting on the throne, then his heavenly counterpart must likewise be the wrong god. Both the apocalyptic and gnostic patterns reflect a situational incongruity: the king is the divine center of the human realm just as the king-god is the center of the cosmos; but the king is the wrong king. What does this portend for the world? What does this imply about the deity? What does this suggest about the archaic, civic rituals of renewal?

This "situation" is only implicit in the Akitu ritual. An archaic omen procedure concerning a native king has been reinterpreted as a *ritual for the rectification of a foreign king*.[22] I suspect that this reinterpretation had its origins in the period of the Assyrian domination of Babylonia[23] and has been "reapplied" in the Seleucid era—with notable success in the case of a figure such as Antiochus I, Sotēr.[24]

This matter of *rectification* is central to the apocalyptic situation and is crucial with respect to other interpretive models for the Akitu ritual. It suggests, on the one hand, that the Akitu festival is not best understood as a ritual of repetition of ahistorical cosmic patterns; and, on the other, that the text should not be reduced through emphasis on its historical dimension to either an instance of nonefficacious propaganda[25] or to an instance of the use of historical realia as *vaticinia ex eventu*.[26] The first slapping of the king in the Akitu festival is not, as is the case with the second slapping, either validated *by* events (as in omen or prophetic traditions) or a validation *of* events (as in archaic rituals), but rather is best understood as a desperate ritual attempt to *influence* events, to set things right. This rectification has both cosmic and human dimensions, as kingship possesses both dimensions.

I have already noted that the cosmic dimension of the ritual is signaled by the recitation of the Enuma elish, but that we need not identify the text referred to in the ritual with the "creation epic" as reconstructed by contemporary scholarship. The fragments of Enuma elish from the second century B.C., those most closely contemporary to the Seleucid Akitu ritual, do not permit confident reconstruction.[27] But a more precious and contemporary source has survived in the fragments of the *Babyloniaka* by Berossus, a priest of Marduk in Babylon (fl. 290–280 B.C.).[28] His work, dedicated to Antiochus I, Sotēr, is an example of the widespread pattern of the paraphrase of archaic, native-language, sacred traditions in Greek during the Greco-Roman period (the closest parallels would be Manetho, Josephus, and the works of Alexander Polyhistor).

The testimonia concerning Berossus divide into two categories: from Greco-Roman authors we learn that he was an astronomer, an astrologer, and related to the sibylline tradition; from Jewish and Christian authors we learn that he was a mythographer and an historian. While these two types of testimonia clearly value different aspects of Berossus and put him to different uses, *taken as a whole* they reveal an overall pattern that closely approaches the apocalyptic: a history of the cosmos and a people from creation to final catastrophe, dominated by astrological determinism.[29] On the basis of the surviving fragments, the *Babyloniaka* appears to have described the history of the world from its creation to its final destruction and offers a periodization of the history of Babylonia which stretches in between. In the former, Berossus draws upon a learned, literate, mythological tradition similar to that represented by Enuma elish and its commentaries; in the latter, on an equally learned, literate, chronicle tradition. A number of elements in Berossus's work parallel motifs found in apocalyptic literature: the tradition of the antediluvian books of Oannes (F1, Jacoby) and the hidden books of Xisuthrus (F4) which contain cosmological and deluge traditions clearly related to those in the Atrahasis epic, Gilgamesh, and Enuma elish; the recording of the deeds of foreign kings including their destruction or restoration of Esagila and the city wall of Babylon (especially, F9 and the parallel locus in Abydenus, Jacoby F6 + 1, which explicitly correlates the building and rebuilding of the walls with the creation of the cosmos);[30] and the correlation of the rule of foreign kings with the rise of idolatry and religious desecration (F11). In the key "apocalyptic" fragment which has survived (F21), beginning and end are clearly correlated. All things will be consumed by fire. The world will be flooded and return to the watery chaos that existed in the beginning.[31] Nevertheless, Berossus and Abydenus should be more properly called *protoapocalypticists*. For, on the basis of what has survived, while there is an explicit cosmic frame of reference, there is no explicit correlation between historical events and the final end, although the pervasive determinism tends toward an implicit correlation. All of the elements of apocalypticism are present, but they do not appear to have been arranged in an apocalyptic schema. But Berossus and Abydenus remain of value to us for suggesting how Enuma elish might have been understood by the learned, priestly circles who developed the Akitu ritual and for enabling us to perceive the movement from prediction to rectification, from cosmogonic to apocalyptic patterns, from apocalyptic situation to apocalyptic text.

It will not be possible to pursue this line of inquiry further without first venturing an interpretation of the Ceramese myth of Hainuwele.

II

The myth of Hainuwele was first collected from the Wemale tribe of West Ceram, one of the Moluccan islands west of New Guinea, in 1927.[32] But the tale was ignored until Adolf Jensen collected several versions of it in 1937–38, and devoted a brilliant and influential series of monographs and articles to its exegesis.[33] Since its publication, many of the most important historians of religion concerned with archaic traditions have written about the Hainuwele myth, and a general consensus has emerged.[34] It is this consensus which needs to be challenged.

The text is too long to quote in its entirety, so I shall offer only a brief summary, partially justified because the only version that Jensen translates strikes me as a composite paraphrase.[35] It begins: "Nine families of mankind came forth in the beginning from Mount Nunusaku where the people had emerged from clusters of bananas," and goes on to narrate how an ancestor (one of the *Dema,* the Marind-anim term for ancestor employed by Jensen as a generic title) named Ameta found a coconut speared on a boar's tusk, and, in a dream, was instructed to plant it. In six days a palm had sprung from the nut and flowered. Ameta cut his finger and his blood dripped on the blossom. Nine days later a girl grew from the blossom and, in three more days, she became an adolescent. Ameta cut her from the tree and named her Hainuwele, "coconut girl": "But she was not like an ordinary person, for when she would answer the call of nature, her excrement consisted of all sorts of valuable articles, such as Chinese dishes and gongs, so that Ameta became very rich." During a major religious festival, Hainuwele stood in the middle of the dance grounds and, instead of *exchanging* the *traditional* areca nuts and betel leaves, she excreted a whole series of valuable articles: Chinese porcelain dishes, metal knives, copper boxes, golden earrings, and great brass gongs. After nine days of this: "The people thought this thing mysterious . . . they were jealous that Hainuwele could distribute such wealth and decided to kill her." The people dug a hole in the middle of the dance ground, threw Hainuwele in, and danced the ground firm on top of her. Ameta dug up her corpse, dismembered it, and buried the cut pieces. From the pieces of her corpse, previously unknown plant species (especially tuberous plants) grew which have been, ever since, the principal form of food on Ceram.

Jensen (like almost all historians of religion who have followed him) understands the tale to describe the origins of death, sexuality, and cultivated food plants. The myth, it is claimed, is a description of human existence as distinct from ancestral times—with the act of killing (in Jensen's phrase, "creative murder") as the means of maintaining the present order. Besides introducing the notion of "creative murder," which I find chilling in a series of essays published in Nazi Germany beginning in 1938, Jensen has demonstrably misread his own text.

I find no hint in the Hainuwele text that sexuality or death is the result of Hainuwele's murder nor that the cultivation of food plants is solely the consequence of her death. Death and sexuality (and their correlation) are already constitutive of human existence in the very first line of the text with its mention of the emergence of man from clusters of bananas. It is a widespread Oceanic tale of the origin of death—found as well among the Wemale in a version collected by Jensen—that human finitude is the result of a choice or conflict between a stone and a banana.[36] Bananas are large, perennial herbs which put forth tall, vigorous shoots which die after producing fruit. The choice, the conflict in these origin-of-death tales, is between progeny followed by death of the parents (the banana) or eternal but sterile life (the stone). The banana always wins. Thus Jensen's interpretation collapses at the outset. Man as mortal and sexual, indeed the correlation of death and sexuality, is the *presupposition* of the myth of Hainuwele, *not* its result. Ameta's dream oracle commanding him to plant the coconut, which occurs before the "birth" of Hainuwele, indicates that the cultivation of plants is likewise present. In fact, Jensen's interpretation rests on only a few details in the myth: that Hainuwele was killed, buried, dug up, and dismembered and that, from the pieces of her body which were then reburied, tuberous plants grew. This is a widespread motif,[37] rendered more "plausible" by the fact that this is the way in which tubers such as yams are actually cultivated. The tuber is stored in the ground, dug up, and divided into pieces; these are then planted and result in new tubers. That tropical yams (such as *Dioscorea alata* or *D. batatas*) can grow to a length of several feet and weigh a hundred pounds only strengthens the analogy with the human body.

If Jensen's exegesis may be set aside on the basis of the evidence he provides, what is the myth about? Here I return to the stratagem I proposed at the outset for gaining a point of entry into the text. Our sense of incongruity is seized by Hainuwele's curious mode of production, the excretion of valuable articles, and it is this act which is explicitly stated as providing the motivation for the central act in the tale, her murder. We share our sense of incongruity with the Wemale, for "they thought this thing mysterious . . . and plotted to kill her."

There is, in fact, a double incongruity, for the objects that Hainuwele excretes are all manufactured goods, goods which are used on Ceram as money (*hárta*). The text clearly cannot antedate the spice trade of the sixteenth and seventeenth centuries (I shall, in fact, argue that it is considerably later).[38] The myth of Hainuwele is not a tale of the origin of death or of yams; it is a tale of the origin of "filthy lucre," of "dirty money."[39]

The myth of Hainuwele is not, as in Jensen's interpretation, primarily concerned with the discrepancy between the world of the *Dema*-ancestors and the world of men. It is, I would suggest, concerned with the discrepancy between the world of the European and the world of the native; it is a witness to the confrontation between native and European economic systems. The text is important not because it opens up a vista to an archaic tuber cultivator culture dominated by a "central mythical idea,"[40] but because it reflects what I would term a *cargo situation* without a cargo cult. It reflects a native strategy for dealing with an incongruous situation, a strategy that draws upon indigenous elements. The myth of Hainuwele is not a primordium, it is a stunning example of what Jensen denigrates as "application."[41]

In order to understand this, we must detour just a bit from the Moluccas to the immediately adjacent island of New Guinea and the Melanesian culture complex. In Melanesian exchange systems, the central ideology is one of "equivalence, neither more nor less, neither 'one up' nor 'one down.' "[42] Foodstuffs and goods are stored, not as capital assets, but in order to be given away in ceremonies that restore equilibrium. Wealth and prestige are not measured by either resourceful thrift or conspicuous consumption, but by one's skill in achieving reciprocity. Exchange goods are familiar. They are local objects which a man grows or manufactures. Theoretically, everyone could grow or make the same things in the same quantity. Difference is, then, a matter of "accident" and must be "averaged out" through exchange.[43]

Foreign trade goods and money function in quite a different way and their introduction into Oceania created a social and moral crisis that we may term the cargo situation.[44] How could one enter into reciprocal relations with the white man who possesses and hoards all this "stuff," whose manufacture took place in some distant land which the native has never seen? How does one achieve equilibrium with the white man who does not appear to have "made" his money? If the white man was merely a stranger (i.e., a nonkinsman), the problem would be serious, but it might not threaten every dimension of Melanesian life. But in Melanesian traditions, the ancestors are white, and, therefore, the native cannot simply ignore the European even if this was a pragmatic possibility. The white man is one of their own, but he refuses to play according to the rules, or is ignorant of them.[45] The problem of reciprocity cannot be avoided. What can the native do to make the white man—his ancestor who has returned on a ship with goods as promised by ancient tradition[46]—admit to his reciprocal obligations?

It is necessary to be quite insistent at this point. The problem of cargo is *not* that the prophecy has failed or that the *parousia* has been delayed. It is rather that the prophecy has been fulfilled, but in an unexpected or "wrong" way. The ancestors *have* returned on a ship, they *have* brought cargo; but they have not distributed it properly in such a way as to achieve equilibrium. As with the Akitu festival, the cargo situation gives rise to myths and rituals concerned with *rectification*. Only the "pressure" is more severe than in the Near East. The center of native culture has not been occupied by a foreign king who does not behave in the required manner, but by one's own ancestor who does not behave in the required manner. "We have encountered the enemy and he is us."

A variety of means have been employed to meet this cargo situation. In explicit Melanesian cargo cults, it is asserted that another ship or airplane will arrive from the ancestors carrying an equal amount of goods for the natives. Or that the goods brought by the Europeans were originally intended for the natives but that the labels have been readdressed. A native "savior" will journey to the land of the ancestors in order either to correct the labels or to bring a new shipment, or the ancestors will redress the injustice on their own initiative.

In other more desperate cargo cults, the natives have destroyed everything that they own, as if, by this dramatic gesture, to awaken the white man's moral sense of reciprocity. "See, we have now given away everything. What will you give in return?" Both of these "solutions" assume the validity of exchange and reciprocity and appeal to it.

Other "solutions," usually not expressed as cargo cults but expressive of the cargo situation, appeal to the mythic resources which underlie the exchange system rather than to the system itself. For example, Kenelm

Burridge, in his classic studies, *Mambu* and *Tangu Traditions,* has demonstrated how the Tangu have reworked a traditional pedagogic tale concerning the relations between older and younger brother so as to reveal that the difference in status between the white man and the native is the result of an accident and is, therefore, in native terms, a situation of disequilibrium which requires exchange.[47]

I should like to appeal to a similar model for the understanding of the myth of Hainuwele. That a cargo situation existed in the Moluccas is beyond dispute. After a period of "benign neglect," the Dutch embarked on a policy of intensive colonialist activities during the years 1902–10, which included the attempt to suppress ancestral and headhunting cults, the destruction of community houses, the use of Amboinese Christians as local administrators, and the imposition of a tax which had to be paid in cash rather than labor exchange.[48] It is this latter innovation which is crucial for my interpretation. While there were some minor revolts and instances of passive resistance in West Ceram,[49] they did not take the form of the nativistic and, at times, cargo cults, collectively known as the Mejapi movements (literally, the ones who hide) of the Central Celebes.[50]

I would date Jensen's version of the Hainuwele tale to the same period. Hainuwele intrudes in an unexpected way on Wemale culture and produces cash (i.e., imported trade goods) in an abnormal and mysterious fashion—objects which have so great a value that no exchange is possible. But the Wemale have a *mythic precedent* for such novelty. In Ceramese myths, in primordial times, when Yam Woman, Sago Woman, or some other similar figure mysteriously produced an unknown form of food (usually by repulsive means), the figure was killed, the food consumed and, thereby, acculturated.[51] The same archaic model, in the Hainuwele myth and under the pressure of the cargo situation, is daringly *reapplied* to the white man and his goods. Murder and eating are means of making something "ours." Furthermore, one might attempt to understand the movement from the living Hainuwele as a producer of cash to the dead Hainuwele as a producer of tubers as an attempt to reverse the situation, an attempt at converting cash into a "cash crop." By being reduced to tubers, Hainuwele provides a proper article for exchange analogous to the areca nuts and betel leaves which she failed to exchange in the myth.

The myth of Hainuwele is an application of this archaic mythologem to a new, cargo situation. The killing of Hainuwele does not represent a rupture with an ancestral age; rather it is her presence which disrupts traditional native society. The setting of the tale is not the mythic "once upon a time" but, rather, the painful, post-European "here and now."

The Ceramese myth of Hainuwele does not solve the problem, overcome the incongruity, or resolve the tension. Rather, it results in thought. It is a testing of the adequacy and applicability of traditional patterns and

categories to new situations and data in the hopes of achieving rectification. It is an act of native exegetical ingenuity, a process of native work.

I have attempted to demonstrate, both by close analysis of text and by
careful attention to historical context, that the Babylonian Akitu festival
and the Ceramese myth of Hainuwele are best described neither in terms
of repetition of the past nor in terms of future fulfillment, but rather in
terms of a difficult and incongruous present; that this present supplies the
chief content of the text and delimits its function; that there is an almost
casuistic dimension to these two documents which may be best described
as "application"; that this incongruity is surprising in light of past precedents; but that it may only be addressed, worked with, and perhaps
even overcome in terms of these same precedents. I have suggested that
both of these texts have in common the attempt at rectification.

To be sure, the Babylonians did not regain their native kingship and
the white man was not brought into conformity with native categories;
he still fails to recognize a moral claim of reciprocity. But this is not how
we judge success in matters of science. We judge harshly those who have
abandoned the novel and the incongruous to a realm outside of the con-
fines of understanding, and we value those who (even though failing)
stubbornly make the attempt at achieving intelligibility, at achieving rectification of either the data or the model.

7 The Devil in Mr. Jones

My starting point in this essay will be three curious titles that are attached by my university to my name: "religion and the human sciences," "religion and the humanities," "history of religions." What might these terms mean? All three set religion within a context. All three suggest limiting perspectives on religion: that it is human and that it is historical (two propositions that I understand to be all but synonymous). All three suggest academic conversation partners for the enterprise of the study of religion: anthropology (in its broadest sense), humanities, and history. These terms locate the *study* of religion. Religion, to the degree that it is usefully conceived as an historical, human endeavor, is to be set within the larger academic frameworks provided by anthropology, the humanities, and history.

All three titles are, as well, highly polemical. Although their daring has been obscured by time, none would have been understood in academic circles a little more than a century ago. Indeed, if understood at all, they would have been thought to embody a contradiction. Although we tend to use the word "humanities" (or the human sciences) as synonymous with liberal learning, with Cicero's *humanitas* and the older Greek *paideia,* and tend to identify its scope primarily with the study of the classical culture of our own past and the more recent works dependent on it, this is not its primary academic sense. When it was revived by the Italian humanists of the fifteenth century, it had a more pointed and argumentative meaning. As first used by Coluccio Salutati, a Florentine chancellor, "humane studies," the "human sciences" were to be contrasted with the "divine sciences"—that is to say, the humanities with theology. Thus, if the study of religion was anything, it was the study of that which was utterly different from the human sciences. The two were perceived to be mutually exclusive.

This was all changed when, on 1 October 1877, the Dutch Universities Act separated the theological faculties at the four state universities (Amsterdam, Groningen, Leiden, and Utrecht) from the Dutch Reformed

Church. For the first time in western academic history, there were established two, parallel possibilities for the study of religion: a humanistic mode within the secular academy and a theological course of study within the denominational seminary. The original draft of the legislation had used a term coined four years earlier, proposing to call the new university department a "Faculty of Religious Sciences," but, after much compromise, the older title, "Faculty of Theology," was retained. Nevertheless, dogmatics and practical theology, the central core of theological education, were removed from the curriculum, to be taught only in the seminaries. Their place in the academy was taken by a new program in history of religions which was assumed to be more "neutral and scientific."

France followed soon after. In 1884 the French Ministry of Education abolished the state Catholic Theological Faculties and a year later replaced them (in the very same building) by the "Fifth Section of Religious Sciences" as part of the École Pratique des Hautes Études. Religious study was added alongside the other four "sections": mathematics, physics and chemistry, natural history and physiology, and the historical and philological sciences. The minister of public instruction charged the new faculty: "We do not wish to see the cultivation of polemics, but of critical research. We wish to see the examination of texts, not the discussion of dogmas."

In 1904 the University of Manchester, which was rare among British universities in being nondenominational and in applying no confessional tests to either students or faculty, established its new Theological Faculty which taught theological subjects and comparative religions but excluded courses in systematic theology and the history of Christian doctrine. All theological students were required to take work in comparative religions. What was intended may be gleaned from the fact that James George Frazer was invited to join the faculty and teach comparative religions. As stated at the inauguration of this new program, this was "the first occasion in this country on which theology, unfettered by [denominational] tests, has been accepted as an integral part of the University organization and has been treated like any other subject."[1] Rarely did any other European country until today follow this pattern. In most of Europe, religious studies were part of the divine sciences.

In the United States, until some twenty years ago, when religious studies were recognized, a sequential pattern prevailed. A doctoral degree in religious studies at a university had as its prerequisite a bachelor of divinity degree from a seminary. It was not until the rise of programs in state universities, a development which followed the 1963 U.S. Supreme Court decision on the *School District of Abington* v. *Schempp,* in which Mr. Justice Goldberg observed, "it seems clear to me . . . that the Court would recognize the propriety of the teaching *about* religion as distin-

guished from the teaching *of* religion in the public schools," that the
parallel course of religious studies in the academy, instituted a century
ago in Holland, became possible in this country.

This political and legislative history, as important as it has been, should
not be allowed to obscure a more fundamental base. Simply put, *the
academic study of religion is a child of the Enlightenment.* This intellectual
heritage is revealed in the notion of generic religion as opposed to historical, believing communities. But it is not this element, as significant
as it was, on which I wish to dwell. Rather it is the mood, the exemplary
Enlightenment attitude toward religion that concerns me.

To put the matter succinctly, religion was domesticated; it was transformed from *pathos* to *ethos*. At no little cost, religion was brought within
the realm of common sense, of civil discourse and commerce. Rediscov-
ering the old tag, "Nothing human is foreign to me," the Enlightenment
impulse was one of tolerance and, as a necessary concomitant, one which
refused to leave any human datum, including religion, beyond the pale
of understanding, beyond the realm of reason.

It was this impulse, this domestication, that made possible the entrance
of religious studies into the secular academy. But the price of this entry,
to reverse the Steppenwolf formula, is the use of our mind. As students
of religion, we have become stubbornly committed to making the attempt
(even if we fail) at achieving intelligibility. We must accept the burden of
the long, hard road of understanding. To do less is to forfeit our license
to practice in the academy, to leave the study of religion open to the
charge of incivility and intolerance.

Against this background, I have deliberately chosen for my topic an
event which is a scandal in the original sense of the word. Such scandals
erupt from time to time and perturb the assumptions of civility. For the
Enlightenment faith in intelligibility, it was the shock over the utter dev-
astation of the Lisbon earthquake on 1 November 1755—reread Voltaire's
Candide![2] For those of us committed to the academic study of religion,
a comparable scandal is that series of events which began at approximately
5:00 P.M., on 18 November 1978 in Jonestown, Guyana. From one point
of view, one might claim that Jonestown was the most important single
event in the history of religions, for if we continue, as a profession, to
leave it ununderstandable, then we will have surrendered our rights to
the academy. The daring and difficult experiment in parallel courses of
religious study begun in Holland a century ago will have concluded in
failure.

One final, preliminary matter. To interpret, to venture to understand,
is not necessarily to approve or to advocate. There is a vast difference
between what I have described as "tolerance" and what is now known
as "relativism." The former does not necessarily lead to the latter. In the

sixteenth century, that great precursor of the Enlightenment, Montaigne, argued in his essay "Of Cannibals":

> Everyone terms barbarity, whatever is not of his own customs; in truth it seems that we have no view of what is true and reasonable, except the example and idea of the customs and practices of the country in which we live. We may call them barbarians, then, if we are judging by the rules of reason, but not if we are judging by comparison with ourselves, who surpass them in every sort of barbarity.[3]

He was stating a principle of toleration, but he was also making a normative claim: we cannot judge another culture by reference to ourselves; we may judge (both another and ourselves), if our criteria are universal "rules of reason." The anthropology of the last century, the study of religions in the academy, has contributed to making more difficult a naive, ethnocentric formulation of the "rules of reason," but this does not require that such "rules" be denied, or suggest that we should slacken in our attempts to formulate them.

It is a far cry from the civility of Montaigne and his Enlightenment heirs to the utter conceptual relativism of D. Z. Phillips when he writes, in *Faith and Philosophical Enquiry:*

> If I hear that one of my neighbors has killed another neighbor's child, given that he is sane, my condemnation is immediate. . . . But if I hear that some remote tribe practices child sacrifice, what then? I do not know what sacrifice means for the tribe in question. What would it mean to say I condemned it when the "it" refers to something I know nothing about? I would be condemning murder. But murder is not child sacrifice.[4]

If the *skandalon* of Jonestown requires that we make the effort of understanding, it requires as well that, as members of the academy, we side with Montaigne against Phillips. For fundamental to the latter's conceptual relativism is the claim that, "what counts as true in my language may not even be able to be described in yours. Translation becomes impossible in principle."[5] But if this be the case, the academy, the enterprise of understanding, the human sciences themselves, become, likewise, impossible in principle since they are fundamentally translation enterprises.

II

The basic facts concerning Jonestown that are matters of public record may be rapidly rehearsed.[6] James Warren Jones was born 13 May 1931 in the small town of Lynn, Indiana. Like many other towns of the region and of the time, Lynn was a seat of both Christian fundamentalism and Ku Klux Klan activity. (The Klan's national headquarters had been in Indianapolis.) There is considerable evidence that by the late forties Jones was deeply committed to the former and had decisively rejected the latter in favor of a vision of racial equality and harmony. In 1950, Jones (now married), moved to Indianapolis and, although not ordained, became a pastor at the Sommerset Southside Church and director of an integrated community center. In difficulty with the Sommerset congregation for his outspoken views on civil rights, he left and, by 1953, had founded his own, interracial Community Unity Church, largely subsidized by his efforts, including the door-to-door peddling of pet monkeys. For a while he also served as associate pastor of the Laurel Street Tabernacle, but, again, his integrationist views forced him out. In 1956, he founded the Peoples Temple, an integrated but predominantly black congregation. He also began the practice of adopting children of various races (he was to adopt a total of seven) and urging his congregants to do so as well. Moving to larger quarters, he began his visits to a variety of evangelists, the most significant being a trip to Philadelphia to talk with Father Divine. By 1960, his efforts in community work had become so well known that he was appointed director of the Indianapolis Human Rights Commission, and articles about him began to appear in the press. In 1961, the Peoples Temple Full Gospel Church became affiliated with the Christian Church (Disciples of Christ), and, in 1964, Jones was ordained a minister by that denomination. In this same period, Jones appears to have introduced more discipline into his congregation (e.g., establishing an "interrogation committee") and to have begun to practice increasingly vivid forms of faith healing; he claimed that he had resurrected a number of dead individuals (by 1972, he would claim to have resurrected more than forty) and that he was able to cure cancer. (This latter led to an investigation by the state of Indiana, but the results were inconclusive.)

In 1965, after reading an article on nuclear destruction in *Esquire Magazine,* Jones predicted the end of the world in a nuclear holocaust which would occur on 15 July 1967. Concerned for the society that would emerge after this event, he sought to find sanctuary for a small, interracial remnant. The magazine mentioned ten places as the safest from destruction, including Belo Horizente, Brazil, and Ukiah, California. Jones visited Brazil, meeting with several of the leaders of messianic cults there as well as stopping off in Guyana on his return. He then moved about 150 members of his congregation from Indianapolis to Ukiah, incorporating the Peoples Temple, Disciples of Christ Church in November 1965. He began a pattern of commuting between his Indianapolis and his California congregations, but increasingly concentrated his activities in Redwood Valley.

By 1967, Jones was an important civic institution in northern California. Several officials had joined his church. He was the chairman of the local Legal Services Society and foreman of the Mendocino Grand Jury.

By 1972, he had expanded his activities, founding churches in San Francisco and Los Angeles. He published a newspaper, *The People's Forum,* which had a press run of 60,000 copies, and had a half-hour radio program, each week, on KFAX. In 1973, he leased 27,000 acres of undeveloped land from the government of Guyana to serve as an "agricultural mission" and a "promised land."

By 1974, his combined California congregations had grown to such a degree that the *Sacramento Bee* declared, "Peoples Temple ranks as probably the largest Protestant congregation in Northern California," and Jones became an important political force. Still combining his preaching of racial equality with services of healing, Jones began to speak to, and attract, a different audience. While still predominantly a black and working class congregation, he also brought into Peoples Temple a new, white, liberal, educated, middle class membership. In 1975, he was named one of the hundred most outstanding clergymen in the United States by *Religion in Life*. He also worked for the political campaign of San Francisco mayor, George Moscone, and entered into the center of West Coast politics. Visibly active in support of freedom of the press causes, he received, in 1976, the *Los Angeles Herald*'s Humanitarian of the Year award. He became active in the presidential campaign of Carter, turning out a huge audience for Rosalynn Carter's appearance; he was later invited by her to the inauguration and corresponded with her in the White House.

Appointed to the San Francisco Housing Authority by Moscone in 1976, he became its chairman in 1977, and received the Martin Luther King Humanitarian of the Year award in San Francisco that year.

Although there had been a few "exposés" of Peoples Temple (most notably a planned eight-part series by Lester Kinsolving in the *San Francisco Examiner* in 1972, which was suppressed after four installments had appeared), it was not until the 1 August 1977 issue of *New West Magazine* with its lurid reports of financial misdealings, beatings, intimidation, brainwashing, and hints of murder that another side of Peoples Temple came into public view. After an unsuccessful attempt to have the story quashed, Jones left for Guyana.

The mission in Guyana had been run, since its establishment, by a skeleton crew. In 1975, there were only 15 members in Jonestown. By 1976, when California's lieutenant governor visited the site, there were some 50 individuals. In May 1977, there were 70 full-time residents. Between late July and December 1977, Jones and some 900 other congregants had moved to Jonestown. A core of about 100 members was left behind to staff the California churches and provide logistical support for the community in Guyana.

Between 1 April and 7 November 1978, there was a flurry of legal actions. Former cult members entered lawsuits against Peoples Temple charging assault and fraud. There were investigations by the San Francisco district attorney's office and by the United States consul in Guyana. Relatives of citizens of Jonestown began making public statements, charging violations of human rights and mistreatment in Jonestown. In June, a former Temple official filed an affidavit to the effect that Jones had assumed "a tyrannical hold over the lives of Temple members," that he had become paranoid and was planning "mass suicide for the glory of socialism." In the same month, James Cobb filed suit against Jones in San Francisco, charging him with planning "mass murder [that] would result in the death of minor children not old enough to make voluntary and informed decisions about serious matters of any nature, much less insane proposals of collective suicide."

On 14 November 1978, Congressman Leo Ryan, of California, left for Guyana to investigate the situation, accompanied by fourteen relatives of Jonestown citizens and representatives of the press. On the afternoon of 17 November, and the morning of the next day, Ryan visited Jonestown and interviewed a number of the Peoples Temple members. A small number indicated that they wished to leave with him, but, in the main, Ryan was positively impressed.

At 4:00 P.M. on the afternoon of 18 November, after having been threatened with a knife in Jonestown, Ryan and four members of his party were shot to death while waiting to board their chartered plane. Eleven members of his party were wounded. Their assailants were members of the Jonestown community.

About an hour later, Jones began the "White Night," an event that had been previously rehearsed, the suicide of every member of Peoples Temple in Jonestown. When it was over, 914 people had died, most by taking a fruit drink mixed with cyanide and tranquilizers; most apparently died voluntarily. (Four individuals, including Jones, died of gunshot wounds. The bodies of some 70 individuals showed puncture wounds which suggest that they were injected with poison—whether voluntarily or not cannot be determined. Two hundred and sixty infants and small children had been administered poison, most by their parents. Dogs, livestock, and fishponds had been poisoned as well.)

Some one hundred of the inhabitants of Jonestown, the majority of whom had been away from the settlement, and a small number who fled the White Night, survived.

With the exception of one Guyanese, all of the dead were American citizens. Most were family groups. The majority were black. Jonestown was a national movement. The birthplaces of the dead were in 39 states and 4 foreign countries. With the exception of one individual from Philadelphia, the last home of all the dead, before Jonestown, was in California with the largest group from the San Francisco Bay area (229), and almost equal numbers from the site of the first Temple in Ukiah–Redwood Valley (139) and Los Angeles (137).

Since the events in Jonestown, I have searched through the academic journals for some serious study, but in vain. Neither in them, nor in the hundreds of papers on the program of the American Academy of Religion (which was in session during the event in 1978 and which meets each year about the time of its anniversary) has there been any mention. For the press, the event was all too quickly overshadowed by other new horrors. For the academy, it was as if Jonestown had never happened.

The press, by and large, featured the pornography of Jonestown—the initial focus on the daily revisions of the body count, the details on the condition of the corpses. Then, as more "background" information became available, space was taken over by lurid details of beatings, sexual humiliations, and public acts of perversion. The bulk of these focused on Jones as a "wrathful, lustful giant": his bisexuality, his mistresses, his all-night sermons on the "curse of his big penis," his questionnaires to adolescent members about their sexual fantasies concerning him, his arrest on a morals charge, his sexual demands on his congregants, including a secretary whose job it was to arrange liaisons for him with male and female members of his congregation, beginning with the formula, "Father hates to do this, but he has this tremendous urge." Everything was sensational. Almost no attempt was made to gain any interpretative framework. According to the journalists Maguire and Dunn, it was an event "so bizarre that historians would have to reach back into Biblical times[!] to find a calamity big enough for comparison."

It was not surprising, I suppose, considering the fact that a major metropolitan daily, the *New York Post,* found it impossible to mention the Ayotollah Khomeni's name without prefacing it by "that madman," that it was the language of fraud and insanity that dominated the accounts. There were several options: he began sincere and went mad; he began a fraud and went mad; he was always a fraud; he was always mad—or, sometimes impossibly, a combination of all of these. Thus *Newsweek* could, in one article, call Jones: "self-proclaimed messiah," "a man who played god," "full of hokum . . . and carnival stuff," "one who mesmerized," "fanatical," "a foul paranoid," "one vulnerable to forces in his own mind," "gifted with a strange power," "victim of darker forces," "a wrathful, lustful giant," "nightmarish," "bizarre." This is the usual language of religious polemics: read the Western biographies of Muhammad! There is neither anything new nor perceptive in this all-but-standard list. There is certainly nothing that will aid understanding. A few journalists of modest literary bent played on his name and made reference to "The Emperor Jones," but little light was shed by that.

More troubling, the newspapers gave a substantial amount of space to other religious leaders and their gyrations in distancing themselves from Jonestown. Perhaps the greatest single scandal in this regard occurred in the *New York Times,* one of whose longer analytical pieces on Jones was an article on the "Op-Ed" page entitled, "Billy Graham on Satan and Jonestown," in which the evangelist fulminated against "false prophets and messiahs," "satanically inspired people," and "the wholesale deception of false messiahs like Jim Jones," concluding:

> One may speak of the Jones situation as that of a cult, but it would be a sad mistake to identify it in any way with Christianity. It is true that he came from a religious background but what he did and how he thought can have no relationship to the views and teachings of any legitimate form of historic Christianity. We have witnessed a false messiah who used the cloak of religion to cover a confused mind filled with a mixture of pseudo-religion, political ambition, sensual lust, financial dishonesty and, apparently, even murder. . . . Apparently Mr. Jones was *a slave of a diabolical supernatural power* from which he refused to be set free.[7]

This is to give way to the forces of unreason. I find Billy Graham's presence on the editorial pages of the *New York Times* a more stunning indication that the faith of the Enlightenment upon which the academy depends is in danger than the events in Jonestown!

The profession of religious studies, when it would talk, privately, within its boundaries, had a different perspective. For many, Jones's declarations that he was a Marxist, a communist, one who rejected the "opiate" of religion, were greeted with relief. He was not, after all, religious. Hence there was no professional obligation to interpret him. Never mind the fact that one of the most important religious phenomena of this century has been the combination of revolutionary Marxism and Roman Catholicism in Latin America, Marxism and Buddhism in southeast Asia, Marxism and Islam in the Middle East.

For others, it was not to be talked about because it revealed what had been concealed from public, academic discussion for a century—that religion has rarely been a positive, liberal force. Religion is not nice; it has been responsible for more death and suffering than any other human activity. Jonestown (and many of the other so-called cults) signaled the shallowness of the amalgamation between religion and liberalism which was, among other things, a major argument for the presence of religious studies in the state and secular universities. Religion was not civil. And so a new term had to be created, that of "cult," to segregate these uncivil phenomena from religion.

But civility is not to be reduced to "nice" behavior. A concomitant of the Enlightenment "domestication" of religion was the refusal to leave any human datum beyond the pale of reason and understanding. If the events of Jonestown are a behavioral *skandalon* to the Enlightenment faith, then the refusal of the academy to interpret Jonestown is, at least, an equivalent *skandalon* to the same faith.

It is remarkable to me that in all the literature on Jonestown that I have read the closest expression of the fundamental mood of the Enlightenment should have come in a sermon preached by a minister to the First United Methodist Church in Reno, Nevada—a minister who lost two daughters and a grandson in the White Night of Jonestown:

> Jonestown people were human beings. Except for your caring relationship with us, Jonestown would be names, "cultists," "fanatics," "kooks." Our children are real to you, because you knew [us]. [My wife] and I could describe for you many of the dead. You would think that we were describing people whom you know, members of our church.[8]

This recognition of the ordinary humanness of the participants in Jonestown's White Night must certainly be the starting point of interpretation. For, "nothing human is foreign to me."

Our task is not to reach closure. Indeed, at present this is factually impossible, for we lack the majority of the necessary data. We know the pornography of Jonestown; we do not know its mythology, its ideology, its soteriology, its sociology—we do not know almost everything we would need to know in order to venture a secure argument. We know, for example, that Jones characteristically held all-night meetings at which he spoke for hours. We know almost nothing of what he said. But we do know enough, as a matter of principle, to refuse to accept prematurely the option of declaring that it is unintelligible and, hence, in some profound sense inhuman. In a situation like this, it is not irresponsible to guess, to imagine Jonestown, for the risk of a model, however tentative, will suggest the kinds of data we might require. And, as enough of the participants are still living and accessible, as enough documentation, including "hundreds of reel-to-reel tapes and cassettes," has been gathered by legal agencies that are incompetent to interpret them, we might hope, in time, to have the data that we need.[9]

How, then, shall we begin to think about Jonestown as students of religion, as members of the academy? How might we use the resources available for thinking about human religious activity within the context of the corporate endeavor of the human sciences? A basic strategy, one that is a prerequisite for intelligibility, is to remove from Jonestown the aspect of the unique, of its being utterly exotic. We must be able to declare that Jonestown on 18 November 1978 was an instance of something known, of something we have seen before. We must perform an act of reduction. We must reduce Jonestown to the category of the known and the knowable.

In a primitive form, this initial move was made in the press which provided lists of suicides for religious and/or political reasons that have occurred in the past. From Masada, a first-century event which has become a foundation myth for the contemporary state of Israel (and which featured the same combination of isolation, homicide, and suicide) to the self-immolation of Buddhist monks and American pacifists during the Viet Nam War, we have seen it and heard about it before. Works such as Foxe's *Book of Martyrs* (1563)—one of the most popular books in the English language—supplied vivid portraits of those who would rather accept death, whether by their own hand or from another's, than renounce their religion. And works by J. Wisse (1933) and the psychiatrist Gregory Zilboorg (1939) supplied lengthy catalogs of corporate suicide among tribal peoples. Then, too, we have not lacked attempts to make such acts comprehensible, to make them less exotic. In studies by a distinguished series of scholars and writers, the act of self-destruction has been rescued from its legal and moral status as irrational. But none of these lists take us very far. Nor are they designed to. They do not allow us to propose an interpretation of Jonestown in its brute specificity. But they do allow us the beginning of reduction, that first glimpse of familiarity that is the prerequisite of intelligibility.

III

In this essay I would like to suggest two models, one quite old, one relatively new, which may illuminate aspects of the White Night of Jonestown. They are necessarily partial. They are far from being final proposals. But they are a beginning at an enterprise of looking at Jonestown rather than staring or looking away. We will have to continue this enterprise. We may, in the end, be frustrated. But not to have attempted an understanding, to allow the pornography of Jonestown to be all that can be thought, is, in a fundamental sense, to have surrendered the academy. It is to deny the possibility of there being human sciences.

The first model we might attempt is exceedingly old. It has been used in Western discourse about religion for close to 2500 years in order to interpret the uncivility of religion. It is a model for which the figure of Dionysus stands as a sign. Regardless of whether it is an adequate understanding of the complex historical development of the vast variety of Dionysiac cults (it is not), the Dionysiac *pattern,* as classically established by Euripides, elaborated by Livy and other Late Antique writers, rediscovered by Nietzsche and the early Rodhe, and, more recently, rediscovered again by René Girard in *Violence and the Sacred* (1972), has proven compelling.

The utility of this model reminds us that the prime purpose of academic inquiry, most especially in the humanities, is to provide *exempli gratia,* an arsenal of classic instances which are held to be exemplary, to provide paradigmatic events and expressions as resources from which to reason, from which to extend the possibility of intelligibility to that which first appears novel. To have discussed Euripides' *Bacchae* is, to some degree, already to have discussed Jonestown.

The *Bacchae* is a complex play. More than many others, it resists univocal interpretation. Here, we are not engaged in studying the *Bacchae*. We are using, perhaps even misusing, Euripides' play for our own, quite particular, purpose. We are using this artifact from 407 B.C. in order to become more familiar with Jonestown.

The play immediately attracts our attention because it takes as one of its themes the introduction of a new religion, that of Dionysus. It focuses, as well, on forms of violence. Dionysus, as he is presented to us in the drama, is one who obliterates distinctions. He is "polymorphous," able to assume any form at will: god, man, beast, male, female, old, young. He abolishes, as well, distinctions among his devotees. They are presented to us as a nameless collective band. They represent a motley mixture of ethnic origins: barbarians, Greco-Asiatics, and Hellenes that have been melded together into a religion that strives for universality, one where no one is excluded, a religion for all mankind. The cult group in the play is exclusively women—although they can act as if they were men. Their chief mode of life is, from their viewpoint, "sober ecstasy." Hence the dualities. They are the "eaters of raw flesh," and they are "devoted to peace." They are the wild "dancers," and they are under strict discipline, being agents of "Justice, principle of order, spirit of custom."

The entrance of Dionysus and his band into a city is perceived, from the point of view of the city, as an invasion, as a contagious plague. It produces civil disorder and madness. Hence its official, civil interpretation will be that it is "alien," that it is founded by a "charlatan and a fraud," one who wishes to profit financially and seduce women. The civil response to such a cult, to its "impostures and unruliness," is expulsion or death. There is *no room* for this sort of religion within *civil space.*

Yet the Messengers give us another, quite different, portrait of the Dionysiac band. Within *their own space,* apart from the city, on a mountain, they live in a paradise of their own making. Here they contravene the civic portrait. They are not "drunk with wine or wandering," but "modest and sober"; Pentheus will see to his "surprise how chaste the Bacchae are." On both occasions when they are spied on by representatives of the city, we see the Bacchae inhabiting *utopian space,* living in gentle, free spontaneity. In each case a Messenger carries this report *back* to the city, a report of the positive aspects of the obliteration of distinctions: not madness, but freedom.

The first Messenger's report is of a sacred and miraculous "peaceable kingdom," where the women tame and suckle wild beasts, where rivers of water, wine, and milk burst forth from the earth, where honey spurts from the wands the women carry. "If you had been there and seen these wonders for yourself, you would have gone down on your knees and prayed to the god you now deny." The second Messenger's report is of domestic peace. "We saw the Maenads sitting, their hands busily moving at their happy tasks."

But the Messengers represent something else. They are not only reporters of Bacchic ethnography, bearing reports on the utopian civil life of the Bacchics within their own space, they are, as well, *invaders* of that space. They are "spies" and intruders. As the Bacchics disorder the city when they "invade," so too the figures from the city disorder paradise when they spy on it and intrude on it. The response in both cases is the same. The Bacchics are instantly transformed into wild figures of violence. The motif of the obliteration of distinctions continues, but now in a way that elicits civil disgust and fear rather than envy and reverence. In the first case, the women tear live, domesticated animals apart with their bare hands. More seriously, they attack civic space. "Like invaders," they swooped down on the border villages, "everything in sight they pillaged and destroyed. They snatched children from their homes"—and they did this with supernatural power, without conventional weapons. When the men of the village fought back, the women routed them with their wands, while the weapons of the men were unable to draw blood. In the second instance, it is a man who is pulled apart by the women's bare hands, a mother who slays her son.[10]

Moving several centuries in time, we find a modulation of the Bacchic paradigm. When, in 186 B.C., the Roman Senate suppressed the Bacchic cults, all of the older elements of religious propaganda were reaffirmed. It was an "invasion" and an "epidemic." It was foreign, fraudulent, characterized by violence and sexual excesses. But the speech that Livy puts in the mouth of the consul Postumius reveals another dimension of our theme. There is no longer a dichotomy between civil space and Bacchic utopian space, the cult now dwells within the city. It lives in *subversive space* where "some believe it to be a kind of worship of the gods; others suppose it a permitted sport and relaxation." Civil understanding has domesticated the Dionysiac cult, and this makes it all the more dangerous. The external utopian space of the Bacchae has become internal, subversive space within the city. The Bacchae now live in a *counterpolis*. In his speech from the Rostra, Postumius declaims:

Unless you are on your guard, Citizens of Rome, this present meeting, held in the daylight, legally summoned by a consul, can be paralleled by another meeting held at night. Now, as individuals, they [the Bac- chics] are afraid of you, as you stand assembled in a united body; but presently, when you have scattered to your houses in the city or to your homes in the country, *they* will have assembled and will be making plans for their own safety and at the same time for your destruction; and then you as individuals will have to fear them as a united body.[11]

But, since the Bacchics are within civil space, they may be dealt with by civil means: trials, executions, banishments, and laws for their suppres- sion.

I suggest no simple parallels. There are profound differences between Dionysiac cults and Peoples Temple Christian Church. Yet the spatial considerations that I have advanced from the one, supply some instances of familiarity when we seek to understand the other.

The fundamental fact about Jones is that he sought to overcome dis- tinctions. At times he termed this impulse, Christianity, at times, socialism or communism, but the effort was the same. While one can point to bisexuality and other forms of liberation and libertinism that bear some resemblance to Dionysiac praxis, these parallels are superficial. The major distinction that Jones labored to overcome was a distinctly modern and American one: it was the distinction of race. This was the consistent theme as he moved from established civil and religious space (the Som- merset Southside Church, the Laurel Street Tabernacle, the Human Rights Commission, the Housing Authority) to a space of his own making. In one of the earliest official reports on Peoples Temple by the district su- perintendent of the United Methodist Church for Oakland and the East Bay, it is described as "a caring community of people of all races and classes. They bear the mark of compassion and justice—compassion for the hungry and jobless, lonely and disturbed, and also for the earth and her offspring."[12] In some sense, the predominance of Blacks in Peoples Temple is equivalent to the predominance of women in the Dionysiac religions.

Prior to Jonestown, Peoples Temple might be described as inhabiting subversive space. It participated in civil activities and won major forms of public recognition for these efforts. But, hidden from public view, it was also a parallel mode of government. Internally, it was a counterpolis. It had its own modes of leadership, its own criteria for citizenship, its own mores and laws, its own system of discipline and punishment. When this was revealed to the public, civil world by disaffected members (as was the Dionysian cult in Rome), the reaction could have been predicted from Livy. An exposé of its founder in terms of fraud and of the Temple in terms of a subversive danger to the community brought legal and legislative remedies to bear: official investigations, lawsuits, criminal charges. Seen in this light, the article in *New West Magazine* is parallel to the speech of Postumius.

Jones's reaction was one of exodus to utopian space, to Guyana. As one reads through the various reports on Jonestown prior to November 1978, the equivalents of the speeches of the Messengers in the *Bacchae,* both those from visitors and those produced by Peoples Temple, there is little doubt that one is reading the language and rhetoric of paradise. One such report, from the summer of 1978, begins by quoting Matthew 25:35–40:

> I was hungry and you gave me food, I was thirsty and you gave me drink, I was a stranger and you welcomed me, I was naked and you clothed me. . . . Truly I say to you, as you did to one of the least of my brethren, you did it to me.

and continues:

> What a miracle it is! Over eight hundred acres of jungle have been cleared since 1974, most of it within the last year. . . . What we found at the cooperative was a loving community in the true New Testament sense. . . . Jonestown offers a rare opportunity for deep relationships between men and women, young and old, who come from diverse racial and cultural backgrounds.[13]

A pamphlet put out by the Temple to extol Jonestown was entitled, "A Feeling of Freedom," and Jones elaborated:

> We enjoy every type of organized sport and recreational games. Musical talents and arts are flourishing. We share every joy and every need. Our lives are secure and rich with variety and growth and expanding knowledge. . . . Now there is peace . . . there is freedom from the loneliness and the agony of racism. . . . We have found security and freedom in collectivism and we can help build a peaceful agricultural nation.[14]

There is little doubt that whatever the "reality," this evaluation *was* shared by the majority of the citizens of Jonestown. It was, to use the title of the Peoples Temple home for retarded children back in Redwood Valley, truly "Happy Acres."

Into this utopian space, figures from the city came to invade and to spy. Congressman Ryan and the press disordered paradise and the result could have been predicted from the *Bacchae*—the rapid shift from peace to terror and the furious murder of the intruders. In the *Bacchae,* the Maenads, after routing the invaders, go on to attack the border villages. At Jonestown, the violence was directed inwards, the White Night, the total destruction of themselves. In part, this was a measure of realism. There was no possible military solution for Jonestown against those they perceived as the aggressors. The Temple lacked the Maenads' supernatural weapons. But, in part, this was as well a spatial reaction. Utopia had been invaded, and it was time for another exodus.

On 15 March 1979, the *New York Times* published the transcript of a tape recording of Jones, during the White Night, exhorting his followers to suicide. It is a remarkable document.[15] Jones clearly interprets the visit of Ryan as an "invasion": they "came after our children." Following the shooting at the airport, more powerful military invaders will return; they will annihilate the community. There is "no hiding place down here." No further terrestrial exodus will serve, there is no utopia, no "nowhere" where they will not be sought out. The tape reiterates: "It's too late for Russia." "There's no plane." So "Let's get gone. Let's get gone. Let's get gone."

The language for death used by Jones and other voices on the tape is consistently spatial—indeed, it suggests a communal rhetoric. "Step over," "step to that other side," "stepping over to another place," "stepping over to another plane," "you have to step across . . . this world was not our home," "if you knew what's ahead of you, you'd be glad to be stepping over." But this language suggests as well the sort of additional data that we need. What was their view of afterlife? Of the "other" world? On the tape there is only a twice-repeated reference to "the green scene thing." But this reference is sufficient to establish a post mortem paradisiacal context, in a place where they will not be followed, where they would not be further intruded upon.

By reading Jonestown in light of the *Bacchae* and Euripides in light of Jonestown, we can begin to understand its utopian logic. We can begin to find Jonestown familiar. Its failure to secure subversive space was predictable, as was a violent conflict when representatives from civil space invaded utopia. By this interpretation, the most proximate responsibility for the events of White Night was Ryan's.

IV

Let me go on to suggest a second option, a second partial interpretation, a second act of making Jonestown familiar.

As I read the various, early press reports of the White Night, my eye was caught by one detail. Not only 914 human deaths, but also all the animals. In the words of the first reporter on the scene:

> I noticed that many of them had died with their arms around each other, men and women, white and black, young and old. Little babies lying on the ground too. Near their mothers and fathers. Dead. Finally, I turned back toward the main pavilion and noticed the dogs that lay dead on the sidewalk. The dogs, I thought. What had they done? Then

I realized that Jones had meant to leave nothing, not even animals, to bear witness to the final horror. There were to be no survivors. Even the dogs and Mr. Muggs, Jonestown's pet chimpanzee, had their place in the long white night into which the Peoples Temple had been ordered by the mad Mr. Jones. The heat and stench were overpowering. There was nothing to drink because Jones had ordered the community water supply contaminated with poison.[16]

Leaving aside Krause's lurid prose and his editorializing, the destruction was intended to be total: men, women, children, animals, fish, and water supply—and this destruction alongside a deliberate presentation of utopian harmony—bodies lying together, "arms around each other," uniting the sexes, age groups, and races.

This, too, has a certain familiarity to the student of religion. Although it is a recent model, rather than an old one that will be called on, the model of the cargo cult. Let me give one specific example from Espiritu Santo in the New Hebrides.[17]

In 1923, a native prophet, Ronovuro, announced that the ancestral dead would return to the island, after a flood, on a ship bearing rice and other foods. This would be distributed to members of his cult if they were fully paid up. (He charged fees for entrance, ranging from 5 shillings to one pound). A stone storehouse was built to hold the cargo. However, Ronovuro prophesied, the Europeans would attempt to prevent the ship from landing and distributing its gifts. Therefore, the natives must rebel. While, eventually, all Whites must be killed, for now, one European was to be singled out. He would serve as a surrogate for the others. In July 1923, a British planter named Clapcott was murdered by Ronovuro's followers. He was shot, and his body was mutilated. According to some reports, parts of it were eaten. The cult was suppressed by military means. Six of the leaders were condemned to death, others were sentenced to prison terms. In 1937, the cult was revived, but was quickly suppressed by the authorities.

In 1944, a new prophet, Tsek, arose and founded the Ronovuro school. It was likewise a cargo cult, but of a somewhat different form. His message, according to J. G. Miller, was:

Destroy everything which you got from the Whites also all [native made] mats and basket-making tools. Burn your houses and build two large dormitories in each village: one for the men and the other for the women. . . . Stop working for the Whites. Slaughter all domestic animals: pigs, dogs, cats, etc.

New social forms were developed. The members of the cult went nude, they spoke a common language although the villages from which they came had originally belonged to different linguistic groups. Tribal friction and quarreling were eliminated in favor of cultic solidarity. A road several miles long, the result of enormous collective labor, was built to the sea, terminating at the site of Clapcott's murder, where the cargo ship would land and discharge the goods.

Again the cult was suppressed, although there are indications that it still continues in modulated forms. Ecstatic speech and healings have been added, and there is a secret room with vines stretched between poles that serves as "wireless belong boy," a place to wait for news of the arrival of the cargo ship.

There are many striking parallels of detail between these cults and Jonestown. But there is so much that is specifically Oceanic in cargo cults that a pursuit of these would be dangerous. Yet there is much, in the general ideology, that is suggestive. In the preceding chapter, I tried to summarize the underlying logic. It need not be rehearsed here. It is sufficient to recall that the central, moral idea was one of achieving exchange reciprocity between the Whites and the natives. A variety of stratagems were employed, the most desperate, such as on Santos, involving a total destruction of everything the natives own as if, by this dramatic gesture, to awaken the White man's sense of obligation to exchange, in order to shame him into a recognition of his responsibilities. "We have now given everything away. What will you give in return?"[18]

I am not suggesting simple parallels. Peoples Temple was not a cargo cult although, if we sought to interpret the religion of Peoples Temple rather than its end, we would be helped immeasurably if we understood it in the context of messianic, nativistic, cargo cults. But Ronovuro and Tsek can help us become familiar with Jones at the moment of the White Night. (Perhaps they could help us become even more familiar with him if we knew more about his religious and political ideologies). Indeed, Jones himself draws a parallel between White Night and native crisis cults. On the transcript, someone protests, and Jones answers:

> It's never been done before you say. It's been done by every tribe in history. Every tribe facing annihilation. All the Indians of the Amazon are doing it right now. . . . Because they do not want to live in this kind of a world.

Alongside the spatial language for death on the last tape from Jonestown, there is another language, the language of "revolutionary suicide" (a term borrowed from the writings of Huey P. Newton). "We are not committing suicide, it's a revolutionary act." "What I'm talking about is the dispensation of judgment, this is a revolutionary—a revolutionary suicide council. I'm not talking about self-destruction." "[Let's] lay down our lives to protest." "We didn't commit suicide. We committed an act of revolutionary suicide protesting the conditions of an inhumane world."

And finally, "I'm sure that they'll—they'll pay for it. This is a revolutionary suicide. This is not a self-destructive suicide. So they'll pay for this. They brought this upon us. And they'll pay for that. I leave that destiny to them." Who are these anonymous figures who will "pay"? Who are "they"? The cargo model suggests Whites.

On the tape, although Jones does refer to the congressman and other external enemies, his primary hostility seems to be directed clearly against defecting members of Peoples Temple, both those who have defected in the past and, more immediately, the small group who left for the airport with Ryan a little more than an hour before.

> That we lay down our lives in protest against what's been done. That we lay down our lives to protest what's being done. The criminality of people. The cruelty of people. Who walked out of here today? Do you know who walked out? Mostly white people. [Voices] Mostly white people.

And, more eloquently, an unidentified woman's voice:

> It broke my heart completely. All of this year the white people had been with us and they're not a part of us [now]. So we might as well end it now, because I don't see. . . . [Music and voices]

Jones and Peoples Temple had labored mightily, at extraordinary cost, to achieve their vision of racial equality. And they had failed. They had failed earlier, even in their internal organization—the leadership group was entirely white. And they failed, most immediately, in the defections. What was left was a gesture—a gesture designed to elicit shame, a gesture that the mixed rhetoric of Jonestown termed a "revolutionary suicide." By destroying all, by giving their all, they sought to call forth a reciprocal action. They would show the world, but most particularly, the defectors. In death, they would achieve a corporate picture of peace and harmony—the picture indelibly recorded by Krause and the news photographers.

They failed, as the cargo cults failed; but we may catch a glimpse of the logic of their deed, aided by familiarity gained from Oceania.

I have by no means supplied a final answer to Jonestown's awesome final solution. But this preliminary attempt has kept faith with the responsibilities attendant on being a member of the academy. It is now for others to continue the task, with Jonestown, or wherever the question of understanding human activities and expression is raised. For if we do not persist in the quest for intelligibility, there can be no human sciences, let alone, any place for the study of religion within them.

Appendixes

Appendix 1

The following original translation of the Io cosmogony by Hare Hongi appeared in the *Journal of the Polynesian Society* 16 (1907): 109–19. I have retained all the typographic details—italics, boldface type, parentheses, brackets, and Hongi's Arabic numerals—but have added new section numbers in Roman numerals. Footnotes have been eliminated. For Johansen's retranslation of section I, see pp. 125–26, below.

[I]

1. **Io** dwelt within breathing-space of immensity.
   The Universe was in darkness, with water everywhere.
   There was no glimmer of dawn, no clearness, no light.
   And he began by saying these words,—
   That He might cease remaining inactive:
   "Darkness, become a light-possessing darkness."
   And at once light appeared.
   (He) then repeated those self-same words in this manner,—
   That He might cease remaining inactive:
   "Light, become a darkness-possessing light."
   And again an intense darkness supervened.
   Then a third time He spake saying:
   "Let there be one darkness above,
   Let there be one darkness below (alternate).
   Let there be a darkness unto Tupua,
   Let there be a darkness unto Tawhito;
   It is a darkness overcome and dispelled.
   Let there be one light above,
   Let there be one light below (alternate).
   Let there be a light unto Tupua,
   Let there be a light unto Tawhito.
   A dominion of light,
   A bright light."
   And now a great light prevailed.
   (**Io**) then looked to the waters which compassed him about,
   and spake a fourth time, saying:
   "Ye waters of Tai-kama, be ye separate.

Heaven, be formed." Then the sky became suspended.
"Bring-forth thou Tupua-horo-nuku."
And at once the moving earth lay stretched abroad.

[II]

2. Those words (of **Io**) became impressed on the minds of our ancestors, and by them were they transmitted down through the generations. Our priests joyously referred to them as being:

> "The ancient and original sayings.
> The ancient and original words.
> The ancient and original cosmological wisdom.
> Which caused growth from the void,
> The limitless space-filling void,
> As witness the tidal-waters,
> The evolved heaven,
> The birth-given evolved earth."

3. And now, my friends, there are three very important applications of those original sayings, as used in our sacred rituals. The first occurs in the ritual for implanting a child within the barren womb. The next occurs in the ritual for enlightening both the mind and the body. The third and last occurs in the ritual on the solemn subjects of death, and of war, of baptism, of genealogical recitals, and such like important subjects, as the priests most particularly concern themselves in.

The words by which **Io** fashioned the Universe—that is to say, by which it was implanted and caused to produce a world of light—the same words are used in the ritual for implanting a child in a barren womb. The words by which **Io** caused light to shine in the darkness are used in the rituals for cheering a gloomy and despondent heart, the feeble aged, the decrepit; for shedding light into secret places and matters, for inspiration in song-composing, and in many other affairs, affecting man to despair in times of adverse war. For all such the rituals to enlighten and cheer, includes the words (used by **Io**) to overcome and dispel darkness. Thirdly, there is the preparatory ritual which treats of successive formations within the universe, and the genealogical history of man himself.

[III]

4. [Ask not of me, thine elder brother, O friend, for a fuller recital of these and kindred matters, I know not the details. I have caught but fragments of them, this I do not conceal; neither may I (indulge your wish) by inventing that which would be false. Yet (albeit it is fragmentary) am I filled with great and mighty things. These may now, for our sojourn in this world draws to a close, be left to others. They may be placed side by side with the (European) law, to become a basis for the history following on after our own time. Thus it is that I, thine elder brother, O friend, who am filled therewith, willingly impart unto you all, these, the wisdom of mine ancestors. Neither shall I, who will shortly die, withhold aught thereof. To-morrow, it may be, I shall suddenly die, and so end. Or, what prospect of war is there? that I should withhold them (as a means of self-defence). Indeed, neither Hone Te Mahu nor Wiremu Tamihana essayed to use them against the *Pakeha* during the Waikato War. For instance, by using the ritual and by plucking out the

heart of a *Pakeha* foe, and offering up the one portion to Uenuku-kai-tangata, the other portion to be eaten by the highest born females. As it happened, it was their own (Maori) hearts which were torn from them by Christian doctrine and (European) law. Why then, need I withhold these sacred rituals? I would not do so in any case; I will disclose them in their numbers and their fragments. (As to the fuller text thereof) a council of Tohungas might successfully weave such together. Meanwhile, it were well to seek out a skilled Maori, well informed in the three rituals under notice, namely: that of child-implanting, the darkness-dispelling, and the cosmology. Here endeth that.]

[IV]

Thus, then, were the primeval waters separated, each unto itself, as we now see their masses. Thus, also, the heaven suspended, apparently (in the first instance) but at a little distance above the moving-earth; thus too, the moving-earth lay outstretched.

[V]

5. And now **Io** caused other reproductions of himself. (Ask me not, my many brethren, "Ha, whom then did **Io** take to wife?" Enough, it is the Maori who speaketh. The Maori who hath no committee of investigation, who, therefore, speaketh thus spasmodically. Who hath no recording ink, therefore relieth upon memory.) As witness the following recital:—

> " 'Tis **Io**
> The A-io-nuku of Motion
> The A-io-rangi of Space
> The A-io-papa of Earth
> The A-io-matua, the Parent
> The Primeval darkness
> The Continuous darkness
> The Groping darkness
> Sleep-impelling-Hine
> The great Firmament (sky-roof)
> The Night
> The Day
> Rangi and Papa, Space and Matter, Sky-father and Earth-mother.

Who begat—No.   1. Tama-rangi-tau-ke, sons of different worlds.
          "   2. Aitua, fate, destiny
          "   3. Rongo and Tane
          "   4. Tane-mahuta
          "   5. Tawhiri-matea
          "   6. Rua-ai-moko
          "   7. Ngana
          "   8. Haumia-tiketike
          "   9. Tu-mata-uenga
          "   10. Tangaroa

When the heaven was poled aloft by Tane-mahuta, he took the sleep-impelling-maid to wife, and begat Makoi-rangi and Pu-whakarere-i-waho.' "

[VI]

As to No. 1, **Tama-a-rangi-tau-ke,** his offspring is primarily the spirit of man. When that spirit leaves the body, it is known as Tama-rangi-tau-ke. The ordure and urine which issues from a dead body, are also referred to as his offspring. These are also known as the Whatu-taka-i-raro, upon which references occur in the rituals concerning the spirit of man.

As to No. 2, **Aitua** (fate, destiny), its offspring is such as the dead body just noticed. None the less, do the genealogical records of the generations pass through such unto Tiki (the first man) and them. Man, the individual, must inevitably die, he cannot live for ever, owing to the action of Pu-whakarere-i-waho. Formerly the days were very short, darkness quickly succeeded dawn, and dawn as quickly succeeding darkness. So it continued down to the generation of Maui-tiki-tiki, when the head of the Sun was beaten, which caused the day to lengthen to what it is at present. At that time although man died he did not utterly perish. He died, as the moon dieth, to be restored to life again by the wonder-working Maui. At length, Maui himself was jammed-to-death, to the laughter of the tiny Fan-tail birds, by his ancestress the Dame-of-darkness-perpetual. He being be-winked and indrawn by the capillaries of Hine-nui-te-po, as a hero died. So man, since then, dieth even unto the great night of Rehua. Maui had essayed to penetrate, by way of the capillaries of Hine-nui-te-po, and to emerge through her mouth, and so subdue her. She proved too powerful, being the elder-sister of Whiro-te-tupua and Tuhi-kai-tangata, sons of Rehua and Rangi-tai-apo, descendents of Pu-whakarere-i-waho. Had Maui conquered her, man would neither die as the moon dieth, nor would he utterly perish in the darkness primeval of Rehua, and the gloomy abyss of Rangi-tai-apo; man would have continued to live forever. He would die neither as the moon or the earth; but, as Maui himself died, so dieth man. Thence it is that we now commiserate each other as to our ultimate end, it is owing to this god-man having died unavenged by the act of his junior, Pu-whakarere-i-waho.

As to No. 3, **Rongo** and **Tane,** the offspring are the *kumara* plants, and such like foods. The various creeping plants which grow, being termed Rongo-mata-aka-wau, the climbing *pikiarero,* the bind-weed tendrils and vines, such as the Taroa, Tamau and Tahua.

As to No. 4, **Tane-mahuta,** his offspring are the trees and the birds.

As to No. 5, **Tawhiri-matea,** his offspring are the winds and the rains. The south wind, the east wind, the north and the west. Those are the progeny of Tawhiri, who gave evidence of their affection for their sky-father who was poled aloft. It is as protesting against this, that Makoirangi and others wage continual warfare, and work evil upon the peculiar children of earth. They, who engage in these evil works, are the progeny of Tawhiri, Makoirangi and Pu-whakarere-i-waho. They continued hostile, the seniors to the juniors, and properly so, for the forcible removal of their sky-father. But, when man uses the rituals for appeasing the anger of the winds, their wrath for the time being is allayed.

As to No. 6, **Rua-ai-moko,** his progeny are the earthquake and volcanic discharge. This son (of the sky-father and earth-mother) is an immature son. Not being fully born, he remains invisible to mortal eye, nor has he any children. It is enough that we are sufficiently acquainted with him as being an earth-shaker.

(By other recitals, earthquakes are explained as caused by his struggles to free himself from his mother's womb. It is said that he can only succeed by destroying his mother, *i.e.,* the earth.)

As to No. 7, **Ngana,** his progeny are the Sun, Moon and Stars. He is the second son of Papa and those who followed Rangi aloft. He, in common with Tama-nui-ki-te-ra (sun-god) and other juniors, sheds his beneficial influence upon earth, and dissipates the hostile energy of Tawhiri-matea (wind-god). Thence, are the warning signs (given to man) of the advent of the year (June), an admonition to the descendants of the eighth (Haumia) on earth here.

As to No. 8, **Haumia-tiketike,** his offspring is the edible root, of which it is said:—"The upstanding ordure of Haumia."

As to No. 9, **Tu-mata-uenga,** his offspring are living men, such as we ourselves (warlike). Thence are the sayings:—Narrow-visaged-Tu: Wrathful-Tu: Raging-Tu: Tu, eater of War parties: and Tu of Shaking-front. Those things which are desired by Tu (the warrior-god) are granted in the potency of the rituals unto god **Io.**

As to No. 10, **Tangaroa,** his progeny are Punga and Ikatere (of the Sea). There is Tu-te-ihiihi and Tu-te-wanawana, in short, all the fish of the ocean, all reptiles of the land.

As to **Pu-whakarere-i-waho,** his offspring is whatever is unjust, death; more particularly calamitous death, which causes extinction of mankind, foods, goods, histories, rituals, and all such like, which concerneth man. These he delighteth to destroy. His dreaded name occurs, as instigator of evil, in propitiatory rituals of the dim past. Rehua and Rangi-taiapo are descendents of Pu-whakarere-i-waho and Makoi-rangi. Thence came the Dame-of-darkness-perpetual, Whiro-te-tupua and Tuhi-kai-tangata.

The following is a retranslation of section I of the original Maori text by J. Prytz Johansen, *Studies in Maori Myths and Rites,* Historisk-filosofiske Meddelelser udgivet af Det Kongelige Danske Videnskabernes Selskab, 37.4 (Copenhagen, 1958), pp. 52–53.

> Io dwelt in the open space of the world.
> The world was dark, there was water everywhere.
> There was no day, no light, nothing concerning light,
> Only dark, water was everywhere.
> It was he who first said this word:
> . . .
> "Night, a day-owning Night."
> Behold! Day had broken.
> Then he spoke in the same way as that word, this word
> . . .
> "Day, a night-owning Day."
> Behold! the time of the great dark returned.
> Then came the third of his words:
> "Let one Night be above
> And one (another) Night below.
> Night, the magician's Night,
> Night, the priest's Night,

A subjected Night.
Let one Day be above
And one (another) Day below.
Day, the magician's Day,
Day, the priest's Day.
A resplendent Day,
A bright Day."
Behold! It had become very bright!
Only now did his eyes seek the waters that surrounded him,
Then his fourth word was uttered, it was this word:
"Te-Wai-ki-Tai-tama, divide the waters,
So that heaven will unfold itself. Heaven has been lifted up.
Te Tupua-horo-nuku is born."
Behold! Papa-tuanuku lay there.

Appendix 2

The following extracts were taken from the transcript of a tape of the final 43 minutes of "White Night," obtained by the *New York Times* from the International Home Video Club, Inc., New York City, and published in the *New York Times,* 15 March 1979.

Jones: I've tried my best to give you a good life. In spite of all that I've tried, a handful of our people, with their lies, have made our life impossible. There's no way to detach ourselves from what's happened today.

Not only are we in a compound situation; not only are there those who have left and committed the betrayal of the century; some have stolen children from others and they are in pursuit right now to kill them, because they stole their children. And we are sitting here waiting on a powder keg.

So, to sit here and wait for the catastrophe that's going to happen on that airplane—it's going to be a catastrophe. It almost happened here. Almost happened when the congressman was nearly killed here. You can't steal people's children. You can't take off with people's children without expecting a violent reaction. And that's not so unfamiliar to us, either, even if we—even if we were Judeo-Christian—if we weren't Communists. The world opinion suffers violence and the violent shall take it by force. If we can't live in peace, then let's die in peace. [Applause]

We've been so betrayed. We have been so terribly betrayed. [Music and singing]

What's going to happen here in a matter of a few minutes is that one of those people on that plane is going to shoot the pilot—I know that. I didn't plan it, but I know it's going to happen. They're gonna shoot that pilot and down comes that plane into the jungle. And we better not have any of our children left when it's over. Because they'll parachute in here on us.

I'm going to be just as plain as I know how to tell you. I've never lied to you. I never have lied to you. I know that's what's gonna happen. That's what he intends to do; and he will do it. He'll do it.

What's with being so bewildered with many, many pressures on my brain seeing all people behave so treasonous—there was just too much for me to put together. But I now know what he was telling me. And it'll happen. If the plane gets in the air even.

So my opinion is that you be kind to children, and be kind to seniors, and take the potion like they used to take in ancient Greece, and step over quietly; because we're not committing suicide—it's a revolutionary act. We can't go back; they won't leave us alone. They're now going back to tell more lies, which means more congressmen. And there's no way, no way we can survive.

Anybody. Anyone that has any dissenting opinion, please speak. Yes. You can have an opportunity, but if the children are left, we're going to have them butchered. We can make a strike, but we'll be striking out against people that we don't want to strike against. We'd like to get the people that caused this stuff; and some—if some people here are prepared and know how to do that, to go in town and get Timothy Stoen, but there's no plane. There's no plane. You can't catch a plane in time.

He's responsible for it. He brought these people to us. He and Deanna Myrtle. The people in San Francisco will not—not be idle. Or would they? They'll not take our death in vain, you know. Yes?

Woman: Is it too late for Russia?

Jones: At this point, it's too late for Russia. They killed. They started to kill. That's why it makes it too late for Russia. Otherwise I'd say, yes, sir, you bet your life. But it's too late. I can't control these people. They're out there. They've gone with the guns. And it's too late. And once we kill anybody—at least, that's the way I've always—I've always put my lot with you. If one of my people do something, that's me.

And they say I don't have to take the blame for this—but I don't live that way. They said, deliver up Ejar; we tried to get the man back here. Ejar, whose mother's been lying on him, and trying to break up this family. And they've all agreed to kill us by any means necessary. Do you think I'm going to deliver them Ejar? Not on your life.

Man: I know a way to find Stoen if it'll help us.

Jones: No. You're not going. You're not going. You're not going. I can't live that way. I cannot live that way. I've lived with—for all. I'll die for all. [Applause]

I've been living on hope for a long time, Christine, and I appreciate—you've always been a very good agitator. I like agitation because you have to see two sides of one issue—two sides of a question.

But what those people are gonna get done; and what they get through will make our lives worse than hell. Will make us—will make the rest of us not accept it. When they get through lying.

They posed so many lies between there and that truck that we are—we are done in as far as any other alternative.

Woman: Well, I say let's make an air—airlift to Russia. That's what I say. I don't think nothing is impossible, if you believe it.

Jones: How are we going to do that? How are you going to airlift to Russia?

Woman: Well, I thought they said if we got in an emergency, they gave you a code to let them know.

Jones: No, they didn't. They gave us a code that they'd let us know on that issue; not us create an issue for them. They said that we—if they saw the country coming down, they'd give us a code. They'd give us a code. We can check on that and see if it's on the code. Did you check with Russia to see if they'll take us in a minute but otherwise we die?

I don't know what else to say to these people. But to me death is not a fearful thing. It's living that's cursed. I have never, never, never, never seen anything like this before in my life. I've never seen people take the law and do—in their own hands and provoke us and try to purposely agitate mother of children. There is no need to finish us; it's not worth living like this. Not worth living like this.

Woman: I think that there were too few who left for 1,200 people to give them their lives for those people that left.

Jones: Do you know how many left?

Woman: Oh, twenty-odd. That's a small—

Jones: Some twenty-odd—

Woman: Compared to what's here.

Jones: Twenty-odd. But what's gonna happen when they don't leave? I hope that they could leave. But what's gonna happen when they don't leave?

Woman: You mean the people here?

Jones: Yeah. What's going to happen to us when they don't leave, when they get on the plane and the plane goes down?

Woman: I don't think they'll go down.

Jones: You don't think they'll go down? I wish I could tell you was right—but I'm right. There's one man there who blames, and rightfully so, Judy Blakey for the murder—for the murder of his mother and he'll—he'll stop that pilot by any means necessary. He'll do it. That plane'll come out of the air. There's no way you can fly a plane without a pilot.

Woman: I wasn't speaking about that plane. I was speaking about a plane for us to go to Russia.

Jones: How—to Russia? You think Russia's gonna want—no—you think Russia's gonna want us with all this stigma? We had some value, but now we don't have any value.

Woman: Well—I don't see it like that. I mean, I feel like that—as long as there's life there's hope. That's my faith.

Jones: Well—some—everybody dies. Some place that hope runs out; because everybody dies. I haven't seen anybody yet didn't die. And I like to choose my own kind of death for a change. I'm tired of being tormented to hell, that's what I'm tired of. Tired of it. [Applause]

To have other people's lives in my hands, and I certainly don't want your life in my hands. I'm going to tell you, Christine, without me, life has no meaning. [Applause] I'm the best thing you'll ever have.

I want—want—I have to pay—I'm standing with [inaudible]. I'm standing with those people. They're part of me. I could detach myself. No. No. No. No. No. No. I never detach myself from any of your troubles. I've always taken your troubles right on my shoulders. And I'm not going to change that now. It's too late. I've been running too long. Not going to change now. [Applause]

Maybe the next time you'll get to go to Russia. The next time round. This is— what I'm talking about now is the dispensation of judgement. This is a revolutionary—a revolutionary suicide council. I'm not talking about self—self-destruction. I'm talking about what we have no other road. I will take your call. We will put it through to the Russians. And I can tell you the answer now, because I am a prophet. Call the Russians and tell them and see if they'll take us.

Woman: I said I'm not ready to die.

Jones: I don't think you are.

Woman: But I know what you meant.

Jones: I don't think you are.

Woman: But I look at all the babies and I think they deserve to live.

Jones: But don't they deserve much more—they deserve peace.

Woman: We all came here for peace.

Jones: And we've—have we had it?

Woman: No.

Jones: I tried to give it to you. I've laid down my life, practically. I've practically died every day to give you peace. And you still not have any peace. You look better than I've seen you in a long while but it's still not the kind of peace that I want to give you.

Woman: I know that. But I still think, as an individual, I have a right to—

Jones: You do, and I'm listening.

Woman: —to say what I think, what I feel. And think we all have a right to our own destiny as individuals.

Jones: Right.

Woman: And I think I have a right to choose mine and everybody else has a right to choose theirs.

Jones: Yes. I'm not criticizing—

Woman: Well, I think I still have a right to my own opinion.

Jones: I'm not taking it from you. I'm not taking it from you.

Man: Christine, you're only standing here because he was here in the first place. So I don't know what you're talking about, having an individual life. Your life has been extended to the day that you're standing there because of him.

Jones: I guess she has as much right to speak as anybody else to—What did you say, Ruby? [Voice, cannot be deciphered.] Well, you'll regret that, this very day if you don't die. You'll regret it if you do though you don't die. You'll regret it.

I saved them. I saved them, but I made my example. I made my expression. I made my manifestation and the world was ready, not ready for me. Paul said I was a man born out of due season. I've been born out of due season, just like all we are—and the best testimony we can make is to leave this goddamn world. [Applause]

Woman: You must prepare to die.

Woman: I'm not talking to her. Will you let—would you let her or me talk?

Jones: Keep talking.

Woman: Would you make her sit down and let me talk while I'm on the floor or let her talk.

Jones: How can you tell the leader what to do if you live? I've listened to you. You asked me about Russia. I'm right now making a call to Russia. What more do you suggest? I'm listening to you. You've yet to give me one slight bit of encouragement. I just now . . . to go there and do that.

[Voices]

Jones: Everybody hold it. We didn't come—hold it. Hold it. Hold it. Hold it.

[Voices]

Jones: Lay down your burden. I'm gonna lay down my burden. Down by the riverside. Shall we lay them down here by the side of Guyana? No man didn't take our lives. Right now. They haven't taken them. But when they start parachuting out of the air, they'll seek some of our innocent babies. I'm not—I don't want. . . . They've got to shoot me to get through to some of these people. I'm not telling them take your child. Can you let them take your child?

Voices: No. No. No.

Jones: I want to see . . .

[Many voices]

Jones: Please. Please. Please. Please. Please. Please Please.

Man: I'm ready to go. If you tell us we have to give our lives now, we're ready—all the rest of the sisters and brothers are with me.

Jones: Some months I've tried to keep this thing from happening. But now I see it's the will—it's the will of Sovereign Being that this happen to us. That we lay down our lives in protest against what's been done. That we lay down our lives to protest at what's being done. The criminality of people. The cruelty of people.

Who walked out of here today? Do you know who walked out? [Voices] Mostly white people walked.

I'm so grateful for the ones that didn't—those who knew who they are. I just know there's no point—there's no point to this. We are born before our time. They won't accept us. And I don't think we should sit here and take any more time for our children to be endangered. Because if they come after our children, we give them our children, then our children will suffer forever.

[Woman's voice, unintelligible]

Jones: What comes now, folks? What comes now?

Man: Everybody hold it.

Jones: Say peace. Say peace. Say peace. Say peace. What's come. Don't let— Take Dwyer on down to the east house. Take Dwyer.

Woman: Everybody be quiet please.

Man: That means sit down. Sit down.

Jones: They know. I tried so very, very hard. They're trying over here to see what's going to happen in Los Angeles. Who is he?

[Voices]

Jones: Get Dwyer out of here before something happens to him. Dwyer. I'm not talking about Ejar. I said Dwyer. Ain't nobody gonna take Ejar. I'm not lettin'em take Ejar.

Woman: At one time, I felt just like [inaudible] . . . but after today I don't feel anything because the biggest majority of the people that left here for a fight and I know it really hurt my heart because—

Jones: Broke your heart, didn't it?

Woman: It broke my heart completely. All of this year the white people had been with us and they're not a part of us. So we might as well end it now, because I don't see—

[Music and voices]

Jones: Well, it's all over, all over. What a legacy, what a legacy. What's the Red Brigade doing, and one's that ever made any sense anyway? They invaded our privacy. They followed us 6,000 miles away. Red Brigade showed them justice. The congressman's dead.

Please get us some medication. Simple. It's simple, there's no convulsions with it. It's just simple. Just, please, get it. Before it's too late. The G. D. F. will be here, I tell you. Get movin', get movin', get movin'.

[Voices]

Jones: Don't be afraid to die. You'll see people land out there. They'll torture some of our children here. They'll torture our people. They'll torture our seniors. We cannot have this.

Are you going to separate yourself from whoever shot the congressman? I don't know who shot him.

Voices: No. No. No.

Jones: Let's make our peace. And those had a right to go, and they had a right to—how many are dead? Aw, God, Almighty God. Huh. Patty Park is dead?

[Voices].

Woman: Some of the others who are . . . long enough in a safe place to write about. . . .

Jones: I don't know how in the world they're ever going to write about us. It's just too late. It's too late. The congressman's dead. The. . . . Many of our . . . are dead. They're all laying out there dead.

Please can we hasten? Can we hasten with our medication? You don't know what you've done. I tried. [Applause and music]

They saw it happen and ran into the bush and dropped the machine guns. Never in my life. But we've got to move. Are you gonna get that medication here? You've got to move. Approximately about forty minutes.

Woman: Do . . . have to know when the people that are standing there in the aisles. Go stand in the radio room yard. Everybody get behind a table and back this way. O.K. There's nothing to worry about. Everybody keep calm; and try and keep your children calm. And all those children that help, let the little children in and reassure them. They're not crying from pain. It's just a little bitter tasting. They're not crying from pain. Annie Miguel, can I please see you back. . . .

Man: So much to do before I came here. So let me tell you about it. It may make a lot of you feel a little more comfortable. Sit down and be quiet, please.

One of the things I used to do—I used to be a therapist. And the kind of therapy that I did had to do with reincarnations in past life situations. And every time anybody had an experience of going into a past life, I was fortunate enough through Father to be able to let them experience it all the way through their death, so to speak. And everybody was so happy when they made that step to the other side.

Woman: I just want to say something for everyone that I see that is standing around, or crying. This is nothing to cry about. This is something we could all rejoice about. We could be happy about this. They always told us that we could cry when you're coming into this world. So we're leaving it, and we're leaving it peaceful. I think we should be—you should be happy about this. I was just thinking about Jim Jones. He just has suffered and suffered and suffered. We have the honor guard and we don't even have a chance to . . . here . . . one more chance. That's few that's gone. There's many more here . . . . That's not all of us. That's not all, yet. That's just a few that have died. I'm looking at so many people crying. I wish you would not cry. [Applause] I've been here one year and nine months. And I never felt better in my life. Not in San Francisco. But until I came to Jonestown. I had a . . . life. I had a beautiful life. We should be happy. At least I am—[Applause]

[Music]

Woman: Good to be alive today. I just like to thank Dad 'cause he was the only one that stood up for me when I needed him. And thank you, Dad.

Woman: I'm glad that you're my brothers and sisters. I'm glad to be here.

[Voices]

Jones: Please. For God's sake, let's get on with it. We've lived—we've lived as no other people lived and loved. We've had as much of this world as you're gonna get. Let's just be done with it. Let's be done with the agony of it. [Applause]

It's far, far harder to have to walk through every day, die slowly—and from the time you're a child till the time you get gray, you're dying.

Dishonest, and I'm sure that they'll—they'll pay for it. They'll pay for it. This is a revolutionary suicide. This is not a self-destructive suicide. So they'll pay for this. They brought this upon us. And they'll pay for that. I leave that destiny to them.

[Voices]

Jones: —wants to go with their child has a right to go with their child. I think its humane. I want to go—I want to see you go, though. They can take me and do what they want—whatever they want to do. I want to see you go. I don't want to see you go through this hell no more. No more. No more. No more.

We're trying. If everybody—relax. The best thing you do to relax and you won't have no problem with this thing. If you just relax.

Man: —a great deal because it's Jim Jones. And the way the children are laying there now. I'd rather see them lay like that than to see them have to die like the Jews did, which was pitiful anyhow. And I just like to thank Dad, who gave them this life, and also death. And I appreciate the fact the way our children are going. Because, like Dad said, when they came in, what they're going to do to our children—they're going to massacre our children.

And also the ones that they take capture, they're gonna just let them grow up and be dummies, just like they want them to be. And not grow up to be a person like the one and only Jim Jones. So I'd like to thank Dad for the opportunity for letting Jonestown be not what it could be, but what Jonestown is. Thank you, Dad. [Applause]

Man: It is not to be feared. It is not to be feared. It is a friend. It's a friend. Sitting there show your love for one another. Take your time—

Jones: Let's get gone. Let's get gone. Let's get gone. We had nothing we could do. We can't separate ourselves from our own people. For twenty years lying in some old rotten nursing home. Taking us through all these anguish years. They took us and put us in chains and that's nothing. This business—that business—there's no comparison to that, to this.

They've robbed us of our land and they've taken us and driven us and we tried to find ourselves. We tried to find a new beginning. But it's too late. You can't separate yourself from your brother and your sister. No way I'm going to do it. I refuse. I don't know who fired the shot. I don't know who killed the congressman. But as far as I am concerned, I killed him. You understand what I'm saying. I killed him. He had no business coming. I told him not to come.

Woman: Right. Right.

[Music]

[Children crying]

Jones: I, with respect, die with the beginning of dignity. Lay down your life with dignity. Don't lay down with tears and agony. It's nothing to death. It's like Mac said, it's just stepping over to another plane. Don't be this way. Stop this hysterics. This is not the way for people who are Socialists or Communists to die. No way for us to die. We must die with some dignity . . . we have no choice. Now we have some choice. Do you think they're gonna allow this to be done? And allow us to get by with this? You must be insane—children, it's just something to put you to rest. Oh God.

[Children crying]

Jones: Mother, mother, mother, mother, mother, please. Mother, please, please, please. Don't do this. Don't do this. Lay down your life with your child. But don't do this.

Free at last. Keep—keep your emotions down. Keep your emotions down. Children, it will not hurt. If you'd be—if you be quiet. If you be quiet.

[Music]

[Children crying]

Jones: It's never been done before, you say. It's been done by every tribe in history. Every tribe facing annihilation. All the Indians of the Amazon are doing it right now. They refuse to bring any babies into the world. They kill every child that comes into the world. Because they don't want to live in this kind of a world.

So be patient. Be patient. Death is—I tell you, I don't care how many screams you hear. I don't care how many anguished cries. Death is a million times preferable to spend more days in this life. If you knew what was ahead of you—if you knew what was ahead of you, you'd be glad to be stepping over tonight.

Death. Death. Death is common to people. And the Eskimos, they take death in their stride. Let's be digni—let's be dignified. If you quit telling them they're dying—if you would also stop some of this nonsense—adults, adults, I call on you to stop this nonsense. I call on you to quit exciting your children, when all they're doing is going to a quiet rest. I call on you to stop this now, if you have any respect at all. Are we black, proud, Socialists—or what are we? Now stop this nonsense. Don't carry this on anymore. You're exciting your children.

All over and it's good. No—no sorrow that it's all over. I'm glad it's over. Hurry, Hurry, my children. Hurry. All I—the hands of the enemy. Hurry, my children. Hurry. There are seniors out there that I'm concerned about. Hurry. I don't want any of my seniors to this mess. Only quickly, quickly, quickly, quickly, quickly. Let's just—Good knowing you.

No more pain, Al. No more pain, I said, Al. No more pain. Jim Cobb is laying on the airfield dead at this moment. [Applause] Remember, the Oliver woman said she—she'd come over and kill me if her son wouldn't stop her. These, these are the people—the peddlers of hate. All we're doing is laying down our lives. We're not letting them take our lives. We're laying down our lives. Peace in their lives. They just want peace.

Man: I'd just like to say that my—my so-called parents are filled with so much hate and treachery. I think you people out here should think about your relatives were and be glad about that the children are being laid to rest. And I'd like to say that I thank Dad for making me strong to stand with it all and make me ready for it. Thank you.

Jones: All they do is taking a drink. They take it to go to sleep. That's what death is, sleep—I'm tired of it all.

Woman: Everything we could have ever done, most loving thing of all of us could have done and it's been a pleasure walking with all of you in this revolutionary struggle. No other way I would rather go than to give my life for socialism, communism. And I thank Dad very, very much.

Woman: Dad's love and nursing, goodness and kindness and bring us to this land of freedom. His love—his mother was the advance—the advance guard to socialism. And his love, his nurses will go on forever unto the fields of—

Jones: —to that, to that, to that, words to that—was the green scene thing.

Woman: Go on unto the sign. And thank you, Dad.

Jones: With the green—and please bring it here so the adults can begin.

—you don't, don't fail to follow my advice. You'll be sorry. You'll be sorry.

We do it, than they do it. Have trust. You have to step across. We used to think this world was—this world was not our home, and it sure isn't—saying, it sure wasn't.

—don't want to tell them. All he's doing—if they will tell them—assure these— can't some people assure these children of the—in stepping over to the next plane. They set an example for others. We said—one thousand people who said, we don't like the way the world is. Take our life from us. We laid it down. We got tired. We didn't commit suicide, we committed an act of revolutionary suicide protesting the conditions of an inhumane world.

[Organ music]

Notes

Introduction

1. The history of the imagination of religion has yet to be written. Perhaps the most useful work, to date, is M. Despland, *La Religion en Occident* (Montreal, 1979), but it is far from adequate.

2. I play, here, with Dilthey's hermeneutic formulation: "Interpretation would be impossible if expressions of life were completely strange. It would be unnecessary if nothing strange were in them. It lies, therefore, between these two extremes" (W. Dilthey, *Gesammelte Schriften* [Stuttgart, 1958]), 7:255.

3. See J. Neusner, ed., *Take Judaism, for Example* (Chicago, 1982) for a volume constructed around the notion of Judaism as providing exempli gratia for religious studies. While I am uncomfortable with the category "world religions" Neusner's enterprise ought to be extended to each of the major traditions in a series of volumes. At minimum, this would make possible the beginning of a responsible undergraduate sequence in "world religions," something impossible with our present textbooks which are either encyclopaedias of trivia or idiosyncratic attempts at synthesis.

4. F. Hutcheson, *An Inquiry into the Original of Our Ideas of Beauty and Virtue in Two Treatises,* 4th ed. (London, 1738), pp. 206–7. The first edition was published anonymously in Dublin in 1725. In the passage quoted, I have modernized both the spelling and punctuation.

5. K. Burke, *The Philosophy of Literary Form,* rev. ed. (New York, 1957), p. 256.

6. V. Shklovsky, "Art as Technique," in L. T. Lemon and M. J. Reis, eds., *Russian Formalist Criticism: Four Essays* (Lincoln, 1965), esp. pp. 13–22.

Chapter 1

1. F. Ponge, *Le Grand Recueil,* vol. 2, *Méthodes* (Paris, 1961), pp. 41–42.

2. For an excellent introduction to the theoretical issues of library classification, see A. Broadfield, *The Principles of Classification* (London, 1946). On alphabetical ordering, see L. W. Daly, *Contributions to a History of Alphabetization in Antiquity and the Middle Ages* (Brussels, 1967).

3. For an initial orientation to taxonomy, see J. Z. Smith, "Animals and Plants in Myths and Legends," *Encyclopaedia Britannica,* 15th ed., 1:916–18.

4. This is a simplification for purposes of illustration. What I have provided, above, is a "key" rather than a "taxonomy." On this distinction, see G. G. Simpson, *Principles of Animal Taxonomy* (New York, 1961), pp. 13–17. For a properly complex discussion of the taxonomy of the *Juglandaceae,* see J. F. Levy, *Etudes sur les Juglandaceae* (Paris, 1955) in the series Mémoires du Muséum National d'Histoire Naturelle, n.s. B, "Botanique," vol. 6.

5. For example, C. Heimsch, Jr., and R. H. Wetmore, "The Significance of Wood Anatomy in the Taxonomy of the Juglandaceae," *American Journal of Botany* 26 (1939): 651–60, and D. R. Whitehead, "Pollen Morphology in the Juglandaceae," *Journal of the Arnold Arboretum* 46 (1965): 369–410.

6. *American College Dictionary,* s.v. "walnut."

7. I am aware that I am raising a controversial matter in equating logical division in definition with taxonomic classification. This equivalence has been asserted on a variety of grounds by scholars as diverse as: H. Daudin, *De Linné à Jussieu: Méthodes de la classification et idée de série en botanique et en zoologie* (Paris, 1926), esp. pp. 6–19; J. Piaget, *Introduction à l'epistémologie génétique* (Paris, 1950), 3:14–15; A. J. Cain, "Logic and Meaning in Linnaeus's System of Taxonomy," *Proceedings of the Linnaean Society of London* 169 (1958): 144–63, and, with most relevance to our concerns, E. Cassirer, *The Problem of Knowledge* (New Haven, 1950), pp. 124–28. The most significant challenge to this point of view is that by J. L. Larson, *Reason and Experience: The Representation of Natural Order in the Work of Carl von Linné* (Berkeley, 1971), esp. pp. 2–3, 22–24 and note 43, 100–101, 143–51.

8. This observation scarcely requires documentation. For an overview, see J. S. L. Gilmour, "The Development of Taxonomic Theory Since 1851," *Nature* 168 (1951): 400–402. The most lucid theoretical contributions remain those of E. Mayr, especially, "The Evolutionary Significance of the Systematic Enterprise," *Uppsala Universitets Årsskrift* 1958:6, pp. 13–20 and *Animal Species and Evolution* (Cambridge, Mass., 1963).

9. M. Adanson, "Préface istorike sur l'état ancien et actuel de la botanike, et une téorie de cette science," in *Familles des Plants* (Paris, 1763), 1:i–cccxxv, esp. pp. cliv–clxv and cccxiii. On Adanson, in addition to the works cited in note 11, below, see A. J. Cain, "Post-Linnaean Development of Taxonomy," *Proceedings of the Linnaean Society of London* 170 (1959): 234–44; D. Floodgate, "Some Comments on the Adansonian Taxonomic Method," *International Bulletin of Bacteriological Nomenclature and Taxonomy* 12 (1962): 171–79.

10. For the logical point here, see W. S. Jevons, *The Principles of Science,* 2d ed. (London, 1877), pp. 682–98.

11. M. Beckner, *The Biological Way of Thought* (New York, 1959), esp. pp. 21–25, 55–80; R. R. Sokol and P. H. A. Sneath, *Principles of Numerical Taxonomy* (San Francisco, 1963), pp. 11–20 et passim; Sneath, "The Construction of Taxonomic Groups," in G. C. Ainsworth and P. H. A. Sneath, eds., *Microbial Classification* (Cambridge, 1962), pp. 289–332. Cf. G. G. Simpson, *Principles of Animal Taxonomy,* pp. 41–57, and E. Mayr, *Principles of Systematic Zoology* (New York, 1969), pp. 82–88.

12. Beckner, *The Biological Way of Thought,* pp. 22–25.

13. Sokol and Sneath, *Numerical Taxonomy,* p. 15; Simpson, *Principles of Animal Taxonomy,* pp. 42–43.

14. See Sokol and Sneath, *Numerical Taxonomy,* chaps. 4–7 and appendix. The best introduction to techniques, with rich bibliography, is N. Jardine and R. Simpson, *Mathematical Taxonomy* (New York, 1971).

15. In addition to the bibliography in Sokol and Sneath, *Numerical Taxonomy,* see D. Harvey, *Explanation in Geography* (London, 1964), pp. 331–48, and R. Needham, "Polythetic Classification: Convergence and Consequences," *Man* n.s. 10 (1975): 349–69. See further, R. Needham, *Reconnaissances* (Toronto, 1980), pp. 6–9, 41–62. I am aware that R. Needham, *Belief, Language, and Experience* (Chicago, 1972), esp. pp. 110–21, insists, on a close relationship between polythetic classification and Wittgenstein's notion of "family resemblance." I find the parallel somewhat superficial. They are built around quite different philosophical presuppositions. For an exceedingly primitive, almost embarrassing, attempt to apply the notion of "family resemblance" to the classification of religions, see R. B. Edwards, *Reason and Religion* (New York, 1972), pp. 14–39. I do applaud Edwards's

conclusion, "There are many sufficient but no necessary conditions for calling something a religion" (p. 38).

16. R. B. Textor, *Cross-Cultural Summary* (New Haven, 1967).

17. I do not intend a false analogy between cultural artifacts and biological species. The latter's capacity for reproduction and inheritance "guarantees" the taxonomic enterprise in a manner impossible for the cultural.

18. See H. Penner and E. Yonan, "Is a Science of Religion Possible?" *Journal of Religion* 51 (1972): 107–33.

19. W. James, *The Varieties of Religious Experience* (New York: Modern Library edition, 1929), p. 10.

20. See the useful overview with bibliography in C. J. Adams, "Religions, Classification of," *Encyclopaedia Britannica,* 15th ed., 15:628–34. See further, J. Z. Smith, "Towards Interpreting Demonic Powers in Hellenistic and Roman Antiquity," in W. Haase, ed., *Aufstieg und Niedergang der romischen Welt* (Berlin, 1978), 16.1: 430–37.

21. G. van der Leeuw, *Religion in Essence and Manifestation* (New York, 1963), esp. pp. 591–649; G. Mensching, *Structures and Patterns of Religion* (Delhi, 1979), esp. pp. 4–56.

22. Some grounds for this enterprise have been laid by the work of A. L. Kroeber. For an early example, see A. L. Kroeber and H. E. Driver, "Quantitative Expressions of Cultural Relationships," *University of California Publications in American Archaeology and Ethnography* 31 (1932): 211–56, and Kroeber's mature essay "Statistics, Indo-European and Taxonomy," *Language* 36 (1960): 1–21.

23. I make this recommendation because of the necessity of taking the historical into account in biological theory. For a preliminary account, M. Beckner, *The Biological Way of Thought* should be required reading for every humanist concerned with methodological questions. S. Toulmin, *Human Understanding* (Princeton, 1972), 1:319–56 et passim, would be a good illustration of a fruitful application of evolutionary theory to the interpretation of humanistic data.

24. F. M. Müller, *Introduction to the Science of Religion* (London, 1873), p. 123.

25. B. Spinoza, *Tractatus Theologico-Politicus,* 3, in C. Gebhard, ed., *Spinoza Opera* (Heidelberg), 1925, 3:56.

26. With most scholars, I take Herodotus's phrase, *Surioi hoi en tē Palistinē* to include, but not be limited to, the Israelites.

27. See the excellent bibliography in A. M. di Nola, "Circoncisione," *Enciclopedia delle Religioni* (Florence, 1970), 2:253–54.

28. A variant of this paradigm, "circumcised but uncircumcised," is raised in an early debate between the two "Houses" in Tosefta and Sifra as to the question of a "second circumcision" for a child born without a foreskin or a proselyte who was already circumcised (Tosefta, Shabbat 3:18 and 15:9; Sifra Tazri'a 1:5 [ed. Weiss, 58b]). There is later Greek tradition concerning this problem being particularly acute in the case of the Samaritans who, from a Jewish point of view, are Israel but not Israel (Migne, *Patrologia Graeca,* 92:625b). I have deliberately excluded Tannaitic materials from this survey. With respect to circumcision (and most other matters), they represent a different horizon of concern.

29. In this discussion, I have assumed the general conclusions of V. Tcherikover, *Hellenistic Civilization and the Jews* (Philadelphia, 1959) for the political rationale of the "hellenistic reform party," and E. Bickermann, *Der Gott der Makkabäer* (Berlin, 1937) for their religious motivations.

30. That the babies were *voluntarily* left uncircumcised by the "reform party" is the understanding in Jubilees 15:33–34; that epispasm was a *voluntary* action by the "reform party" is the understanding in 1 Macc. 1:15 (cf. Josephus *Ant.* 12.241). 1 Macc. 1:48, 60–61 and 2 Macc 6:10 (cf. Josephus *Ant.* 12.254) interpret the babies left uncircumcised as being by foreign decree; the Latin *Testament of Moses* 8:3 views their epispasm as being imposed

by force on Jewish youths by Syrian officials. The alternative understanding of 1 Macc. 2:46 to that offered above would be that force was applied against the Syrian officials who sought to prevent circumcision. See Josephus *Ant.* 12.278. Such an interpretation, in Maccabees, seems unlikely on the basis of context.

31. Cf. R. Kraft, "Judaism on the World Scene," in S. Benko and J. J. O'Rourke, *The Catacombs and the Colosseum* (Valley Forge, 1971), pp. 81–98, esp. pp. 84–85. Kraft's essay, in many ways, parallels the concerns of this essay.

32. The classic studies of the relevant Greco-Egyptian papyri remain R. Reitzenstein, *Zwei religionsgeschichtlichen Fragen* (Strassburg, 1901), pp. 1–46, and U. Wilcken, "Die ägyptische Beschneidungsurkunden," *Archiv für Papyrusforschung* 2 (1903): 4–13. New material continues to be uncovered. See, among others, M. Stracmans, "A propos d'une texte relatif à la circoncision égyptienne," *Annuaire de l'Institut de Philologie, d'Histoire orientale et slave d'Université de Bruxelles* 13 (1953): 631–39.

33. It is striking that most of the scholars from G. F. Moore to E. P. Sanders, who have pursued the mirage of "normative Judaism" (see below, chap. 2), have failed to note the majority of the passages and options considered above.

34. This is not to make some facile argument that the inscriptions provide a "window" into popular Judaism as opposed to the elitist texts. In fact, the majority of the inscriptions are relentlessly elitist.

35. For the Jewish inscriptions from Rome, I have used J.-B. Frey, *Corpus Inscriptionum Judaicarum* (Rome, 1936), vol. 1, numbers 1–532, with the important corrections by B. Lifshitz in the reprint of this volume (New York, 1975). I have also compared Frey's texts with their reediting in H. J. Leon, *The Jews of Ancient Rome* (Philadelphia, 1960), pp. 263–346. The numeration is the same in all three. I have designated these Roman inscriptions *CIJ*.

36. For the Jewish inscriptions from Beth She'arim, I have used M. Schwabe and B. Lifshitz, *Beth She'arim*, vol. 2, *The Greek Inscriptions* (New Brunswick, 1974), designated *BS*, and the important section on the Hebrew and Aramaic inscriptions from catacombs 12–14 and 20 in N. Avigad, *Beth She'arim*, vol. 2, *The Excavations, 1953–1958* (New Brunswick, 1976), pp. 230–58, designated *BSa*.

37. For the Jewish inscriptions from Egypt, I have used J.-B. Frey, *Corpus Inscriptionum Judaicarum* (Rome, 1952), vol. 2, numbers 1424–1539, as reedited by D. M. Lewis in V. Tcherikover, A. Fuks, and M. Stern, *Corpus Papyrorum Judaicarum* (Cambridge, Mass., 1964), 3:138–66. I have designated these inscriptions, *CPJ*.

38. See F. Hauck, *"Hosios, Hosiōs,"* *Theological Dictionary of the New Testament* (Grand Rapids, 1964–), 5:489–92, for the basic bibliography and summaries of the various scholarly conclusions.

39. S. Lieberman, *Greek in Jewish Palestine* (New York, 1942), pp. 69–78, esp. p. 71. L. H. Feldman, "Jewish 'Sympathizers' in Classical Literature and Inscriptions," *Transactions of the American Philological Association* 81 (1950): 200–208, esp. 204–5, discussing *hosios*, but not in funerary inscriptions, sets forth the odd notion that there were people who were "simply and literally 'pious' Jews in the general and not the technical sense." I have no notion of the two senses of pious to which he alludes.

40. There is no necessity for a full set of references. R. Lattimore, *Themes in Greek and Latin Epitaphs* (Urbana, 1962), pp. 266–300, esp. pp. 290–99, provides an excellent overview.

41. *CPJ* 1452–54, 1456, 1458, 1460, 1466, 1468–71, 1473–76, 1480–87, [1491], 1492, 1494–1504, 1514, 1519, 1521, 1523, 1525–27, 1530.

42. This is to support Frey's contention (*Corpus,* 1:lxxvi) that the synagogue of the Hebrews belonged, at least at its origin, to a community which came from Judea in contradistinction to the "Vernacular" Synagogue which he understands to have been formed by "indigenous" Jews, born in Rome. I find this more compelling than the alternative,

linguistic understanding which is forcefully argued by A. Momigliano, "I nomi delle prime 'sinagoghe' romane e la condizione giuridica della communità in Roma sotto Augusto," *Rassegna Mensile di Israël* 6 (1931): 283–92, esp. 290–91.

43. F. E. Williams, *"The Vailala Madness" and Other Essays* (Honolulu, 1977), pp. 404–5.

Chapter 2

1. On these handbooks, see H. Hadju, *Das mnemotechnische Schriften des Mittelalters* (Vienna, 1932); P. Rossi, *Clavis Universalis arti mnemoniche e logica combinatoria da Lullo a Leibniz* (Milan and Naples, 1960); F. Yates, *The Art of Memory* (Chicago, 1966). I should note that I was led to take the starting point in memory for this essay by rereading the classic study by M. Halbwach, *Les cadres sociaux de la mémoire* (Paris, 1952).

2. E. B. Tylor, *Researches into the Early History of Mankind,* 3d ed. (London, 1878), p. 130. See also Tylor, *Primitive Culture,* 2d ed. (New York, 1889), 1:115–16.

3. J. G. Frazer, *The Golden Bough,* 3d ed. (New York, 1935), 1:53, see also, 1:221–22.

4. Note that David Hume, in his discussion of the Laws of Association in the third chapter of *An Enquiry Concerning Human Understanding,* writes of the similarity between words in different languages "even where we cannot suspect the least connection or communication," and thus moves from association as a matter of individual psychology, to association as an anthropological issue (in the edition by C. W. Hendel [Indianapolis, 1955], the passage quoted occurs on p. 32).

5. E. O'Gorman, *La idea del descumbrimiento de América* (Mexico City, 1951). Compare his own English language version, *The Invention of America: An Inquiry into the Historical Nature of the New World and the Meaning of Its History* (Bloomington, 1961). I have oversimplified O'Gorman's important argument as to the nature of invention. He maintains that the "New World" was invented over time as explorers came to realize that it was a world that their traditional world view had not anticipated. See further, W. Washburn, "The Meaning of 'Discovery' in the Fifteenth and Sixteenth Centuries," *American Historical Review* 68 (1962): 1–21.

6. *The Works of Samuel Taylor Coleridge* (New York, 1854), 2:31.

7. Ihab H. Hassan, "The Problem of Influence in Literary History: Notes toward a Definition," *Journal of Aesthetics and Art Criticism* 14 (1955): 66–76. I quote p. 68. At the present, comparative law and comparative literature are the only two humanistic enterprises that function in such a way as to merit the title discipline. The question of "influence" has been much debated in comparative literature. In addition to Hassan, I have been much influenced by C. Guillén, "Literatura como sistema: Sobre fuentes, influencias y valores literarios," *Filologia romanze* 4 (1957): 1–29, in its clarification of the psychological nature of the postulation of influence—although, I dissent from the conclusions he reaches.

8. H. Bergson, *Matter and Memory,* 5th ed. (Garden City, N.Y., 1959), p. 152.

9. J. Z. Smith, *Map Is Not Territory: Studies in the History of Religion* (Leiden, 1978), pp. 240–64.

10. C. Lévi-Strauss, *Structural Anthropology* (New York, 1963), 1:14.

11. B. Malinowski, *Crime and Custom in Savage Society* (Paterson, 1964), p. 126.

12. J. H. Steward, *Theory of Culture Change: The Methodology of Multilinear Evolution* (Urbana, 1955); S. Toulmin, *Human Understanding* (Princeton, 1972), 1:133–44 et passim.

13. F. Boas, "The Limitations of the Comparative Method of Anthropology," *Science* n.s. 4 (1896): 901–8. I quote pp. 907 and 903–4.

14. See F. Eggan, "Social Anthropology and the Method of Controlled Comparison," *American Anthropologist* 56 (1964): 743–63 for a useful overview.

15. HRAF comparison is embodied in G. P. Murdock's classic *Social Structure* (New York, 1949) and his proposal "World Ethnographic Sample," *American Anthropologist* 59 (1957): 664–87. For the methodology, see F. W. Moore, ed., *Readings in Cross-Cultural*

Methodology (New Haven, 1961), and R. L. Merritt and S. Rokkan, eds., *Comparing Nations: The Use of Quantitative Data in Cross-National Research* (New Haven, 1966). The encyclopaedic nature of the enterprise will become apparent to even the most casual reader of these works. This is not surprising inasmuch as the first proposal for such a study was made by E. B. Tylor, "On a Method of Investigating the Development of Institutions," *Journal of the Royal Anthropological Institute* 18 (1889): 245–72 (see the important note by F. Galton on p. 272). Within the sociological literature chiefly concerned with intrasocietal comparison, see, among others, G. Sjöberg, "The Comparative Method in the Social Sciences," *Philosophy of Science* 22 (1955): 106–17, and R. M. Marsh, *Comparative Sociology: A Codification of Cross-Societal Analysis* (New York, 1967).

16. H. Pinard de la Boullaye, *L'Etude comparée des religions* (Paris, 1922), 1:385 and 387.

17. Hence, their sharp critique of the evolutionary school.

18. Hence, their sharp critique of the naturist school. See further, J. Z. Smith, "Myth and Histories," in H. P. Duerr, ed., *Mircea Eliade Festschrift* (Frankfurt, 1982).

19. H. Winckler, *Altorientalische Forschungen* (Leipzig, 1900), 3:274.

20. A. Jeremias, *Das Alte Testament im Lichte des Alten Orients* (Leipzig, 1904). For the historian of religion, the most important edition of this work is not one of the three German editions (Leipzig, 1904, 1906, 1916), but rather the English translation by C. L. Beaumont, *Old Testament in Light of the Ancient East* (London, 1911), vols. 1–2, with new materials added by Jeremias. The bulk of vol. 1 constitutes a major essay by Jeremias on the *Weltbild* which was not incorporated into the German version.

21. Jeremias, *Old Testament*, 1:4, n.2.

22. Ibid.

23. Jeremias, *Old Testament*, 1:4.

24. On the debt to the Pan-Babylonian school, see, among others, B. S. Childs, *Myth and Reality in the Old Testament* (London, 1960), p. 74.

25. See G. F. Moore, "Christian Writers on Judaism," *Harvard Theological Review* 14 (1921): 243–44, and Moore, *Judaism in the First Centuries of the Christian Era: The Age of the Tannaim* (Cambridge, Mass., 1927–30), vols. 1–3, esp. 1:129 and n. 1.

26. Moore, *Judaism,* 1:16, 115, 135; 2:295; 3:vii-viii. It should be understood that the passages in Moore cited in notes 26–33 are intended as clear examples of the point in question and do not constitute exhaustive lists.

27. Moore, *Judaism,* 1:22 and n. 1, 110, 220, 281, 323, 386; 2:22, 395.

28. Moore, *Judaism,* l:ix, 23–27, 44, 119; 2:154.

29. Moore, *Judaism,* 2:279–395, esp. pp. 289, 292–95, 394–95. Cf. 1:404.

30. Moore, *Judaism,* 1:551.

31. Moore, *Judaism,* 1:332, 417, 544–46. Whether this is Protestant bias or a caution of his own formulation of the "church" of Judaism, or "catholic (universal) Judaism" (1:111)— a formulation which is derived from S. Schechter—I cannot determine. I suspect the former.

32. Moore, *Judaism,* 1:460, 476, 515; 2:65, 88 n.l.

33. Moore, *Judaism,* 2:394–95.

34. R. Horton, "African Conversion," *Africa* 41 (1971): 85–108.

35. J. L. Borges, *Ficciones* (New York, 1962), esp. p. 49.

36. Moore, *Judaism,* 1:21–22 (emphasis mine). Note that the first sentence is a statement of the doctrine of "survivals," on which see 2:8.

37. Moore, *Judaism,* 1:viii.

38. G. F. Moore, *History of Religions* (New York, 1913–19), vols. 1–2. See the pungent remarks on this work in J. Baillie, *The Interpretation of Religion* (London, 1928), pp. 130–31.

39. E. R. Goodenough, *Jewish Symbols in the Greco-Roman Period* (New York, 1953–70), vols. 1–12. The quote is taken from 12:vii.

40. In my attempt to construct a synthetic account of Goodenough's model, I have drawn on Goodenough's essays: "Symbolism in Hellenistic Jewish Art: The Problem of Method," *Journal of Biblical Literature* 56 (1937): 103–14; "The Evaluation of Symbols Recurrent in Time," *Eranos Jahrbuch* 20 (1951): 285–319; "Symbols as Historical Evidence," *Diogenes* 44 (1963): 19–32, as well as on the relevant sections in *Jewish Symbols,* 1:3–32; 4:3–70; 11:3–21, 64–67; 12:64–77.

41. I have combined two passages, one from "Evaluation of Symbols," p. 298, the other from *Jewish Symbols,* 8:220.

42. J. Neusner, "Comparing Judaisms," *History of Religions* 18 (1978): 177–91.

43. E. P. Sanders, "Patterns of Religion in Paul and Rabbinic Judaism: A Holistic Method of Comparison," *Harvard Theological Review* 66 (1973): 455–78.

44. E. P. Sanders, *Paul and Palestinian Judaism: A Comparison of Patterns of Religion* (Philadelphia, 1977), p. 16.

45. Sanders, *Paul,* pp. 16–18.

46. Neusner, "Comparing Judaisms," p. 178.

47. Ibid., p. 179.

48. On the problem of defining and classifying early Judaisms, see chap. 1, above.

49. J. Neusner, *The Talmud as Anthropology* (New York, 1979), p. 28, n. 33.

50. L. Wittgenstein, *Philosophical Investigations,* 3d ed. (London, 1958), p. 84e (no. 215).

Chapter 3

1. J. Neusner, "Judaism in the History of Religions," in J. Helfer, ed., *On Method in the History of Religions* (Middlebury, 1968), esp. pp. 38–39.

2. M. Black, *Models and Metaphors* (Ithaca, 1962), esp. pp. 236–38; M. B. Hesse, *Models and Analogies in Science* (Notre Dame, 1966), esp. pp. 164–65.

3. R. Firth, *Elements of Social Organization,* 3d ed. (London, 1962), p. 216.

4. K. Popper, *The Logic of Scientific Discovery,* rev. ed. (New York, 1965), p. 27.

5. M. E. Spiro, "Religion: Problems of Definition and Explanation," in M. Banton, ed., *Anthropological Approaches to the Study of Religion* (London, 1966), p. 89.

6. Cicero, *De natura deorum* 2.72.

7. The familiar, alternative definition based on a derivation from *religare,* "to bind" in Lactantius, *Divinae institutiones* 4.28 is likewise suspect. See J. B. Kätzler, "*Religio:* Versuch einer Worterklärung," *Jahresbericht des Bischöflichen Gymnasiums Paulinum in Schwaz* 20 (1952–53): 2–18 for a review of the present state of the discussion, and an argument for derivation from the root *lig-,* "to pay attention to, to take care to." See further, G. Lieberg, "Considerazioni sull' etimologia e sul significato di *religio,*" *Revista di Filologia e di Istruzione classica* 102 (1974): 34–57; R. Muth, "Römische *religio,*" in *Serta Philologica Aenipotana* in the series Innsbrucker Beiträge zur Kulturwissenschaft, 8–9 (1962): 247–71; R. Muth, "Vom Wesen römischer 'religio,' " in W. Haase, ed., *Aufstieg und Niedergang der römischen Welt* (Berlin, 1978), 16.1:342–51.

8. S. Freud, "Obsessive Acts and Religious Practices," in J. Strachey, ed., *The Standard Edition of the Complete Psychological Works of Sigmund Freud* (London, 1959), 9:117–27. It is also available in the Collier edition of *The Collected Papers of Sigmund Freud,* edited by P. Rieff in the volume entitled *Character and Culture* (New York, 1963), pp. 17–26. In the latter edition, the passages quoted occur on pp. 17–19 and 25, with emphasis added.

9. In this paper, I focus on the exegetical. See chap. 4, below, for a preliminary redescription of ritual.

10. Pindar, fragment 169 as quoted in Herodotus 3.38.

11. M. A. Amerine, "Wine Making," *Encyclopaedia Britannica,* 15th ed., 9:877–78.

12. M. Eliade, *Patterns in Comparative Religion* (New York, 1958), pp. 11–12.

13. I have taken these quotations from A. E. Jensen, *Myth and Cult among Primitive Peoples* (Chicago, 1963), pp. 5–6, 66, 171, 174, 176, 194.

14. For example, a substantial fraction of the recovered documents from the ancient Near East are lists. For a bibliography of primary materials, see R. Borger, *Handbuch der Keilschriftliteratur* (Berlin, 1975), 3:36–37 (secs. 18–20), 64–65 (sec. 66), 66 (sec. 68), 99–108 (sec. 92), 108–9 (sec. 94), 110–42 (secs. 96–111), 117–19 (sec. 116). This does not include the large class of economic documents which are largely in list form.

15. H. Kenner, *Flaubert, Joyce, and Beckett: The Stoic Comedians* (Boston, 1962), pp. xiii, xviii-xix, 1–4. This is one of the rare works of literary criticism to reflect on the aesthetics of the list. J. Goody, *The Domestication of the Savage Mind* (Cambridge, 1977), esp. pp. 80–111, offers an extensive study of the list. R. Harbison, *Eccentric Spaces* (New York, 1980), pp. 153–62, offers a fascinating meditation on the aesthetics of the museum catalog.

16. Kenner, *Flaubert, Joyce, and Beckett*, p. 2.

17. A. H. Gardiner, *Ancient Egyptian Onomastica* (Oxford, 1948), 1:8.

18. We still lack a full history of encyclopaedias. R. Collison, *Encyclopaedias: Their History throughout the Ages*, 2d ed. (New York, 1966), is the most accessible. G. A. Zischka, *Index lexicorum: Bibliographie der lexicalischen Nachschlagewerke* (Vienna, 1959), contains much of value. P. A. Lyon, "Encyclopaedia," *Encyclopaedia Britannica*, 9th ed., 8:190–204, offers an excellent overview. B. Wendt, *Idee und Entwicklungsgeschichte der enzyklopädische Literatur* (Wurzberg, 1941), is of value as a checklist. H. J. de Vleeschauwer, *Encyclopédie et bibliothèque* (Pretoria, 1956), has some useful illustrative materials. On classical encyclopaedias, see 0. Jahn, "Uber römische Encyclopädien," *Berichte der königlich sächsischen Gesellschaft der Wissenschaften* (1850), phil.-hist. Klasse 2:4, 263–87; H. Nettleship, *Lectures and Essays on Subjects Connected with Latin Literature and Scholarship*, lst series (Oxford, 1885), esp. pp. 205–6, 283–86; F. della Corte, *Enciclopedisti latini* (Genoa, 1946). On Christian medieval encyclopaedias, see the standard works by C. V. Langlois, *La connaissance de la nature et du monde au moyen âge* (Paris, 1911), and L. Thorndike, *A History of Magic and Experimental Science* (New York, 1926), vol. 2. See further, M. de Bouard, "Encyclopédies medievales," *Revue des questions historiques* 112 (1930): 258–304, and M. T. Hodgen, *Early Anthropology in the Sixteenth and Seventeenth Centuries* (Philadelphia, 1964), esp. pp. 49–77. Encyclopaedias provide a useful and illuminating genre for study of lists and modes of exegesis.

19. Unfortunately, only the English translation exists in a critical edition. M. C. Seymour, ed., *On the Properties of Things: John Trevisa's Translation of Bartholomaeus Anglicus De Proprietatibus Rerum: A Critical Text* (Oxford, 1975), vols. 1–2. The 1601 Frankfurt edition of *De proprietatibus rerum* has been reprinted (Frankfurt, 1964), but not collated with the previous 11 editions. I know of no recent edition of the French translation.

20. G. Bateson, *Naven*, 2d ed. (Stanford, 1968), pp. 6–7.

21. A. Alt, "Die Weisheit Salamos," *Theologische Literaturzeitung* 76 (1951): 139–44.

22. C. Lévi-Strauss, *Elementary Structures of Kinship* (Boston, 1969), pp. 494–95, and n. 2. Note that the list, as given in Lévi-Strauss, is a composite from several ethnographic sources.

23. For example, K. Burridge, *Tangu Traditions* (Oxford, 1969), pp. 198–99.

24. N. D. Munn, *Walbiri Iconography* (Ithaca, 1973).

25. G. Bochet, "Le Poro des Dieli," *Bulletin de l'Institut français d'Afrique noire* 21 (1959): 76.

26. See, among others, M. Griaule and G. Dieterlen, *Signes graphiques soudanais* (Paris, 1951), and C. Calame-Griaule, *Ethnologie et langage: La Parole chez les Dogon* (Paris, 1965).

27. H. Maine, *Ancient Law* (London, 1917), chap. 2. See further the excellent review of this notion in L. L. Fuller, *Legal Fictions* (Stanford, 1967), esp. pp. 5–10, 38–40, 56–80.

28. I have summarized the account in V. Turner, *Ndembu Divination* (Manchester, 1961).

29. B. Ray, *African Religions* (Englewood Cliffs, 1976), pp. 107–8, summarizing W. Bascom, *Ifa Divination* (Bloomington, 1969).

Chapter 4

1. F. Kafka, "Reflections on Sin, Hope, and the True Way," in Kafka, *The Great Wall of China* (New York, 1970), p. 165.

2. Plutarch *De vitioso pudore* 534C.

3. For a familiar example, the Israelites at the time of their exodus from Egypt did not have time to leaven their bread. This domestic accident—assuming for the moment the historicity of the account in Exod. 12:39—was "discovered" to have significance (i.e., nothing of the old year carried over into the new) and was regularized as part of a spring New Year festival, later developed into Passover.

4. Pausanias I.26.6. See further, C. J. Herington, *Athena Parthenos and Athena Polias* (Manchester, 1955).

5. For example, Leviticus Rabbah, 34. See further, J. Z. Smith, *Map Is Not Territory* (Leiden, 1978), pp. 113–14 for other examples.

6. b. Shabbat 21b and scholion Megillat Ta'anit 25 Kislev. This story is not known to the authors of the books of the Maccabees. See 1 Macc. 4:36–59 and J. A. Goldstein, *I Maccabees* (Garden City, 1976), pp. 273–84.

7. The action appears to be attributed to Alexander Jannaeus in Josephus *Ant.* 13.372. It is attributed to an anonymous Sadduccean priest in rabbinic texts, e.g., M. Sukka 4.8; Tosefta Sukka 3.16 [197]; b. Sukka 48b. For a comparison of these two interpretations, see J. Derenbourg, *Essai sur l'histoire et la géographie de la Palestine* (Paris, 1867), 1:96–101. For a sociological interpretation, see L. Finkelstein, *The Pharisees*, 3d ed. (Philadelphia, 1962), 2:700–708.

8. A. van Gennep, *Les Rites de passage* (Paris, 1909), p. 16.

9. Herodotus 2.172. I have adapted the standard translation by G. Rawlinson.

10. The story is explicitly cited by Minucius Felix *Octavius* 22.4; Theophilus *Ad Autolycum* 1.10 and elsewhere. It seems to lie behind texts such as Philo *Contemp.* 7; Justin *I Apologia* 9.3; Arnobius *Adversus Nationes* 6.12.

11. Isaiah 44:14–17.

12. Horace *Satires* I.8.1–3.

13. E.g., Wisdom of Solomon 13:11–14:8; Tertullian *De idolatria* 8.

14. Tertullian *Apologia* 13.4.

15. S. Freud, "Obsessive Acts and Religious Practices," in J. Strachey, ed., *The Standard Edition of the Complete Psychological Works of Sigmund Freud* (London, 1959), 9:117–27. Compare L. Wittgenstein, "Remarks on Frazer's 'Golden Bough,' " *Human World* 3 (1971): 32, "The ceremonial (hot or cold) as opposed to the haphazard (lukewarm) is a characteristic of piety."

16. J. L. Borges, *Ficciones* (New York, 1962), p. 130.

17. For an archaic example, see T. Save-Söderberg, *On Egyptian Representations of Hippopotamus Hunting as a Religious Motif* (Lund, 1953).

18. For this complex within the circumpolar region, see I. Paulson, *Schutzgeister und Gottheiten des Wildes (der Jagdtiere und Fische) in Nordeurasien* (Stockholm, 1961).

19. A. I. Hallowell, "Bear Ceremonialism in the Northern Hemisphere," *American Anthropologist* 28 (1926): 1–175; E. Lot-Falck, *Les Rites de chasse sur les peuples sibériens* (Paris, 1953).

20. Lot-Falck, *Rites,* pp. 117–38; Hallowell, "Bear Ceremonialism," p. 32, n. 80.

21. Hallowell, "Bear Ceremonialism," pp. 43–53; Lot-Falck, *Rites,* pp. 103–6.

22. Hallowell, "Bear Ceremonialism," pp. 41–42; Lot-Falck, *Rites,* pp. 139–40, 143–51.

23. *Suomen Kansen Vahat Runot* (Helsinki, 1908–43), 9.4:1101, as translated by C. M. Edsman, "The Hunter, the Game, and the Unseen Powers: Lappish and Finnish Bear Rites," in H. Hvarfner, ed., *Hunting and Fishing* (Luleå, 1965), p. 176.

24. See, from quite different perspectives, K. Kindaichi, "The Concepts behind the Ainu Bear Festival," *Southwestern Journal of Anthropology* 5 (1949): 345–50; A. Slawik, "Zur Etymologie des japanischen Terminus marebito 'Sakraler Besucher,' " *Wiener Völkerkundliche Mitteilungen* 2 (1954): 44–58; J. M. Kitagawa, "Ainu Bear Festival (Iyomante)," *History of Religions* 1 (1961): 95–151, and I. Goldman, *The Mouth of Heaven: An Introduction to Kwakiutl Religious Thought* (New York, 1975), esp. chaps. 1, 7–8.

25. Hallowell, "Bear Ceremonialism," pp. 53–54; Lot-Falck, *Rites,* pp. 151–61.

26. D. Zelenin, *Kult ongonov v Sibiri* (Moscow and Leningrad, 1936), p. 209. I have followed the French translation by G. Welter, *Les Cultes des idoles en Sibérie* (Paris, 1952), p. 143. Cf. Lot-Falck, *Rites,* p. 153.

27. Hallowell, "Bear Ceremonialism," pp. 54–61; Lot-Falck, *Rites,* pp. 170–73.

28. *Suomen Kansen Vahat Runot,* 6.2:4883, in Edsman, "The Hunter," p. 186.

29. *Suomen Kansen Vahat Runot,* 1.4:1244, in Edsman, "The Hunter," p. 185.

30. Lot-Falck, *Rites,* pp. 173–85.

31. J.Teit, *The Lillooet Indians* (Leiden, 1906), p. 279, in the series American Museum of Natural History Memoirs, 4, Jessup North Pacific Expedition, 2.1.

32. See, M. Eliade, *Shamanism* (New York, 1964), pp. 158–64, and the literature he cites.

33. Hallowell, "Bear Ceremonialism," pp. 61–106; Lot-Falck, *Rites,* pp. 186–213.

34. In the translation by J. M. Crawford, *The Kalevala* (Cincinnati, 1898), 2:661–78.

35. Hallowell, "Bear Ceremonialism," p. 54, citing L. von Schrenck, *Reisen und Forschungen im Amurlande in den Jahren 1854–1856,* vol. 3.1, *Die Völker des Amurlandes* (St. Petersburg, 1891), p. 561.

36. Hallowell, "Bear Ceremonialism," pp. 33–42. Cf. M. G. Levin and L. P. Potapov, *The Peoples of Siberia* (Chicago, 1964), pp. 213, 254, 447, 520, 553, 590, 738, 770.

37. W. Jochelson, *The Koryak* (Leiden and New York, 1905–08), p. 142, in the series American Museum of Natural History Memoirs, 5, Jessup North Pacific Expedition, 7. Cf. Hallowell, "Bear Ceremonialism," p. 38.

38. Hallowell, "Bear Ceremonialism," p. 39, quoting E. G. Ravenstein, *The Russians on the Amur* (London, 1861), p. 379.

39. R. P. Trilles, *Les Pygmées de la forêt équatoriale* (Paris and Munster i. Wein, 1925), p. 325.

40. Ibid., pp. 460–61 and 358.

41. Hallowell, "Bear Ceremonialism," pp. 106–35. For a useful comparative treatment, see H. J. R. Paproth, "Das Bärenfest der Ketó in Nordsiberien in Zusammenhang gebraucht mit den Bärenzeremonien und Bärenfesten anderer Völker der nördlichen Hemisphäre," *Anthropos* 55 (1962): 55–88. It is to be regretted that, since the study by W. Koppers, "Der Bärenkult in ethnologischer und prähistorischer Beleuchtung," *Palaeobiologica,* 1933, pp. 47–64, the study of bear ceremonialism has been linked with the attempt to reconstruct paleolithic religion. See the careful review articles by K. J. Narr, "Interpretation altsteinzeitlicher Kunstwerke durch völkerkundliche Parallelen," *Anthropos* 50 (1955): 513–45, and especially, Narr, "Bärenzeremoniell und Schamanismus in der Alteren Steinzeit Europas," *Saeculum* 10 (1959): 233–72.

42. Cf. Hallowell, "Bear Ceremonialism," p. 132, who argues that the bear festival "is only an extension of the rite which is observed at the slaughter of every bear."

43. The desire for a bloodless killing seems to be behind the strangulation. Note that L. von Schrenck, *Die Völker des Amurlandes,* p. 711, records that the Gilyak (i.e., the Nivkhi) immediately cover with snow any blood that is spilled during the ritual kill. On this detail,

see further Hallowell, "Bear Ceremonialism," p. 115, n. 484, and C. Coon, *The Hunting Peoples* (New York, 1976), pp. 380–81.

44. I can find no unambiguous evidence for this among northern hunters. See its appearance among Philippine Negritos as described in K. Stewart, *Pygmies and Dream Giants* (New York, 1954), p. 65.

45. Lot-Falck, *Rites,* p. 154 et passim.

46. I. Lissner, *Man, God, and Magic* (London, 1961), p. 246.

47. S. Reinach, "L'Art et la magie," *L'Anthropologie* 14 (1903): 257–66.

Chapter 5

1. The traditional dichotomy of "myth and history" seems to me to be more usefully expressed as a distinction between "past" and "history" as adumbrated by J. H. Plumb, *The Death of the Past* (Boston, 1971), esp. pp. 11–17. Plumb's suggestive distinction requires more systematic elaboration.

2. The work of the Africanists is summarized with considerable methodological rigor and rich bibliography in J. Vansina, *Oral Tradition* (London, 1965). Useful orientation may be gained by the various articles in the collective volumes edited by J. Vansina, R. Mauny, and L. V. Thomas, *The Historian in Tropical Africa* (London, 1964); D. F. McCall, *Africa in Time Perspective* (Boston, 1964), and cf. D. F. McCall, "Anthropology and History: The African Case," *Journal of Interdisciplinary History* 1 (1970): 139–47; T. O. Ranger, *Emerging Themes of African History* (Nairobi, 1968). I would call particular attention to the writings of Luc de Heusch, especially his magisterial volume, *Le Rwanda et la civilisation interlacustre* (Brussels, 1966), for an exemplary instance of rigorous historical inquiry set in the context of a rich theory of myth which develops themes of central importance to historians of religion. For the same issues with respect to Oceanic materials (the culture area on which this chapter concentrates), see the superb review article by P. M. Mercer, "Oral Tradition in the Pacific: Problems of Interpretation," *Journal of Pacific History* 14 (1979): 130–53. Most interesting, for its evaluations and its rigor with respect to both written and oral materials, is A. R. Tippett, *Aspects of Pacific Ethnohistory* (Pasadena, 1973).

3. See pp. 90–91.

4. For the full text, see Appendix 1, p. 121–25.

5. For example, R. Pettazzoni, *Dio: Formazione e sviluppo del monoteismo nella storia delle religioni* (Rome, 1922), 1:173–76 et passim; see further, Pettazzoni, "Io and Rangi," in *Pro Regno, Pro Sanctuario: Festschrift G. van der Leeuw* (Nijkerk, 1950), pp. 359–65 (reprinted in Pettazzoni, *Essays on the History of Religions* [Leiden, 1954], pp. 37–42), and Pettazzoni, *L'omniscienza di Dio* (Turin, 1955), pp. 510–12; C. Clemen, "Der sogennant Urmonotheismus der Primitiven," *Archiv für Religionswissenschaft* 27 (1925): 290–333, esp. p. 320; P. Radin, *Primitive Man as Philosopher* (New York, 1927), pp. 292–328, 335–39, and cf. Radin, *Primitive Religion* (New York, 1938), pp. 265–66; F. R. Lehmann, "Io, die hochste Gottheit der Maori," *Ethnologische Studien* 1 (1931): 271–92; M. Eliade, *The Myth of the Eternal Return* (New York, 1954), pp. 24, 82–84 (both these passages are lacking in the first French edition [Paris, 1949], but are inserted in the second French edition [Paris, 1969], pp. 27–28, 100–101); see further, Eliade, "Structure et fonction du mythe cosmogonique," in *La Naissance du monde* (Paris, 1959), pp. 472–75, and Eliade, *Myth and Reality* (New York, 1963), pp. 30–33; H. Baumann, *Das doppelte Geschlecht* (Berlin, 1955), pp. 231–34; C. Long, *Alpha: Myths of Creation* (New York, 1963), pp. 155–59, 172–74.

6. Eliade, *Myth and History,* pp. 30 and 32. See my study of Eliade's treatment of the Io myth, set against a background of intellectual history, J. Z. Smith, "Myth and Histories," in H. P. Duerr, ed., *Mircea Eliade Festschrift* (Frankfurt, 1982).

7. A. W. Howitt, "On Some Australian Beliefs," *Journal of the Royal Anthropological Institute* 13 (1884): 185–98 and "The Jeraeil, or Initiation Ceremonies of the Kurnai Tribe,"

ibid. 14 (1885): 301–27, are the most significant. The scattered materials were drawn together and supplemented in Howitt, *Native Tribes of South-East Australia* (London, 1904). The history of the Australian data for "High God" is exhaustively reviewed in W. Schmidt, *Der Ursprung der Gottesidee*, (Münster i. Wein, 1925–55), vols. 1–12, especially vols. 1 and 3. It has been brilliantly summarized by M. Eliade, *Australian Religions* (Ithaca, 1973), esp. pp. 3–24.

8. A. Lang, *The Making of Religion* (London, 1889), esp. pp. 193–229.

9. See above, notes 5 and 7.

10. E. B. Tylor, "The Limits of Savage Religion," *Journal of the Royal Anthropological Institute* 21 (1891): 283–301.

11. See Schmidt, *Ursprung*, 1:211–487, esp. pp. 256–73.

12. R. Horton, "African Conversion," *Africa* 41 (1971): 85–108; Horton, "On the Rationality of Conversions," ibid. 45 (1975): 219–35, 373–99. Cf. J. Goody, "Religion, Social Change and the Sociology of Conversion," in J. Goody, ed., *The Changing Social Structure in Ghana* (London, 1975), pp. 91–106. Horton's proposal deserves the most serious study by historians of religion.

13. H. Hongi, trans., "A Maori Cosmogony," *Journal of the Polynesian Society* 16 (1907): 109–19 (abbreviated here *JPS*). See Appendix 1.

14. J. Prytz Johansen, *Studies in Maori Rites and Myths* (Copenhagen, 1958), p. 50, in the series Historisk-filosofiske Meddelelser udgivet af Det Kongelige Danske Videnskabernes Selskab, 37.4). Johansen's study and those by Lehmann (above, n. 5), Buck, and Barrière (below, n. 27) are the only treatments of Io that are of value.

15. Johansen, *Studies*, pp. 52–53. See Appendix 1.

16. See Gudgeon's obituary notice in *JPS* 21 (1920): 20–21, and the brief article in G. H. Scholefield, ed., *A Dictionary of New Zealand Biography* (Wellington, 1940), 1:335.

17. Hare Hongi was declared to be "not quite reliable" by E. Best. In transcribing Maori texts, he changed their dialect and "made some alterations to make certain statements agree with his own views." (Best, cited in D. Simmons and B. Biggs, "The Sources of the 'Lore of the Whare-wānanga,' " *JPS* 79 [1970]: 24–25 and n. 14). S. Percy Smith, in an editorial note to Hare Hongi's article, "The Gods of Maori Worship," *JPS* 21 (1920): 24, states, "on the first page of each number of the *Journal* is printed the following sentence: Authors are responsible for their respective statements—Mr. Hare Hongi is responsible for the views set forth in this interesting paper." I know of no other such specific warning prefaced to an article in *JPS*. Thus, the two figures most important in the subsequent publication of Io materials, both agree that Hare Hongi is untrustworthy.

18. I have added Roman numerals in brackets to the text reprinted in Appendix 1 to facilitate the reader's reference. I may add that in this text, as in most other published Maori materials, the division into lines and verses by editors and/or translators is arbitrary. See Johansen, *Studies*, p. 50.

19. Eliade has persistently held that section II is a statement by Hare Hongi—in fact, the translator. I can find no justification for this extraordinary error. See Eliade, *Myth of the Eternal Return*, p. 82; *Patterns in Comparative Religion*, p. 410; "Structure et fonction," p. 473; *Myth and Reality*, p. 31.

20. Hongi, "A Maori Cosmogony," p. 118.

21. Eliade, in the works cited above, n. 5, and in *From Primitives to Zen* (London, 1967), pp. 86–87; Long, *Alpha*, pp. 172–74.

22. J. C. Andersen, *Myths and Legends of the Polynesians* (London, 1928), pp. 353–54.

23. W. E. Gudgeon had briefly mentioned the text and the deity two years before the 1907 publication, in "Mana Tangata," *JPS* 14 (1905): 51–53, and "Maori Religion," ibid., pp. 108–9.

24. E. Best, "The Cult of Io, the Concept of a Supreme Being as Evolved by the Ancestors of the Polynesians," *Man* 13 (1913): 98–108. See further, Best, "Ceremonial Performances Related to Birth," *Journal of the Royal Anthropological Institute* 44 (1914): 127–62; "The Maori Genius for Personification," *Transactions of the New Zealand Institute* 53 (1921): 1–3; *Maori Religion and Mythology* (Wellington, 1924), esp. pp. 36–39, 88–101; *The Maori as He Was* (Wellington, 1924), esp. 1:32–33, 40–41, 63–65. Other materials in Best seem unrelated to the Matorohanga-Whatahoro tradition, for example, Best, *Tuhoe: The Children of the Mist* (New Plymouth, 1925), pp. 1026–40, esp. pp. 1026 and 1028; "Notes on Rituals, Customs and Beliefs," *JPS* 35 (1926): 8, and "Irihia," *JPS* 36 (1927): 335.

S. Percy Smith, *The Lore of the Whare-wānanga*, vol. 1, *Te Kauae Runga or Things Celestial* (New Plymouth, 1913), in the series Memoirs of the Polynesian Society, vol. 3; the text has recently been reprinted (New York, 1978). This contains a Maori text with a heavily edited English "translation" and notes by Smith. Indeed, Simmons and Biggs charge that "much of the English text is not found in Maori at all; conversely, some of the Maori text is not translated or is translated badly" (Simmons and Biggs, "Sources," p. 35; see below, n. 25). There are Io materials scattered throughout the volume, especially in chap. 2, p. 105 (2 titles), p. 107 (3 titles, Io "the origin of all things"), p. 108 (1 title, relation of Io to Rangi and Papa), pp. 110–12 (a section entitled, "Io, the Supreme God," mainly devoted to exegeting 16 titles). Elsewhere in the volume, Io is mentioned on pp. 92–93 (5 titles in a *karakia*), p. 96 (3 titles in a *karakia*), pp. 116, 122, 125 (all three have one line references to the "heaven of Io" in relationship to the ascent of Tane), pp. 129–30 (a dialogue between Io and Tane), pp. 140, 148 (both refer to Io in an anthropogonical context), p. 158 (1 title). There is no Io cosmogony analogous to the 1907 text. To this complex of materials should be added S. P. Smith and Te Whatahoro, "The Maori Philosophy of Life according to the Teaching of Nepia Pohuhu," *JPS* 32 (1923): 1–9, esp. pp. 7–8, and *Lore*, vol. 2, *Te Kauae Raro or Things Celestial* (New Plymouth, 1915), in the series Memoirs of the Polynesian Society, vol. 3 (reprinted, New York, 1978), pp. 18 (2 titles in a *karakia*, cf. the original publication as "Lore of the Whare-wānanga, Part II," *JPS* 22 [1913]: 19–21) and p. 207 (3 titles in a *karakia*).

25. The earliest reference to Whatahoro and his relationship with Matorohanga, in print, that I am familiar with is T. W. Downes, "On the Whatu Kura," *JPS* 19 (1910): 218–21. The "canonical" account of the transmission is in Smith, *Lore*, 1:i–ii. This can be supplemented by other materials, largely drawn from Augustus Hamilton, then director of the Dominion Museum, in H. W. Williams, "The Maruiwi Myth," *JPS* 44 (1937): 107; E. W. G. Craig, *Man of the Mists: A Biography of Elsdon Best* (Wellington, 1964), pp. 146–47; D. Simmons and B. Biggs, "The Sources of the 'Lore of the Whare-wānanga,' " *JPS* 89 (1970): 24. Hamilton was certainly deceived in his judgment that Whatahoro was an "aged and learned Maori chief of the Wairapa and Wanganui" (Craig, *Man of the Mists*, p. 146). For the important detail concerning Whatahoro's deficient abilities in Maori, see Williams, "Maruiwi Myth," pp. 105–8 and Craig, *Man of the Mists*, p. 148. The various copies of the Whatahoro manuscripts are cataloged and evaluated in Simmons and Biggs, "Sources," pp. 24–33.

26. Craig, *Man of the Mists*, pp. 148, 150, 156–57. Most interesting is the quotation from Best: "A matter of great importance is the way in which questions are put to the native. In this respect, one has to be extremely cautious for you can get any information required from a native if you can put certain leading questions in a certain way. . . . By asking the same questions within intervals of some months between questionings, I have got totally different answers from Whatahoro" (Craig, *Man of the Mists*, p. 150).

27. The first critical treatment of the Matorohanga-Whatahoro tradition that I am aware of is that by H. W. Williams, "Maruiwi Myths," esp. pp. 105–8, which focuses on the "historical" materials. For critical approaches to the Io traditions within these materials, see P. Buck (Te Rangi Hiroa), *The Coming of the Maori*, 2d ed. (Wellington, 1950), pp.

16–18, 433–538, esp. 526–36; T. Monberg, "Ta'aroa in the Creation Myths of the Society Islands," *JPS* 65 (1956): 256–58; D. B. Barrière, "Revisions and Adulterations in Polynesian Creation Myths," in G. A. Highland, ed., *Polynesian Cultural History: Festschrift K. P. Emory* (Honolulu, 1967), esp. pp. 107–8. Johansen, *Studies,* pp. 40–43, while cautious, is more positive in his evaluation of the tradition. Cf. J. P. Johansen, *The Maori and His Religion in Its Non-Ritualistic Aspects* (Copenhagen, 1954), pp. 275–76.

28. Craig, *Man of the Mists,* p. 168.

29. Simmons and Biggs, "Sources," p. 41, cf. p. 36. Chapter 2 was most probably added after 1908, that is, after the 1907 publication of Gudgeon's text. (See below, n. 68.)

30. I have not been able to locate a substantial early printed example of European skepticism. That such arguments were made, especially claiming dependence by the Maori on Christianity for the notion of Io, is clear from defensive notes by Best and Smith. Best, who dates the traditions as "neolithic" and whose subtitle for his 1913 publication, "The Concept of a Supreme Being as Evolved *by the Ancestors of the Polynesians*" (emphasis mine) indicates his view of the high antiquity of the deity, argues: "Inasmuch as this name [Io] and conception have caused doubt in certain minds that attribute them to missionary influence and teaching . . . [concluding, therefore, that it is] a pious fraud. . . . We know that mission teachings have influenced the Maori and that the present day native may mix native with Christian myths, but no Bible teaching resembles the old Maori cult of Io" (Best, "Some Place Names of Islands in the Society Group," *JPS* 26 [1917]: 114). Smith, likewise, defends the antiquity of the traditions. "It will possibly be thought that the idea of Io . . . is derived from the Christian teachers of the Maori people, and that it has been engrafted on to Maori beliefs in modern times since Christianity was introduced . . . there is no foundation for such an idea. The doctrine of Io is evidently a *bona-fide* relic of very ancient times, handed down with scrupulous care generation after generation" (Smith, *Lore,* 1:vii). And, again, Smith: "It has been reported that doubt has been expressed on the genuineness of this supreme god creator [Io], and it has been said that the Maori priests have adopted the idea from the Scriptures and tacked the whole idea on to their original beliefs. To us this idea is an absurdity" (Smith, Prefatory Note, *JPS* 29 [1920]: 139). Best's frequent references to Andrew Lang, *Making of Religion* (e.g., "The Cult of Io," p. 98; *Tuhoe,* p. 1024) suggest some knowledge of the Lang-Tylor debate (see above, notes 8, 10–11). It is in this context that we must understand the interest in Best's work by the Royal Anthropological Institute (see Craig, *Man of the Mists,* pp. 168–69). Of the positive European responses (reviewed below), one that strikes a quaint contemporary note is that by Anna Kingsford, a "well known ethnographer" who objected to the title God as expressing only the male principle. "The only word that expresses the dual principle in God is Io" ("Notes and Queries," *JPS* 27 [1918]: 95).

31. For expressions of Maori pride, see the letter from Te Haupapa-o-Tane to S. Percy Smith, printed under the title, "Io, the Supreme God and Other Gods of the Maori," *JPS* 29 (1920): 140–43. See also the eulogy upon Best's death by T. Wi Repa in *JPS* 41 (1932): 12–15.

32. For example, E. S. C. Handy, *Polynesian Religion* (Honolulu, 1927), esp. pp. 94–98, for a collection of sources and quotations. This contextless anthology continues to be cited as the main authority for Io by many historians of religion (see below, n. 34).

33. A. Earle, *Narrative of a Nine Months Residence in New Zealand in 1827* (London, 1832), p. 142. Cf. R. A. Cruise, *Journal of a Ten Month Residence in New Zealand,* 2d ed. (London, 1824), 2:116. For a review of some of this early travel literature, see Lehmann, "Io," pp. 72–73.

34. E. Tregear, *The Maori Race* (Wanganui, 1904), pp. 450–51. Note that this account was given new circulation by Handy, *Polynesian Religion,* pp. 95–96, and, through him, continued currency (e.g., Eliade, *From Primitives to Zen,* pp. 14–15). One of the important

elements in evaluating the early group of New Zealanders working on Io is the observation of their close associations. Not only were most of them founding members of the Polynesian Society and connected with the Dominion Museum, but there were also more intimate connections. Thus Tregear's book is dedicated to E. Best and has a preface by S. P. Smith. Best was W. E. Gudgeon's brother-in-law, and so on. This provided a means of mutual reinforcement that muted the possibility of critical distance for this "Io circle." It makes it impossible for subsequent scholarship to claim the work of any of them as independent witnesses. (For other names of this group, see below, n. 50. For another close association, see below, n. 70.)

35. In traditional Maori cults, the *tuahu* or *tūāahu*. In the cult of Io, pronunciation of the name is associated primarily with an open body of water. See Best, "The Cult of Io," p. 99. For these general taboos, see Smith, *Lore* 1:85–86.

36. C. O. Davis, *The Life and Times of Petuone, the Celebrated Ngapuhi Chief* (Auckland, 1876), p. 13. This passage is cited in Tregear, *Maori Race*, p. 450; Gudgeon, "Mana Tangata," p. 52; Smith, *Lore*, 1:viii. I doubt Johansen's surprising conjecture that the priest "one hundred miles away" might have been Te Matorohanga! (*Studies*, p. 40).

37. Davis, *Petuone*, pp. 132–33. Lehmann, "Io," p. 292, terms Davis's text, "der älteste veroffentlichte Spruch (*karakia*) in dem Io erwähnt wird."

38. Buck, *Coming of the Maori*, pp. 532–33. Cf. Johansen, *Studies*, p. 38.

39. J. White, *The Ancient History of the Maori: His Mythology and Traditions* (Wellington, 1887), 2:2. This statement has attained all but canonical status. The chapter, "The God Io," occupies 2:1–19; only pp. 1–5 are relevant.

40. White, *History*, 2:1–2. Compare the refrain in G. Grey, *Ko nga Moteatea, me nga Hakirara o nga Maori* (Wellington, 1853), p. 253 (line 51).

41. White, *History*, 2:2–5. Cf. the *takiri* omens in G. Grey, *Polynesian Mythology* (London, 1855), p. 197. For an early attempt to relate Io to *io*, see J. C. Andersen, *Maori Life in Aotea* (Wellington, 1907), p. 535, where Io is defined as "the supreme being, his presence was felt in twitchings of various parts of the body;" cf. pp. ix, 34, 183–84 (where White is cited). See further, J. M. Brown, *Maori and Polynesian* (London, 1907), p. 132.

42. Buck, *Coming of the Maori*, p. 532. Cf. Best, *Tuhoe*, p. 1026.

43. White, *History*, 1:32. Compare the striking tradition recorded by S. Savage, "The Rarotongon Version of the Story of Rata," *JPS* 19 (1910): 144, 159: "Rata was also a descendent of Mū who cohabited with the god Io, for it is said, *No rato mai a Rata-Ariki ia Mū ma Io* (Rata was a descendent of Io and Mu). This is a part of our sacred karakia and only recited on special occasions . . . I may say that the god Io was an *Atua-mekameka* (god of good) and the ancient priests, my ancestors, always ended up the special karaki with this chant: *Io-Io-te atua ki-te-rangi-tua-tini-tini*, Io, the great god of the vast heavens." This sexual conception of Io clearly represents a different mythologem from that of the asexual Io who created heaven and earth. See Johansen, *Studies*, pp. 48–50.

44. White, *History*, 3:230.

45. Note that in largely ritual contexts concerned with making a woman fruitful or in childbirth, it is alleged that Io is invoked. H. Hongi, "Maori Cosmogony," p. 114 (i.e., section II in Appendix 1), states the fact, which Eliade has interpreted as a homology with creation (*Myth and Reality*, pp. 31–32). In "native" exegesis, the analogy is based on Io's having vivified (though not formed) the first woman (i.e., Hinenuitepo or Hineahuone). See Smith, *Lore* 1: 140–41; Best, "Ceremonial Performances," esp. pp. 127–33; Best, *Maori Religion and Mythology*, p. 76; Best, *The Whare Kohunga and Its Lore* (Wellington, 1929), p. 6. In White, *History*, 1:158, the first woman is called Iowahine, but no association appears with Io. Pettazzoni, "Io and Rangi," treats this theme through a web of associations that lacks validity.

46. E. Tregear, *The Maori-Polynesian Comparative Dictionary* (Wellington, 1891), p. 106, s.v. "Io."

47. Tregear, *Dictionary*, p. 669. According to Tregear's note, this genealogy was collected by Shand. Shand subsequently published the genealogy in "The Moriori People of Chatham Islands; Part IV, Morioro Genealogy," *JPS* 4 (1895): 33–46, in which he names Minarapa Tamahiwiki as his informant from whom he collected the tradition in 1868 (p. 33). After giving the genealogy, without commenting on Io, Shand (p. 45) compares it with a Maori one from Grey, *Nga Moteatea*, p. 423. Focusing on the relevant segment:

Moriori	Maori
Tiki	Tiki
Uru	Uru
Ngangena	——
Io	——
Iorangi	Waionuki
Waiorangi	Waiorangi

There are close parallels to the genealogy cited above (n. 43). In both instances, there would appear to have been an insertion of Io into one of the traditional genealogies. See Johansen, *Studies*, pp. 49–50 for other examples.

48. Tregear, *Dictionary*, p. 667. Mair is named as one of Tregear's oral sources (p. xii). Compare the Ngati Maniapoto genealogy inserted (by S. P. Smith?) in Best, "Lore of the Whare-kohunga," *JPS* 14 (1905): 210, and in J. Cowan, *The Maoris of New Zealand* (Christ Church, 1910), pp. 103–4, and Cowan, *The Maori of Yesterday and Today* (London, 1930), pp. 52–55. In this genealogy, attributed to Wahanui, Io appears original.

49. "An Ancient Maori Poem Attributed to Tuhoto-Araki," *JPS* 16 (1907): 43–60, esp. pp. 50–51. The text was translated by G. H. Davis and J. H. Pope, with notes by H. T. Whatahoro. Cf. E. Best, "The Maori Concept of the Spirit World," *JPS* 25 (1916): 174, who writes of this text that the English is not a translation but a paraphrase of the freest nature [with] sentences that one looks for in vain in the original." Buck, *Coming of the Maori*, p. 534, rates the poem highly as "authentic evidence in support of Io" and retranslates several lines. The attribution to Tuhoto-Ariki is, most certainly, false. For the same myth in the Matorohanga-Whatahoro tradition, see Smith, *Lore*, 1:127–31.

50. I have omitted consideration of synthetic accounts such as Tregear, *Maori Race*, pp. 456–57, and Andersen, *Maori Life*, p. 535, as these are based entirely on secondary sources. Unfortunately, I have also had to omit names cited as having early information on Io, apparently oral reports, for which no further information is given, for example, Judge Manning and C. E. Nelson in Smith, *Lore*, 1:viii, and an editorial note by Smith in *JPS* 29 (1920): 139. I cite one bit of speculation by Nelson, below, n. 58.

51. This appears as an editor's footnote to T. G. Hammond, "Atua Maori," *JPS* 8 (1899), 90, after Hammond quotes J. White, "Io is really the god" (*History*, 2:2). The editors were Tregear and Smith. The statement is most likely by Smith and appears with slight emendation in *Lore* 1:viii as well.

52. K. Sinclair, "The Election of the Maori King," which appears as an appendix to Sinclair's reedition of J. E. Gorst, *The Maori King* (Oxford, 1959), pp. 263–74, esp. p. 269; cf. p. 264, where Tamihana's "explanation" is interpreted by Sinclair as an example of his "arrogance," a notion which eludes me. I know of no discussion of this text in relation to Io.

53. Burrow's account was the source of a pamphlet by T. Buddle, *The Maori King Movement in New Zealand* (Auckland, 1860), which I have been unable to obtain.

54. See, for example, Smith and Whatahoro, "Teachings of Nepia Pohuhu," pp. 8–9, on the various sorts of *mana* in the hands of Io, and Buck's retranslation of the poem attributed to Tuhoto-Ariki cited above, n. 49.

55. For early accounts of this practice, see J. S. Polack, *Manners and Customs of the New Zealanders* (London, 1840), 1:37–38 and 2:126–27; E. Tregear, "The Maoris of New Zealand," *Journal of the Royal Anthropological Institute* 19 (1890): 123.

56. See below, notes 85–93.

57. I refer to the sort of diffusion accounts associated with the British preoccupation with "solar mythology." See, R. M. Dorson, "The Eclipse of Solar Mythology," in T. A. Sebeok, ed., *Myth: A Symposium* (Bloomington, 1958), pp. 25–63. New Zealand mythology played a minor role in this, made accessible through the works of G. Grey and W. W. Gill. See R. M. Dorson, *The British Folklorists* (Chicago, 1968), pp. 372–74.

58. For the first example, Gudgeon, "Maori Religion," p. 109; for the second, Andersen, *Myths and Legends,* p. 351; for the third, "Notes and Queries," *JPS* 27 (1918): 95; and for the fourth, C. E. Nelson, as quoted in J. Cowan, *The Maori of Yesterday and Today,* p. 216.

59. E. de Bovis, "Etat de la société Taitienne à l'arrivé des Européens," *La Revue maritime et coloniale* (1855), which I have not seen. De Bovis's essay was reprinted in *Annuaire des Etablissements français de l'Océanie* (Papatee, 1863; reprinted Paris, 1893), p. 95, and as a separate article, under the title, *Etat de la société Tahitienne à l'arrivée des Européens* (Papatee, 1909), p. 45.

60. Cited by Tregear, *Dictionary,* p. 106, s.v. "Ioio"; Tregear, *Maori Race,* p. 456; and the prefatory note to H. Hongi, "Maori Cosmogony," p. 109. This formed a plank in Tregear's "philological" arguments for Io as a pan-Pacific deity. De Bovis's text was already cited by A. Fornander, *An Account of the Polynesian Race* (London, 1878), 1:64, in support of his Semitic diffusion theory.

61. The refutation of Tregear was accomplished with brilliance by K. P. Emory, "The Tahitian Accounts of Creation by Mare," *JPS* 47 (1938): 48. For further Society Islands "evidence," see E. Best, "Some Place Names of Islands of the Society Group," *JPS* 26 (1917): 114, who reports that the title *Io i te rahi naro* (Io of the hidden place), occurs which he compares with the Maori, *Io mata ngaro* (Io of the hidden face). The two titles are not parallel (see Best, "Cult of Io," p. 100, and Smith, *Lore,* 1:6 and 16). As Best's source is contemporary, it may be used for suggesting diffusion of Io after 1907–13, but, despite his eloquent defense, cannot be used as unimpeachable evidence for a pan-Oceanic deity, "from time immemorial whose name was brought hither by the Maoris."

61. See T. Henry, *Ancient Tahiti* (Honolulu, 1928), pp. 10–31. See the early native biblical myths in W. Ellis, *Polynesian Researches* (London, 1827), 2:38.

62. A similar argument could be made for the report that the natives of Rarotonga, "most appropriately and beautifully transfer the name of the living god, Io-ora, to Jehovah," in W. Gill, *Myths and Songs from the Pacific* (London, 1876), p. 28. The "transfer" seems to me to have been the other way around.

63. On Kiho, see J. F. Stimson, *Tuamotuan Religion* (Honolulu, 1933), esp. pp. 69–89, which compares Io and Kiho, including a comparison of Kiho with H. Hongi, "A Maori Cosmogony" (Stimson, pp. 75–77) and Stimson, *The Cult of Kiho-Tumu* (Honolulu, 1933). For the Hawaiian 'Io, see Aheuna (Mrs. E. D. Taylor), "The Cult of Iolani," *Paradise of the Pacific* 44:12 (1931): 78. She reports an esoteric tradition of 'Io, "the Holy Spirit of the ancient Maolis of Hawaii . . . believed to be akin to Io of the Maori . . . who left Hawaii . . . [for] New Zealand." She concludes, "Io to us is Jehovah to other peoples."

64. The criticial evaluation of the informants for the Kiho cult has been the special contribution of K. P. Emory, "The Tuamotuan Creation Charts by Paiore," *JPS* 48 (1939): 22–26; "Tuamotuan Concepts of Creation," *JPS* 49 (1940): 116–26, 132–36 and notes 151–71; *Tuamotuan Religious Structures* (Honolulu, 1947), esp. pp. 5–7. Cf. R. Piddington in his

edition of R. W. Williamson, *Essays in Polynesian Ethnology* (Cambridge, 1939), pp. 293–301. Emory demonstrated that Stimson's informants, who admitted to having either "lied" or "to have made it up as a joke," were influenced by what Stimson told them about the Maori Io cult, including specific materials from Smith's *Lore* ("Creation Charts," pp. 24 and 29, n. 53; "Concepts of Creation," p. 120). Emory concludes that the informants were led "to invent Kiho after hearing [from Stimson] of the Maori esoteric cult of Io" ("Concepts of Creation," p. 116). E. S. C. Handy, "The Hawaiian Cult of Io," *JPS* 50 (1941): 136 and 158–59, reviewed Aheuna's claim with caution. While accepting the notion that an esoteric cult had been revealed, centering around a superior god (Io/Uli), he concluded: "Let's not rush to enthrone Io as a Supreme Being in Hawaii: the evidence only proves that he was a superior protective deity." K. P. Emory, "The Hawaiian God Io," *JPS* 51 (1942): 202 and 206, was more critical. "The informant who revealed the 'cult of 'Io' was obviously striving to show that the Hawaiians had a cult equivalent to the Maori cult of Io." He traced the impetus for the creation of the Hawaiian deity to 1920, when a group of Mormon Maoris visited Hawaii and discussed Io (largely based on the *Lore*) at several parties and receptions which Aheuna attended. It should be noted that the Maori Mormons have incorporated Io into their theology (see P. H. de Bres, *Religion in Atene* [Wellington, 1971], pp. 18 and 52). This incorporation deserves further study. (I have omitted Handy and Emory's discussion of 'Io in relation to the hawk's cry, *io*, as it is not relevant to our concerns.)

65. See the excellent reviews of the literature and critical summaries in Buck, *Coming of the Maori*, pp. 526–36 and Barrière, "Revisions and Adulterations," pp. 103–19.

66. This is the conclusion of Buck and Barrière (see n. 65). See further, T. Monberg, "Ta'aroa in the Creation Myths of the Society Islands," *JPS* 65 (1956): 256–58, 280–81. Johansen, *Studies,* recognizes that the majority of the traditions are "post-European," but suggests the possibility of a pre-European "core" (pp. 38–39, 42–43, 47, 51, 56, 190–91), before concluding, "all things considered, there is the greatest probability that Io became a high god after the Europeans came to New Zealand" (p. 193).

67. See above, n. 52.

68. Simmons and Biggs, "Sources of the 'Lore of the Whare-wānanga,' " pp. 26, n. 17, 36, and 41, trace the Io materials in chap. 2 of the *Lore* to a manuscript in the collection of the Polynesian Society (MSS Smith-Whatahoro III). The bulk of this manuscript is concerned with genealogies. Smith copied the Whatahoro manuscript in 1911; *however,* it had already been copied by T. W. Downes in 1908. Downes's copy includes *no* Io materials. "It seems likely that everything Smith copied . . . in 1911 had been added after Downes made his copy in 1908." I draw the most negative of the possible inferences from their study: that the materials on Io were added *as a result of* the 1907 publication of the "Maori Cosmogony." See the account of the Io materials in *Lore* given in n. 24, above. It consists mainly of a set of titles and a few details—all of which give the impression of having been inserted into already existing traditional materials.

69. See above, n. 23.

70. T. W. Gudgeon, *The History and Doings of the Maoris from the Year 1820 to the Signing of the Treaty of Waitangi in 1840* (Auckland, 1885). Note that pp. 95–225 consist of an essay by J. White on "Maori Customs and Superstitions." I have taken the information as to W. E. Gudgeon's actual authorship of his father's work from his obituary notice in *JPS* 29 (1920): 21, and the entry in the *Dictionary of New Zealand Biography,* 1:335.

71. The two occurrences on the South Island are puzzling, even though one has been identified as "possibly European" (see above, n. 44). The identification of Whatahoro's traditions with the Ngati Kahunguna should be disregarded, for none of his Io traditions can be traced back to the Matorohanga transmission.

72. Note that Hare Hongi has inserted in parentheses "(European) law" in his translation. This may not be correct. It is possible that the reference could be to the Old Testament. Compare the reference to "doctrine" (*whakapono*) and "law" (*ture*) later in the same section.

73. Best, "Cult of Io," pp. 101–2. Cf. Craig, *Man of the Mists*, pp. 170–71.

74. Johansen, *Studies*, p. 41; A. Ngata, "The Religious Situation," in I. L. G. Sutherland, ed., *The Maori People Today* (Oxford, 1940), p. 335.

75. See Johansen, *Studies*, pp. 56–57.

76. Best's consistent dating of the Io traditions was that they were "neolithic" (e.g., "Cult of Io," p. 98). See above, n. 30.

77. The only scholar that I have read to hint at a connection is Johansen, *Studies*, p. 41: "The time of its [the *Lore*] genesis is also suggestive. It was a time when there was religious and political unrest among the Maoris which also appeared in the Hauhau movement." However, he does not pursue this argument to any causal conclusions or to critical reflections with respect to the Io cult. For general background of the period, I have relied on J. Cowan, *The New Zealand Wars: A History of the Maori Campaign and the Pioneering Period* (Wellington, 1923), vols. 1–2; A. J. Harrop, *England and the Maori Wars* (London, 1937); J. K. Cunningham, "The Maori-Pakeha Conflict, 1858–1885: A Background to Political Geography," *New Zealand Geographer* 12 (1956): 12–31; K. Sinclair, *The Origins of the Maori Wars* (Wellington, 1957); H. G. Miller, *Race Conflict in New Zealand, 1814–1865* (Auckland, 1960); B. J. Dalton, *War and Politics in New Zealand, 1855–1870* (Sydney, 1967); T. Gibson, *The Maori Wars: The British Army in New Zealand, 1840–1872* (London, 1974). See further, the useful bibliography by R. A. Adams, *The Maori Wars* (Wellington, 1961).

78. See J. C. Beaglehole, *The Discovery of New Zealand*, 2d ed. (Oxford, 1961).

79. The studies by J. M. R. Owens are fundamental, especially, "Christianity and the Maoris to 1840," *New Zealand Journal of History* 2 (1968): 18–40 (cf. J. Binney, "Christianity and the Maoris to 1840: A Comment," ibid. 3 [1969]: 143–65); *The Unexpected Impact: Wesleyan Missionaries and the Maoris in the Early Nineteenth Century* (Auckland, 1973); *Prophets in the Wilderness: The Wesleyan Mission to New Zealand, 1819–1827* (Auckland, 1974).

80. The most useful overview is H. M. Wright, *New Zealand, 1769–1840: Early Years of Western Contact* (Cambridge, Mass., 1967). See also, J. M. Ward, *British Policy in the South Pacific, 1786–1893* (Sydney, 1950); J. O. Miller, *Early Victorian New Zealand: A Study of Racial Tension and Social Attitudes, 1839–1852* (Oxford, 1958); P. R. May, *The West Coast Gold Rush*, 2d ed. (Christchurch, 1962); I. M. Woods, *The Shadow of the Land: A Study of British Policy and Racial Conflict in New Zealand, 1832–1852* (Wellington, 1968).

81. Prior to the first census by F. D. Fenton, *Observations on the State of the Aboriginal Inhabitants of New Zealand* (Auckland, 1859), all figures for the Maori population of New Zealand are impressionistic estimates. The various early estimates are carefully reviewed, compared, and evaluated in D. I. Pool, *The Maori Population of New Zealand, 1769–1971* (Auckland, 1971), esp. pp. 52–60, 234–37.

82. For these statistics, see Auckland University College, Department of Economics, *Statistics of New Zealand for the Crown Colony Period, 1840–1852* (Auckland, 1954). I have also used various volumes of the *New Zealand Official Handbook* (1893-); the articles by W. Gill, "New Zealand," *Encyclopaedia Britannica*, 9th ed., 17:466–71, and W. P. Reeves, "New Zealand," *Encyclopaedia Britannica*, 11th ed., 19:624–31; and a note in R. Firth, *Elements of Social Organization* (London, 1951), p. 103, n. 1. An excellent overview may be gained from K. B. Cumberland, "A Land Despoiled: New Zealand about 1838," *New Zealand Geographer* 6 (1950): 13–34.

83. See T. L. Buck, *The Treaty of Waitangi*, 3d ed. (New Plymouth, 1936), and R. Firth, *Economics of the New Zealand Maori*, 2d ed. (Wellington, 1959), esp. pp. 438–57. Much

useful information can be gleaned from N. Smith, *Native Custom and Law Affecting Native Land* (Wellington, 1942).

84. See K. Burridge, *New Heaven and New Earth: A Study of Millenarian Activities* (New York, 1969), esp. pp. 37–39 and 115, cf. pp. 15–22.

85. The classic account remains the contemporary one by J. E. Gorst, *The Maori King, or Our Quarrel with the Natives of New Zealand* (London, 1864), which has been reprinted in an edition by K. Sinclair (Hamilton, 1959). I have also used the contemporary account of "Gore Brown to Newcastle, 22 May 1860," *Great Britain: Parliamentary Papers,* 1860/552, pp. 1–13, and the important materials in J. H. Kerry-Nicholls, *King Country or Journeys in New Zealand* (London, 1884). See further, K. Sinclair, *The Maori Land League: An Examination into the Source of a New Zealand Myth* (Auckland, 1950), and cf. Sinclair, *Origins of the Maori Wars,* pp. 61–84; P. Te Huranui (Jones), *An Account of the Life and Times of Potatau Te Wherowhero, The First Maori King* (Carterton, 1960); M. P. K. Sorrenson, "The Maori King Movement, 1858–1885," in R. Chapman and K. Sinclair, eds., *Studies of a Small Democracy: Festschrift W. Airey* (Auckland, 1963), pp. 33–55, 257–61.

86. Compare the traditional story of Wherowhero's receiving the kingship in Hurinui, *King Potatau,* pp. 183–266.

87. Tamihana in Gorst, *Maori King* (1959), p. 267.

88. Gorst, *Maori King* (1864), pp. 163–82.

89. See the use of both biblical passages and Christian hymns in Tamihana's account, and compare the public utterances of Wherowhero and other traditional chiefs in Gorst, *Maori King* (1959), pp. 265–67 with those on pp. 270–73. Sorrenson, "Maori King Movement," pp. 45–47, is useful on this tension.

90. See above, n. 52.

91. See above, notes 39 and 48.

92. I cannot identify Hone Te Mahu in section III.

93. In some Io texts, it appears that the King Movement's political structure has been transposed to the political structures of Io's realm (e.g. Best, *Maori Religion and Mythology,* pp. 251–52), but this will require further study.

94. The chief studies are F. Vaggioli, *Storia della Nuova Zelanda* (Parma, 1896), 2:356–457; S. Babbage, *Hauhauism: An Episode in the Maori Wars, 1863–1866* (Dunedin, 1938); W. Greenwood, "The Upraised Hand," *JPS* 51 (1942): 1–81; R. W. Winks, "The Doctrine of Hauhauism," *JPS* 62 (1953): 199–236; V. Lanternari, *The Religions of the Oppressed* (New York, 1965), pp. 200–210; K. Burridge, *New Heaven and New Earth,* pp. 15–21; B. R. Wilson, *Magic and the Millennium* (London, 1973), pp. 245–52. *All* of these studies are now superseded by P. Clark, *Hauhau: The Pai Marire Search for Maori Identity* (Auckland, 1975). W. E. Gudgeon has given an interesting account of Hauhau in "Maori Superstition," *JPS* 14 (1905): 171–76.

95. Clark, *Hauhau,* p. 12.

96. Clark, *Hauhau,* p. 10.

97. The Ua Rongopai manuscript, marginal numbers 27, 29, and 35 as translated in Appendix 1 to Clark, *Hauhau,* pp. 113–31 (quotations from pp. 123–25).

98. Clark, *Hauhau,* p. 61, quoting a letter from a Ngati Ruani chief to Tamihana urging him to join Pai Marire.

99. Clark, *Hauhau,* pp. 80, 90–93, 97, 117–18 et passim, has given particular emphasis to the role of the *karakia.* He is dependent, in part, on M. McLean, "Maori Chant: A Study in Ethnomusicology" (diss., University of Auckland, 1965), which I have not seen. In relation to the thesis that the *karakia* were intended to supplant the Christian Bible, note that a number of earlier Maori cults had, likewise, sought to replace the Bible and the missionary with a more direct form of relationship. See, for example, the coastal Taranaki "Warea Delusion" (1845, a period when Te Ua was in Taranaki), which claimed to have done away

with books and missionaries because, now, "god dwelt within them" (i.e., the natives). See R. Taylor, *The Past and Present of New Zealand with Its Prospects for the Future* (London, 1868), pp. 41–43; Clark, *Hauhau*, p. 105.

100. Clark, *Hauhau*, p. 122 and n. 21; for the millennium in Pai Marire, see Clark, p. 88.

101. At the annual meeting for 1894 of the Polynesian Society, (*JPS* 3:ix), it is reported, Tiwai Paraone of Miranda, Auckland, was elected a corresponding member of the society. His name is carried on subsequent membership lists until 1913, being omitted in 1914 and all later lists. There is no obituary notice, contrary to usual procedure, for Tiwai Paraone in any of the annual reports. Further archival research may clarify the matter. But this is a proper concern of an historian, not of an historian of religion attempting to preinterpret the 1907 text. The general thesis of the relationship of the cult of Io and the Io texts to Maori nativistic syncretism is not affected by the identification.

102. E. Best, "Sacerdotal Terms," *JPS* 38 (1929): 53. Compare the Ngati Kahungunu tradition that associates Io-whenua with volcanic activity in Best, "Sacerdotal Terms," *JPS* 37 (1928): 68. Johansen's arguments, *Studies*, p. 193, are, unfortunately, not convincing.

103. A. T. Ngata, *Nga Moteatea* (Hastings, 1928-), no. 115, which I have not seen. I have used the quotation in Johansen, *Studies*, pp. 191–92.

104. This appears to be an adaptation of the traditional conflict narrative between two brothers in connection with the separation of Rangi and Papa. See Grey, *Polynesian Mythology*, p. 7, and J. White, "Maori Customs and Superstitions," in T. W. Gudgeon, *History and Doings of the Maori*, p. 97. Note a variant tradition which declares both brothers to be evil in J. White, *History*, 1:36. See the version of this traditional conflict, related to Io, in Smith, *Lore*, 1:20, 123, et passim.

105. Compare the enigmatic saying by Te Ua in the Ua Rongopai MSS, 28: "Indeed, what is it that rests in the midst of peace, calm and heaven-sent light? . . . a Maori woman" (translated in Clark, *Hauhau*, p. 123).

106. See, already, the early use of the Bible in the Pai Marire, "Lament for King Tawhiao," edited and translated as Appendix 2 in Clark, *Hauhau*, pp. 132–37.

107. See Buck, *Coming of the Maori*, pp. 446–47.

108. Ibid., pp. 433–35.

109. See above, n. 47, for similar insertions of Io into traditional genealogies.

110. See above, n. 12. For a more speculative version, see P. Radin, *Primitive Man as Philosopher*, pp. 292–328.

111. See above, n. 5, for Eliade's treatment of the text.

112. Johansen's translation, *Studies*, p. 57.

113. The deities in *karakia* 4 cannot be identified. Does this suggest a new mythology?

114. See the comparisons in Johansen, *Studies*, pp. 58–61. Unfortunately, the argument he develops is vitiated by the unreliable nature of the materials in *Lore*. Thus, despite his assumptions, he is comparing the 1907 text with traditions that cannot be assumed to antedate it.

115. An historian of religion who seeks to undertake the tasks of preinterpretation on a variety of texts *must* become involved in the study of traditions for which he has no expertise. I am deeply indebted to a set of bibliographical resources without which the decade's labor which resulted in this essay could not have been undertaken. I would particularly acknowledge: J. Collier, *The Literature Relating to New Zealand: A Bibliography* (Wellington, 1889); A. Hamilton, "Handlist of Certain Books and Papers Containing Information Relating More or Less Directly to the Maori of New Zealand," *Transactions of the New Zealand Institute* 33 (1900): 515–37 (offprint: Wellington, 1911); T. M. Hocken, *A Bibliography of the Literature Relating to New Zealand* (Wellington, 1909); H. W. Williams, *Bibliography of Printed Maori to 1900* (Wellington, 1924); L. Jore, *Essai de bibliographique du Pacifique* (Paris, 1931); R. S. Duff and R. Allan, *Selected Bibliography of the Anthropology of New Zealand, 1900–1948*

(Christchurch, 1949); C. R. H. Taylor, *A Select List of Books Relating to New Zealand and Certain Pacific Islands, 1912–1945* (Wellington, 1949); J. Harris, *A Guide to New Zealand Reference Materials*, 2d ed. (Dunedin, 1950); C. R. H. Taylor, *A Pacific Bibliography* (Wellington, 1951); I. E. Leeson, *A Bibliography of Bibliographies of the South Pacific* (Oxford, 1954); J. O. Wilson, *A Finding List of British Parliamentary Papers Relating to New Zealand, 1817–1900* (Wellington, 1960); R. A. Adams, *The Maori Wars: A Bibliography* (Wellington, 1961); R. O. Reilly and R. Tessier, *Tahitians: Répertoire bio-bibliographique* (Paris, 1962); F. M. Camack and S. Saito, *Pacific Island Bibliography* (New York, 1962); S. J. Cauchi, ed., *A Bibliography of New Zealand Bibliographies: Preliminary Edition* (Wellington, 1967); E. Reiner, *Geographischer Literaturbericht Neuseeland, 1962–1972* (Cologne, 1974).

Chapter 6

1. On cargo, nativistic, and revitalization movements, see the extensive descriptive bibliography in W. La Barre, "Materials for a History of Studies of Crisis Cults," *Current Anthropology* 12 (1971): 3–44. For the use of these materials for the interpretation of Jewish traditions, see, among others, S. Isenberg, "Millenarianism in Greco-Roman Palestine," *Religion* 4 (1974): 26–46; in Christian tradition, see, among others, J. Gager, *Kingdom and Community* (Englewood Cliffs, 1975), esp. chap. 2.

2. For another aspect of incongruity, see J. Z. Smith, *Map Is Not Territory* (Leiden, 1978), pp. 190–207.

3. In this chapter, I have drawn freely on two previously published essays, Smith, *Map Is Not Territory*, pp. 67–87 and 289–309.

4. I have altered the standard English translation (see below, n. 5) at this point from "subordinate" to "protected citizen," of Babylon. In rendering the text in this manner, I have followed the interpretation of W. F. Leemans, "Kidinnu: Une symbole de droit divin babylonien," in M. David, B. A. van Groningen, and E. M. Meijers, eds., *Symbolae ad jus et historiam antiquitatis: Festschrift J. C. van Oven* (Leiden, 1946), pp. 31–61, esp. pp. 54–59. In relatively late materials (listed in Leemans, p. 54, n. 80), "les ṣābē kidinni ne sont mentionnés que dans certaines villes babyloniennes: Babylone, Borsippa, Sippar, Nippur et Uruk . . . ces villes mentionnés . . . sont toutes des vieux centres du culte des dieux. Les ṣābē kidinni de ces villes furent les citoyens [p.55] . . . le kidinnu fut un embleme divin, les ṣābē kidinni furent les citoyens qui se rangeaient sous cet emblème" [p. 56]. Leemans goes on to argue that ṣābē kidinni is a term which refers to the protection of the privileges of the citizens of ancient Babylonian cities *by Assyrian monarchs* against, "les inhabitants de la compagne" and marauders such as the Chaldeans and Arameans. "Après l'effondrement de la domination assyrienne il n'est plus jamais question de ṣābē kidinni ou de kidinnūtu en matière de droit publique. C'est seulement en matière religieuse [p. 57, citing the Akitu festival text] . . . c'était particulièrement les rois assyriens qui protégeaient les ṣābē kidinni. Ce titre ils pouvaient le trouver dans les fonctions de l'autorité cléricale supreme, dans lesquelles ils furent précisément reconnus pars les prêtres qui régnaient dans les villes anciennes; c'est comme tels qu'ils étaient les exécuteurs de la protection divine. C'est dans cette éxécution qu'ils usaient de toutes sortes de privilèges séculiers" [p. 59]. Leemans cites several Assyrian royal texts which reestablish certain tax exemptions and other fiscal benefits *(andurāru)* for the "citoyens opprimés de Babylone, en particulier les ṣābē kidinni, les protégés d'Anu et d'Enlil" [p. 59]. See further A. L. Oppenheim, *Ancient Mesopotamia* (Chicago, 1964), pp. 120–22. While altering the translation of line 426, I have retained the standard English translation, "dependents," in line 444.

5. Translation by A. Sachs, in J. B. Pritchard, ed., *Ancient Near Eastern Texts Relating to the Old Testament*, 2d ed. (Princeton, 1955), p. 344, of F. Thureau-Dangin, *Rituels accadiens* (Paris, 1921), p. 144.

6. P. Lambrechts, "Les fêtes phrygiennes de Cybèle et d'Attis," *Bulletin de l'Institut belge de Rom* 27 (1952): 141–70; *Over griekse en oosterse mysteriengodsdiensten: De sogenannte Adonismysterien* (Brussels, 1954); "La resurrection d'Adonis," *Annuaire de l'Institut de philologie et d'histoire orientales et slaves* 13 (1955): 207–40; *Attis, van herdersknaap tot god* (Brussels, 1962); *Attis en het feest der Hilariën* (Amsterdam, 1967). Alongside Lambrechts, with particular reference to the Babylonian materials, see the crucial article by W. von Soden, "Gibt es ein Zeugnis dafür, dass die Babylonier an die Wiederauferstehung Marduks geglaubt haben?" *Zeitschrift für Assyriologie*, n.s., 17 (1955): 130–66.

7. A useful bibliography of older studies in which each of these options may be found is in I. Engnell, *Studies in Divine Kingship in the Ancient Near East* (Oxford, 1967), pp. 201–2. For the historian of religion, the most balanced treatments remain A. J. Wensinck, "The Semitic New Year and the Origin of Eschatology," *Acta Orientalia* 1 (1923): 159–99, and G. Furlani, "L'umiliazione del re durante la festa di Capodanno a Babele," *Studi e materiali di storia delle religioni* 4 (1928): 5–16 and 305–7. There are some judicious remarks in J. J. Stamm, *Das Leiden des Unschuldigen in Babylon und Israel* (Zurich, 1946), esp. pp. 30–32, and a useful typology in V. Lanternari, *La grande festa: Storia del Capodanno nelle civiltà primitive* (Milan, 1959), pp. 441–67.

8. A remote parallel has been suggested in the beating of the king in the archaic Indian *rājasūya* ritual (see *Śatapatha-brāhmana* V.4 and *Kātyāyana-śrautasūtra* XV.7 in A. Weber, *Über die Königsweihe: Den Rājasūya* [Berlin, 1893], p. 63), by R. Pettazzoni, *La confessione dei peccati* (Bologna, 1935), 1:94–95, and J. C. Heesterman, *The Ancient Indian Royal Consecration* (The Hague, 1957), p. 156, and cf. pp. 4–5 and 141. While I remain unconvinced by the parallel, I have been influenced in my general approach to the Akitu festival by Weber's interpretation of the *rājasūya* ritual.

9. For a detailed study of the well-known "negative confession" in the Egyptian Book of the Dead, chap. 125, see C. Maystre, *Les déclarations d'innocence* (Cairo, 1937). For a comparison between the Egyptian and Babylonian negative confessions, see Pettazzoni, *La confessione dei peccati*, 2:1–24 and 88–103. Both Maystre's and Pettazzoni's interpretations are flawed by the use of the rubric "magic."

10. A. K. Grayson, *Babylonian Historical-Literary Texts* (Toronto, 1975), pp. 56, 69–71. On the matter of Seleucid "copies" of more archaic texts, see J. Z. Smith, *Map Is Not Territory*, pp. 71–72.

11. H. W. F. Saggs, *The Greatness That Was Babylon* (New York, 1962), p. 385. I regret that S. K. Eddy, *The King Is Dead: Studies in Near Eastern Resistance to Hellenism, 334–31 B.C.* (Lincoln, 1961), p. 107, whose interpretation of the religious history of the period has been fundamental for the point of view expressed in this chapter, shares the same presumption.

12. See von Soden, "Gibt es ein Zeugnis?" pp. 131, 158, 161–66. Cf. F. M. Th. de Liagre Böhl, "Die Religion der Babylonier und Assyrier," in F. König, ed., *Christus und die Religionen der Erde* (Freiburg, 1951), 2:477; G. van Dreel, *The Cult of Aššur* (The Hague, 1974).

13. See, for example, the texts in D. D. Luckenbill, *The Ancient Records of Assyria* (Chicago, 1927), 2:70 and 127.

14. See above, n. 5. The texts are cited in Leemans, "Kidinnu," p. 54 and n. 80 (texts c and d).

15. The standard edition is W. Dittenberger, *Orientis Graeci Inscriptiones Selectae* (Leipzig, 1903), 1:253. See the new restoration and full discussion in M. Zambelli, "L'ascesa al trono di Antioco IV Epifane di Siria," *Rivista di filologia e di istruzione classica* 38 (1960): 363–89, esp. pp. 374–80. See further, O. Mørkholm, *Antiochus IV of Syria* (Copenhagen, 1966), pp. 118–22, 132.

16. See T. H. Gaster, *Thespis,* 2d ed. (Garden City, 1961), p. 33, who supplies comparative material (largely drawn, without attribution, from J. G. Frazer, *The Golden Bough,* 3d ed. [London, 1935], 7:248–50) and hints at such an interpretation of the second slapping of the king at the Akitu festival. F. F. Hvidberg, *Graad og Latter i det Gamle Testamente* (Copenhagen, 1938), p. 11, while providing much valuable material for Israelitic and Canaanite traditions, misses this text in the Akitu festival, being thoroughly under the sway of the "dying-rising" pattern.

17. *KAR* 143:34 and 219:8/*VAT* 9555 and 9538 in S. Langdon, *The Babylonian Epic of Creation* (Oxford, 1923), p. 41. See the entire translation (pp. 34–49) and Langdon's discussion (pp. 50–59). The text was first discussed, in connection with the "dying-rising" pattern, by H. Zimmern, "Zum babylonischen Neujahrsfest: Zweiter Beitrag," *Berichte über die Verhandlungen der Königliche Sächsischen Gesellschaft,* philol.-hist. Klasse, 70 (1918): 2–20, and, most explicitly from this point of view, in S. H. Hooke, *Babylonian and Assyrian Religion* (New York, 1953), pp. 111–14. This interpretation collapses before von Soden's careful analysis of the text in "Gibt es ein Zeugnis?" (see the pages cited above, n. 12). See further, G. Meier, "Ein Kommentar zu einer Selbstprädikation des Marduk aus Assur," *Zeitschrift für Assyriologie,* n.s. 13 (1942): 241–46, esp. p. 245, and W. G. Lambert, "The Great Battle of the Mesopotamian New Year: The Conflict in the Akitu House," *Iraq* 25 (1963): 189–90.

18. Thureau-Dangin, *Rituels accadiens,* p. 136 (lines 279–84).

19. S. A. Pallis, *The Babylonian Akitu Festival* (Copenhagen, 1926), p. 232.

20. W. G. Lambert, "A New Look at the Babylonian Background of Genesis," *Journal of Theological Studies,* n.s. 16 (1965): 291.

21. Compare the bilingual text from Sippar, which describes the creation of the world by Marduk as a process of temple construction. A. Heidel, *The Babylonian Genesis,* 2d ed. (Chicago, 1951), pp. 61–63.

22. To this construct might be compared the materials published by A. K. Grayson and W. G. Lambert, "Akkadian Prophecies," *Journal of Cuneiform Studies* 18 (1964): 7–30; W. W. Hallo, "Akkadian Apocalypses," *Israel Exploration Journal* 16 (1966): 231–42; R. D. Biggs, "More Akkadian Prophecies," *Iraq* 29 (1967): 117–32; H. Hunger and S. A. Kaufman, "A New Akkadian Prophecy Text," *Journal of the American Oriental Society* 95 (1975): 371–75. In this series, one Seleucid text has been published (Biggs, "More Akkadian Prophecies," pp. 128–32) possibly from Babylon. A new Seleucid composition, "The Dynastic Prophecy," has been published by A. K. Grayson, *Babylonian Historical-Literary Texts,* pp. 24–37.

23. See above, n.4, and the important text published by F. M. Th. de Liagre Böhl, *Der babylonische Fürstenspiegel* (Leipzig, 1937), on which see W. G. Lambert, *Babylonian Wisdom Literature* (Oxford, 1960), pp. 110–15, and I. M. Diakonoff, "A Babylonian Political Pamphlet," *Studies in Honor of Benno Landsberger* (Chicago, 1965), pp. 343–50.

24. Pritchard, *Ancient Near Eastern Texts,* p. 317.

25. See, for example, Eddy, *The King Is Dead,* pp. 159–60. I regret Eddy's interpretation, as he is one of the few scholars to insist on the importance of the decline of native kingship.

26. See the important article on this theme by E. Osswald, "Zum Problem der *vaticinia ex eventu,*" *Zeitschrift für die alttestamentliche Wissenschaft* 75 (1963): 27–44.

27. Texts cited in R. Labat, *Le poème babylonien de la création* (Paris, 1935), p. 18.

28. See the edition of the fragments of Berossus in F. Jacoby, *Die Fragmente der griechischen Historiker* (Berlin, 1923–), 3C:364–97 (no. 680), and the older edition by P. Schnabel, *Berossus und die babylonisch-hellenistische Literatur* (Leipzig, 1923), pp. 250–75. Schnabel's work is the only substantial monograph on Berossus. Most works are consecrated to a recovery of historical realia. I have been much stimulated by the recent study by R.

Drews, "The Babylonian Chronicles and Berossus," *Iraq* 37 (1975): 39–55. The following paragraphs on Berossus have been adopted from J. Z. Smith, *Map Is Not Territory,* pp. 68–70.

29. Jacoby, *Fragmente,* is unable to accept this totality and splits Berossus in two! The historian described by Jewish and Christian authors is identified by Jacoby as Berossus of Babylon; the astrological material transmitted by Greek and Latin authors is attributed to "pseudo-Berossus of Cos," wholly an invention by Jacoby. See Drews, "Babylonian Chronicles and Berossus," pp. 51–54.

30. Jacoby, *Fragmente,* has sundered this correlation by assigning Abydenus's cosmic material to F1 and his "historical" account to F6. They occur together in Eusebius *Praeparatio evangelica* 9.41, and in the Armenian translation of the *Chronicle* 49 (pp. 18–19).

31. On Berossus, F21 (= Seneca *Naturales Quaestiones* 3.29), see J. Bidez, "Bérose et la grande année," *Mélanges P. Fredericq* (Brussels, 1904), pp. 9–19; P. Schnabel, "Apokalyptische Berechnung der Endzeiten bei Berossos," *Orientalistische Literaturzeitung* 13 (1910): 401–2 and *Berossos* pp. 94–109; W. Gundel in F. Boll and C. Bezold, *Sternglaube und Sterndeutung,* 4th ed. (Leipzig and Berlin, 1931), pp. 200–205 (cf. W. and H. G. Gundel, *Astrologumena* [Wiesbaden, 1966], pp. 45–46 and n. 14); B. L. van Waerden, "Das grosse Jahr und die ewige Wiederkehr," *Hermes* 80 (1952): 129–55; B. Sticker, "Weltzeitalter und astronomische Perioden," *Saeculum* 4 (1953): 241–49; V. Nikiprowetsky, *La troisième sibylle* (Paris, 1970), pp. 88–122; M. Hengel, *Judaism and Hellenism* (Philadelphia, 1974), 1:191–93; and J. J. Collins, *The Sibylline Oracles of Egyptian Judaism* (Missoula, 1974), pp. 101–7 et passim.

32. G. de Vries, *Bij de Berg-Alfoeren op West-Seran: Zeden, Gewoonten en Mythologie van een Oervolk* (Zutphen, 1927), pp. 152–57. In this version, the protagonist is a miraculous male child!

33. A. E. Jensen, "Eine ost-indische Myth als Ausdruck einer Weltanschauung," *Paideuma* 1 (1938–40): 199–216, and, with H. Niggemeyer, *Hainuwele: Völkerzählungen von der Molluken-Insel Ceram* (Frankfurt am Main, 1938), esp. pp. 59–65. These early treatments established the basic lines of Jensen's interpretation which he was to repeat in a variety of works. See especially, "Das Weltbild einer frühen Kultur," *Paideuma* 3 (1944): 1–83; *Die drei Ströme: Züge aus dem geistigen Leben der Wemale* (Leipzig, 1948), esp. pp. 88–92, 98–101, 114–16; *Das religiöse Weltbild einer frühen Kultur* (Stuttgart, 1948); "Das mythische Weltbetrachtung der alten Pflanzervölker," *Eranos-Jahrbuch* 17 (1950): 421–73; *Mythos und Kult bei Naturvölkern* (Wiesbaden, 1951), with an English translation, *Myth and Cult among Primitive Peoples* (Chicago, 1963), which was the subject of an intensive review and discussion in *Current Anthropology* 6 (1965): 199–215; "Der Ursprung des Bodenbaus in mythologischer Sicht," *Paideuma* 6 (1956): 169–80; "Prometheus und Hainuwele-Mythologem: Eine Apologie," *Anthropos* 58 (1963): 145–86.

34. For a statement of the consensus portrait, see J.Z. Smith, "Dema Deities," *Encyclopaedia Britannica,* 15th ed., 3:454. The most suggestive challenge to Jensen, thus far, is V. Lanternari, *La grande festa,* esp. chap. 4. The most important extension of Jensen's work is O. Zerries, "Die kulturgeschichtliche Bedeutung einiger Mythen aus Südamerika über den Ursprung der Pflanzen," *Zeitschrift für Ethnologie* 77 (1952): 62–82, and, especially, "Entstehung oder Erwerb der Kulturpflanzen und Beginn des Bodenbaus im Mythos der Indianer Sudamerikas," *Paideuma* 15 (1969): 64–124. See further the use of the "Hainuwelemythologem" in P. J. Raats, "A Structural Study of Bogobo Myths and Rites," *Asian Folklore Studies* 29 (1970): 1–132, esp. pp. 62–81, and cf. 22–23, 53–56 et passim. I find the debate between C. Schmitz, "Die Problematik der Mythologem 'Hainuwele' und 'Prometheus,' " *Anthropos* 55 (1960): 215–37, and Jensen, "Prometheus und Hainuwele Mythologem," unilluminating.

35. The full narrative is given in German translation in Jensen, *Hainuwele*, pp. 59–65 (no. 11), and *Das religiöse Weltbild*, pp. 34–38. There is an English translation in J. Campbell, *The Masks of God: Primitive Mythology* (New York, 1959), pp. 173–76.

36. The banana-stone tale is one variant of Thompson motif A1335.3, *Origin of Death from an Unwise Choice* (S. Thompson, *Motif-Index of Folk-Literature*, 2d ed. [Bloomington, 1955–58]). The Wemale version is somewhat atypical in that it is not choice by the ancestors, but a violent contest between the banana and a stone. See the text in Jensen, *Hainuwele*, pp. 39–43 (no. 1), esp. pp. 39–40. For a more typical version from the neighboring Central Celebes, see J. G. Frazer, *The Belief in Immortality and the Worship of the Dead* (London, 1913), 1:74–75.

37. Thompson motifs A2611, *Plants from Body of Slain Person*, and A2611.0.1, *Plants from Grave of Slain Person*. Cf. B. F. Kirtley, *A Motif Index of Traditional Polynesian Tales* (Honolulu, 1971), pp. 105–6; R. E. Mitchell, *The Folktales of Micronesia* (Nagoya, 1971), pp. 245–46. Regrettably, no similar index exists for the Indonesian culture complex, but see G. Hatt, "The Corn Mother in America and Indonesia," *Anthropos* 46 (1951), esp. pp. 844–91 for a rich collection. Raats, "Structural Study of Bogobo Myths," pp. 44–45, adds useful parallels from the Malay Archipelago.

38. For early reports of *hárta*, see the texts cited in W. P. Groeneldt, "Notes on the Malay Archipelago and Malacca Compiled from Chinese Sources," *Verhandelingen van het Koninklijk Instituut voor de Taal-, Land-, en Volkenkunde van Nederlandisch-Indië* 39 (1880): 102, 119; W. W. Rockhill, "Notes on the Relations and Trade of China with the Eastern Archipelago and the Coasts of the Indian Ocean during the Fourteenth Century," *T'oung Pao* 16 (1915): 257, 260; and M. A. P. Meilink-Roelofsz, *Asian Trade and European Influence in the Indonesian Archipelago between 1500 and about 1630* (The Hague, 1962), pp. 99, 158 et passim. Meilink-Roelofsz notes that "the inhabitants of the Moluccas gave higher prices [in spices] for Chinese porcelain than could be obtained anywhere else" (p. 99). Compare the early European reference to the use of Chinese porcelain, brass, and copper as "money" in the Moluccas in Gonzalo Fernandez de Oviedo de Valdes, *Historia general y natural de las Indias y tierra firme del mar oceano* (Seville, 1535) in the edition of D. José Almador de los Rios (Madrid, 1852), 1:100–105, and appendix, plate 1, fig. 1, on which, see D. Lach, *Asia in the Making of Europe* (Chicago, 1965), 1.2:600–601.

Jensen quite rightly notes that the word *hárta* (of Malaysian derivation) signifies all imported articles (*Die drei Ströme*, p. 59) and that "Hárta ist 'Heiratsgeld' aber auch eine Sammelbezeichnung für nicht-ceramesischen Kulturgut, das einen besonderen Vermögenwert darstellt, wie chinesische Teller, Gongs und andere Metallsachen" (*Hainuwele*, p. 50), but he fails to perceive its significance, arguing only that, because of the pristine, archaic mentality of the Wemale and their holistic way of life, *hárta* is "not perceived as everyday imported wares, but rather as a divine gift which had been given to man in primordial times" (*Die drei Ströme*, p. 248). In keeping with his tendency to archaize his data, Jensen notes a homology between *hárta* and the head taken in headhunting (*Die drei Ströme*, p. 246) on the basis of inconclusive evidence from E. Stresemann, "Religiöse Gebräuche auf Seran," *Tijdschrift voor Indische Taal-, Land-, en Volkenkunde* 62 (1923): 308, 346. Hatt ("Corn Mother," p. 889) attempts a similar identification, on the basis of Jensen's tale 21 (*Hainuwele*, p. 71) and argues for a general Indonesian pattern of jewels and wealth being symbolically equivalent to food.

To the Hainuwele narrative should be compared Jensen's tale 45 (*Hainuwele*, pp. 101–2) which shares a number of motifs, and, especially, his tale 264 (*Hainuwele*, pp. 299–300), in which an eel instructs a young man to slay him; from his eyes come tall trees (cf. Thompson motif A2611.3), and from their leaves, Chinese porcelains and gongs.

39. Compare the materials on anal creation and the interrelation of *Geld, Gold und Kot* in A. Dundes, "Earth Diver: Creation of the Mythopoeic Male," *American Anthropologist*

64 (1962): 1032–51; and the useful anthology edited by E. Borneman, *The Psychoanalysis of Money* (New York, 1976).

40. See the summary of Jensen's position regarding "die zentrale mythische Idee" in *Die drei Ströme*, p. xi.

41. See, among other loci, Jensen, "Spiel und Ergriffenheit," *Paideuma* 2 (1942): 124–39; *Die drei Ströme*, pp. 275–77; *Myth and Cult*, pp. 4–6, 59–79, et passim. Note that, in general conformity to the presuppositions of the Frobenius school, Jensen consistently devalues "application" as a "depletion." For a further discussion and critique of Jensen's notion of "application," see chap. 3, above.

42. K. Burridge, *Mambu: A Study of Melanesian Cargo Movements and Their Social and Ideological Background* (New York, 1970), pp. 82–85.

43. The classic study of exchange and reciprocity remains M. Mauss, *Essai sur le don* (Paris, 1925). Perhaps the most useful recent treatment (with rich bibliography) is M. Sahlins, "On the Sociology of Primitive Exchange," in M. Banton, ed., *The Relevance of Models in Social Anthropology* (London, 1965), pp. 139–236.

44. Cf. K. Burridge, *New Heaven and New Earth: A Study of Millenarian Activities* (New York, 1969), pp. 145–49 et passim.

45. The theme of the white ancestors appears to be a subtype of the widespread motif that the ancestors/dead are the reverse of the living. See J. Z. Smith, *Map Is Not Territory*, pp. 157–58, n. 31. It is possible to advance the proposition: no tradition that ancestors are white, no cargo cult.

46. It has been the special merit of V. Lanternari to insist on the relationship of the archaic motifs of white ancestors, the ship of the dead, and the return of the dead at New Year festivals to the cargo cults. See V. Lanternari, "Origini storiche dei culti profetici melanesiani," *Studi e materiali di storia delle religioni* 27 (1956): 77–82; *La grande festa*, pp. 411–40 et passim, and *The Religions of the Oppressed* (New York, 1963), pp. 166–67, 185–87.

47. Burridge, *Mambu*, pp. 154–76, and Burridge, *Tangu Traditions* (Oxford, 1969), pp. 113–14, 229–30, 330, 400–411.

48. Despite Jensen's insistence that, unlike the coastal peoples (*Die drei Ströme*, pp. 6–10), the inland and highland tribes escaped the impact of the European—he, in fact, documents each of these nativistic elements (*Die drei Ströme*, pp. 35–45)—although not to the degree of the Christianized or Islamized coast. On the latter, see the work of Jensen's colleague, J. Roder, *Alahatala: Die Religion der Inlandstämme Mittelcerams* (Frankfurt am Main, 1948) and note the role of the Christian Ceramese in the abortive 1950 rebellion (on which see J. M. van der Kroef, "The South Moluccan Insurrection in Indonesia," *Journal of East Asiatic Studies* 1 [1954]: 1–20, and the apologia by G. Decker, *Republik Maluku Selaten* [Göttingen, 1957]). The Moluccan rebellion against the Dutch continues.

49. Jensen, *Die drei Ströme*, pp. 42–43. One suspects that, if Jensen's interest in the topic had been greater, much more could have been reported.

50. For the classic description of the Mejapi movements, see A. C. Kruyt and N. Adriani, "De Godsdienstig-Politeke Beweging 'Mejapi' op Celebes," *Bijdragen tot de Taal-, Land-, en Volkenkunde van Nederlandsch-Indië* 67 (1913): 135–51. For a brief English description, see J. M. van der Kroef, "Messianic Movements in the Celebes, Sumatra, and Borneo," in S. L. Thrupp, ed., *Millennial Dreams in Action* (New York, 1970), esp. pp. 80–91. To be sure, the Kakihan association was preeminently considered to be a political movement by colonial administrators and missionaries in Ceram until the pioneering work by J. G. F. Riedel, *De sluik- en kroesharige Rassen tusschen Selebes en Papua* (The Hague, 1886), esp. pp. 107–11, recognized its nature as a native, religious, secret society. See further the important dissertation by J. P. Duyvendak, *Het Kakean-Genootschap van Seran* (Almelo, 1926), who stresses the Melanesian parallels. For colonial attempts at suppression, see Jensen, *Die drei Ströme*, p. 42.

51. See, among others, Jensen, *Hainuwele,* pp. 69–71 (nos. 17–22) and de Vries, *Bij de Berg-Alfoeren,* pp. 257–58. For a most elaborate example from the neighboring Lesser Sunda Islands, see P. A. Burger, "Manggaraise verhalen over het ontstann van der rijst en de mais," *Tijdschrift voor Indische Taal-, Land-, en Volkenkunde* 81 (1941): 411–23.

Chapter 7

1. For this brief historical narrative, I have drawn on the convenient account in E. J. Sharpe, *Comparative Religion: A History* (London, 1975), pp. 119–43.

2. For the role of the Lisbon earthquake in the European history of ideas, see T. D. Kendrick, *The Lisbon Earthquake* (Philadelphia, 1957).

3. Montaigne, "Of Cannibals," in *The Complete Works of Montaigne,* trans. D. M. Frame (Stanford, 1958), pp. 152–53.

4. D. Z. Phillips, *Faith and Philosophical Enquiry* (London, 1970), p. 237, as quoted in R. Trigg, *Reason and Commitment* (Cambridge, 1973), p. 22.

5. Trigg, *Reason and Commitment,* pp. 24–25.

6. In addition to contemporary press accounts, I have used J. Maguire and M. L. Dunn, *Hold Hands and Die* (New York, 1978), M. Kilduff and R. Javers, *The Suicide Cult* (New York, 1978); C. Krause, *Guyana Massacre* (New York, 1978) and the useful collection of source materials in S. Rose, *Jesus and Jim Jones* (New York, 1979). I have also made use of the Report of a Staff Investigative Group to the Committee on Foreign Affairs, U.S. House of Representatives, *The Assassination of Representative Leo J. Ryan and the Jonestown Guyana Tragedy* (Washington, D.C., 1979). Despite a number of more recent works, published since 1980, I have not seen cause to alter this essay in either matters of fact or, especially, in conclusions.

7. *New York Times,* 5 December 1978.

8. *United Methodist Reporter,* December 1978, as quoted in Rose, *Jesus and Jim Jones,* p. 186.

9. Subsequent to the original presentation of this essay (1980), J. L. Reston, Jr., gained access to 900 hours of these tapes through a freedom-of-information suit. Reston's book, *Our Father Who Art in Hell* (New York, 1981), makes little use of this precious material. A 90-minute selection from the tapes was played over National Public Radio in April 1981. While the editing and selection were savagely contrived, there is enough in this selection (including Jones interpreting himself by means of a full-blown gnostic myth) to indicate that a careful study of the entire collection of tapes by a trained and sensitive historian of religion would yield valuable results.

10. Euripides *Bacchae,* especially lines 672–768.

11. Livy *History* 39. 16.

12. J. Moore, as quoted in Rose, *Jesus and Jim Jones,* p. 132.

13. Ibid., p. 162.

14. J. Jones, as quoted in Rose, *Jesus and Jim Jones,* pp. 30 and 32.

15. See Appendix 2 for the full text.

16. Krause, *Guyana Massacre,* p. 132.

17. For factual material, I have used J. G. Miller, "Naked Cults in Central West Santos," *Journal of the Polynesian Society* 57 (1948): 330–41; J. Guiart, " 'Cargo Cults' and Political Evolution in Melanesia," *South Pacific* 5 (1951): 128–29; Guiart, "Forerunners of Melanesian Nationalism," *Oceania* 22 (1951): 81–90. My interpretation of the exchange ideology of total destruction is quite different from the understanding of this radical act in M. Eliade, *The Two and the One* (New York, 1965), pp. 125–28.

18. J. Z. Smith, *Map Is Not Territory* (Leiden, 1978), pp. 305–7, and chap. 6, above.

Index